Odious Praise

Odious Praise
Rhetoric, Religion, and Social Thought

ERIC MACPHAIL

The Pennsylvania State University Press
University Park, Pennsylvania

Library of Congress Cataloging-in-Publication Data

Names: MacPhail, Eric, author.
Title: Odious praise : rhetoric, religion, and social thought / Eric MacPhail.
Description: University Park, Pennsylvania : The Pennsylvania State University Press, [2022] | Includes bibliographical references and index.
Summary: "Reassesses the genre of epideictic rhetoric from antiquity to the Renaissance by looking at a series of texts that exploit the potential of praise to undermine consensus and to challenge the normative values of society. The authors covered range from Isocrates, Plato, and Aristotle to Erasmus, Machiavelli, and Montaigne"—Provided by publisher.
Identifiers: LCCN 2021054131 | ISBN 9780271092331 (hardback)
Subjects: LCSH: Rhetoric, Ancient. | Rhetoric. | Praise in literature. | Praise—Religious aspects. | Epideictic rhetoric
Classification: LCC PA3038 .M33 2022 | DDC 809/.93353—dc23/eng/20220106
LC record available at https://lccn.loc.gov/2021054131

Copyright © 2022 Eric MacPhail
All rights reserved
Printed in the United States of America
Published by The Pennsylvania State University Press,
University Park, PA 16802–1003

The Pennsylvania State University Press is a member of the Association of University Presses.

It is the policy of The Pennsylvania State University Press to use acid-free paper. Publications on uncoated stock satisfy the minimum requirements of American National Standard for Information Sciences—Permanence of Paper for Printed Library Material, ANSI Z39.48–1992.

CONTENTS

vii | Acknowledgments
viii | List of Abbreviations

1 | Introduction: Isocrates and the Genealogy of Odious Praise

11 | 1. Platonic Values: Polycrates and the Politics of Epideictic

39 | 2. Ciceronian Values: Cicero and the Praise of Latin

65 | 3. Church Values: Lorenzo Valla and the Praise of Thomas Aquinas

83 | 4. Religion and the Limits of Praise: Isocrates and the Praise of Superstition

111 | Conclusion

115 | Appendix: Sperone Speroni, "Discorso dei lodatori"
118 | Notes
135 | Bibliography
142 | Index

ACKNOWLEDGMENTS

I would like to acknowledge the generous assistance of the College Arts and Humanities Institute of Indiana University and also to express my gratitude for the hospitality shown me by the Centre d'Études Supérieures de la Renaissance of Tours.

Portions of chapter 4 originally appeared in "Jean Bodin and the Praise of Superstition," *Rhetorica* 36, no. 1 (2018): 24–38, published by University of California Press, and "Montaigne and the Theatre of Conscience," *French Studies* 68 (2014): 465–76, published by Oxford University Press.

ABBREVIATIONS

The following abbreviations are used to cite the works of Erasmus.

Allen   P. S. Allen et al., eds. *Opus epistolarum Desiderii Erasmi Roterodami.* 12 vols. Oxford: Oxford University Press, 1906–58. References are to letter and line number.

ASD   *Opera omnia Desiderii Erasmi Roterodami.* In progress. Amsterdam: Elsevier, 1969–. References are to ordo, volume, and page number.

CWE   *Collected Works of Erasmus.* In progress. Toronto: University of Toronto Press, 1974–. References are to volume and page number, except for letters: letters use only Allen letter numbers with line numbers of the English translation.

Ep.   A letter in any edition using Allen numbers.

LB   Jean Le Clerc, ed. *Desiderii Erasmi Roterodami opera omnia.* 10 vols. Leiden: P. Van der Aa, 1703–6. References are to volume, column, and column section number.

Introduction
Isocrates and the Genealogy of Odious Praise

Busiris is the hero of this story. He's the legendary king of Egypt who slaughtered his guests at the altar of the gods and then ate them. He finally bit off more than he could chew when he tried to pull the same trick on Hercules. In this final encounter, as one Renaissance commentator remarked, he paid the price for his inhospitality.[1] Despite his many eccentricities, we can sympathize with Busiris, for he was in fact the inaugural victim of odious praise, an encomium pronounced by the sophist Polycrates, which we know only from Isocrates's attempts to redeem Busiris from the damage done to his reputation by the earlier encomium. In his oration, known simply as *Busiris*, Isocrates reproaches Polycrates for praising the king in such a way that he looks worse than if Polycrates had blamed him.

Isocrates's oration is intermittently concerned with the achievements of its eponymous subject but more nearly concerned with denouncing the ethical and artistic confusion of Polycrates's praise of Busiris. Addressing his rival, Isocrates insists, "although you claim to be defending Busiris, you have not only not freed him from the defamation that he is already facing, but you have even implicated him in such enormous crimes that no one could invent any more terrible. Others who have attempted to malign him have only slandered him for sacrificing the strangers that visited him. You even accuse him of cannibalism" (11.5).[2] In effect, Polycrates substitutes calumny for praise, which is an ethical and artistic confusion in violation of the very laws of praise (11.33). Polycrates's speech is less a defense or ἀπολογία than an admission of guilt or ὁμολογία (11.44). Worst of all, he gives rhetoric a bad name, which it will endeavor to maintain indefinitely. His praise is so odious that it is a reproach to the teaching of eloquence (11.49). To recapitulate, in Isocrates's view, and we'll have to take his word for it, Polycrates's encomium of Busiris casts odium on the one who praises, the one who is praised, and the art of praise itself.

This sophistic dispute over the reputation of a mythological tyrant did not fail to leave its mark on the Latin grammatical tradition, especially in its engagement with Virgil's *Georgics*. At the outset of book 3 of his agricultural poem, Virgil invokes a series of mythological commonplaces, asking if there is anyone who has not heard of harsh Eurystheus, who imposed the labors of Hercules, or of the altars of unpraised Busiris: "quis aut Eurysthea durum / aut inlaudati nescit Busiridis aras?"[3] In his philological miscellany entitled *Attic Nights*, the second-century Latin author Aulus Gellius reports that ancient grammarians were not pleased by Virgil's choice of the epithet *illaudatus* or "unpraised" to characterize so notorious a tyrant (and so precocious a violator of international law). This characterization struck the grammarians as something of an understatement, and they vented their grammatical indignation in hostile glosses on the offending passage from the *Georgics*. In rebuttal, Gellius argues that Virgil could not have used a harsher term than *illaudatus* since to be unpraised is the very limit of badness.[4]

The same epithet continued to provoke some resistance among Renaissance commentators, who usually gloss *illaudatus* with *illaudabilis* or "unworthy of praise." One commentator who devoted more ingenious attention to the problem was Pierio Valeriano, who considers various meanings of *illaudatus* before invoking the testimony of Isocrates's *Busiris* as a decisive intertext for the *Georgics*. Isocrates, Valeriano reminds us, criticized his rival for making Busiris seem even more worthy of odium by virtue of his praise: "But among all these interpretations [of the epithet *illaudatus*], the best seems to be the speech of Isocrates saying that the person who had attempted to praise Busiris only managed to make him seem more odious and blameworthy through his praise."[5] In other words, Virgil called Busiris *illaudatus* because, as we know from Isocrates, even his praise turns to blame. You can't praise him even if you want to, for the more you praise him, the worse he seems. This paradox, we may add, did not prevent Isocrates from writing his own alternative praise of Busiris as the legendary founder of Egypt and its venerable traditions. It seems that, for the grammatical tradition so hastily summarized here, Busiris represents something of a limit case for epideictic rhetoric or the rhetoric of praise and blame.

His notoriety raises the question of what lies beyond praise. Is anything or anyone so universally abhorred as to remain immune to praise? Similarly, are there any universal values, shared by all orators and all audiences, or only relative ones? Moreover, keeping in mind Gellius's argument that *illaudatus* marks the limit or *finis* of immorality, how does praise define or set the boundaries of the normative values of society? What if praise transgresses the confines of social consensus?

The praise for which Isocrates reproached Polycrates is an interesting test of social consensus. Everyone agrees that cannibalism is wrong, except for those who disagree, like Michel de Montaigne in his essay "Des Cannibales." Already in antiquity, Petronius imagined a scenario that might inspire some reevaluation of cannibalism. In the final episode of his fragmentary novel the *Satyricon*, Petronius has his picaresque hero Eumolpus pose as a rich old man without family in order to live at the expense of the *captatores* or legacy hunters who are drawn by the lure of his supposed wealth and frailty. This *tragoedia* or imposture can only last so long before the *captatores* grow restless, and, in the final numbered section of the text, one of Eumolpus's accomplices admonishes him that their luck is running out. The text then offers what must be an excerpt from Eumolpus's will that specifies under what conditions his heirs will be able to claim their share of the inheritance: they will have to eat his dead body in public before witnesses.[6] We all know, proclaims the will in a brilliant parody of sophistic ethnology, that there are peoples who conserve the custom of eating the remains of their dead relatives so that sometimes those who get sick before they die are accused of spoiling the meat.[7] Therefore, exhorts the testator, go ahead and eat my body with as good a will as you used to curse my spirit. At this point, greed seems to overwhelm the social stigma against cannibalism, and one of the obliging heirs steps forward to earn his portion. His name? Gorgias, a not so subtle tribute to the legacy of sophistic rhetoric, a legacy that Petronius found more than palatable. The last excerpt of the text cites some famous instances of cannibalism, presumably to whet the appetite of the *captatores*. Some of these examples reappear in Montaigne's essay on cannibals, such as the Saguntines, who, when besieged by Hannibal, ate human flesh, even though, Petronius reminds us, they didn't have an inheritance to look forward to.[8] These examples from Polycrates, Petronius, and others suggest that even such a universally reviled practice as cannibalism is not immune to praise. What then can be *illaudatus*?

One of the most interesting testimonies to the power of odious praise can be found in a very prominent work of vernacular prose from the late sixteenth century, *Les six livres de la République* by Jean Bodin. Book 4, chapter 7 of this masterpiece of political philosophy begins with an axiom: faction and sedition are bad for every kind of republic. If we are going to praise sedition, faction, and civil war, Bodin asks, what's next? Should we praise disease like the sophist Favorinus of Arles? Such perverse praise would confound good and evil, profit and loss, vice and virtue; in short, it would mix fire and water, heaven and earth.[9] Such a mixture is known as chaos, the original state of matter evoked in the opening lines of Ovid's *Metamorphoses*. Bodin's vision of chaos reveals the potency of odious praise, which threatens our sense of order and coherence. Odious praise can turn everything upside down. At the same time, it can highlight the uncomfortable proximity of *le bien* and *le mal*, as if to remind us of how arbitrary our moral values really are. No system of values is safe from odious praise.

If praise can be odious, so can neologism. So I will hasten to point out that I didn't make up the expression "odious praise." I found it in a sonnet by the French Renaissance lyric poet Joachim Du Bellay. In sonnet 143 of *Les Regrets et autres œuvres poëtiques* from 1558, the poet claims to choose encomium over satire. He would rather flatter than antagonize in verse, since even praise is often odious: "Veu que le loüer mesme est souvent odieux" (v. 14).[10] How can praise be odious? As we have seen, praise can be odious when it is a disguise for blame. It can also provoke hatred through envy. The odious potential of praise was already well recognized in antiquity, as Laurent Pernot reminds us in his recent primer on epideictic rhetoric, where he invokes the tradition of "figured speech," in which "the orator uses false pretenses to disguise his real intent, or speaks obliquely in order to get to his point indirectly."[11] Pernot quotes an interesting example from the beginning of Pliny the Younger's *Panegyric* of Emperor Trajan, where the panegyrist says that the risk he runs is not the danger of underpraising a conceited tyrant but rather the indiscretion of overpraising a modest and clement ruler. Trajan's panegyrist need not fear that when he speaks of *humanitas*, his audience will understand *superbia*, or when he speaks of *frugalitas*, they will think he means *luxuria*, or when he says *clementia*, they will hear *crudelitas*, and so forth (*Panegyricus* 3.4). This elaborate prologue suggests the possibility of a kind of code of ironic epideictic, where each virtue stands for its corresponding vice and praise has to excuse itself. Under the rubric of "the psychopathology of the encomium," Pernot marshals further examples that bring us closer to Du Bellay's vernacular usage. From Euripides, he retrieves two characteristic and, in some respects, aphoristic sentences: "for indeed to praise too much is hateful" and "when the good are praised, in some fashion they hate their praisers if they praise to excess."[12] Another example, and for the Renaissance a more familiar one, comes from Lucian's *How to Write History*, which warns inept encomiasts how little their efforts will profit them, for "those they praise hate them."[13] Thus, by the time Du Bellay wrote that praise is often odious, his claim, though paradoxical, was something of a commonplace.

I propose to revise this commonplace slightly and to focus not on vindictive or defamatory praise but on something more unsettling, something that is less personal and more institutional in its scope. In this study, "odious praise" is understood to encompass the uses of praise that challenge the constituent elements of collective identity, such as the ethical, cultural, and spiritual values shared by the members of a community. Understood in this admittedly broad sense, odious praise can be a tool of analysis and an antidote to all forms of chauvinism. If we reflect with Montaigne on how our cultural identity inhibits our critical faculties, we may come to appreciate the therapeutic effects of odious praise. In his essay on custom, Montaigne explains how custom invades conscience and makes us applaud our own conformity to society's values. "The laws of conscience, which we say are born of nature, are born of custom. Each man, holding in inward veneration the opinions and behavior approved and accepted around him, cannot break loose from them without remorse, or apply himself to them without self-satisfaction."[14] When we venerate the ambient values of our society, "the opinions and behavior approved and accepted around us," we affirm our collective identity, and this identity is what Montaigne calls later in the same essay a prejudice or "violent prejudice" (84). In its adversarial relationship to collective identity, odious praise can help to overcome this prejudice.

Before we investigate how praise can undermine the normative values of society, I suppose we ought to acknowledge the more conventional assumption that praise reinforces those values. This view achieved renewed prominence in an article coauthored by Chaïm Perelman and Lucie Olbrechts-Tyteca, which formed the nucleus of their frequently reedited treatise on argumentation known as *La nouvelle rhétorique*.[15] Here the authors insist that the epideictic genre of rhetoric deals with value judgments and seeks to reinforce adhesion to consensus values in society rather than simply to display the virtuosity of the orator.[16] They fear that Aristotle may not have grasped this dimension of epideictic, but Barbara Cassin dismisses this apprehension in her own discussion of how praise can create as well as conserve social values.[17] For the Renaissance, John O'Malley reminds us that "epideictic is 'dogmatic' oratory. That is to say, it assumes agreement on the point at issue, and its purpose is to arouse deeper appreciation for an accepted viewpoint."[18] Virginia Cox sums up a venerable and authoritative tradition when she contrasts epideictic with the other two genres: "Demonstrative oratory, by contrast—something of a poor relation in the ancient world, though of signal importance in the less politicized rhetoric of later times—is exercised in celebratory contexts such as funerals and the opening of games and serves the end rather of ritually enforcing collective values than of swaying an audience to a practical decision."[19] Though we may doubt whether rhetoric has grown less politicized, this ritual enforcement of consensus values seems to be the task assigned to praise in Aristotle's *Rhetoric* and in the long tradition that it has sponsored in Western thought.

Book 1, chapter 9 of Aristotle's *Rhetoric* reviews the topics of praise and blame and offers a classification of the virtues that overlaps with their treatment in the *Nicomachean Ethics*.[20] At first glance, the topics of praise seem to be the same as the topics of ethics, making praise an instrument of ethical training. However, when in the course of his chapter Aristotle explains how the orator can best use these topics to his advantage, the discussion veers into the territory of the sophists and may even help us to theorize odious praise. Here Aristotle exploits the proximity of vice and virtue in order to teach us how to praise a weakness as a strength or conversely, to blame a strength as a weakness. For instance, we can call the angry man "straightforward" (ἁπλοῦν) and the arrogant "high-minded" (μεγαλοπρεπῆ), or the rash "courageous" and the spendthrift "liberal" (1367a32–b3). Quintilian summarizes this guide to euphemism as follows: "ut pro temerario fortem, prodigo liberalem, avaro parcum vocemus" (*Institutio oratoria* 3.7.25).[21] This may be precisely what Pliny has in mind at the outset of his *Panegyric* when he disavows such an abuse of language. Then Aristotle reminds the epideictic orator that he must consider the audience before whom he delivers his speech of praise, for different audiences have different value systems, such as the Scythians, the Spartans, and the philosophers (1367b7–11). The Renaissance commentator Johann Sturm immediately recognized the sophistic nature of Aristotle's argument in *Rhetoric* 1.9, and he has a keen commentary on Aristotle's examples of different audiences with radically different values: "He posits three types of people, and the first is the worst, namely the Scythians, for whom it was praiseworthy to kill their guests. The Spartans are the second type, because they respected war but allowed theft and didn't condemn it. And there is no race of men among whom something cannot be praised."[22] So Sturm derives from the Aristotelian-sophistic principle of the relativity of values the lesson that nothing is *illaudatus*: there is no conduct so deplorable that it cannot be praised somewhere. Conversely, whatever we praise to one audience may prove odious to another. Praise doesn't travel since values change from place to place. On the basis of this fairly conventional insight, we want to examine the tension between competing value systems within Renaissance culture and the role of epideictic in fomenting this tension. To do so, we first need to propose a schematic typology of Renaissance values.

Therefore, as an organizing principle, not a philosophical one, we will attempt briefly to classify those values that constitute the collective identity of Renaissance readers, writers, and critics of epideictic works. The classes within this classificatory scheme can correspond to different corporate identities within Renaissance culture such as humanists and scholastics. The first class in our classification, a classification intended as a gloss on our table of contents rather than as a new explanation of the European Renaissance, encompasses Platonic values. Plato's dialogues stage a confrontation between Socrates and the sophists, as the archetypes of the philosopher and the antiphilosopher. Socrates represents the positive value and the sophists the negative value. These values are so fully assimilated by the Renaissance that to praise the sophists or to blame Socrates can only be odious praise. Yet Socrates was condemned by his own contemporaries, not only in court but also in epideictic prose, and the lost *Accusation of Socrates* by the infamous Polycrates launched an enduring challenge to the politics of Platonic values. In the sixteenth century, Platonic values come under particularly corrosive scrutiny in the vernacular discourses of Sperone Speroni, who by turns attacks and defends both Socrates and his adversaries the sophists and even equates the two at times. We can discern some similar impulse in the Latin declamations of Girolamo Cardano, who claims that Socrates is overrated (and Nero underrated). Finally, Michel de Montaigne revisits the politics of praise in his essays on Socrates and Sparta and in his neo-Socratic challenge to humanism.

The next class of values is Ciceronian values, and these values are challenged and affirmed through the praise of language. Cicero engages in a sort of odious praise when he prefers Latin to Greek, as he does in his dialogue *De finibus* and elsewhere, and Renaissance writers extend the debate from the classical languages to the vernacular, as does Joachim Du Bellay in his *Deffence et Illustration de la Langue Françoyse*. In the Renaissance, linguistic identity is closely entwined with one of the most odious forms of epideixis, the praise and dispraise of Cicero, of which a spectacular but not unique example is Erasmus's *Dialogus Ciceronianus*. A more representative but less-known example is the *Apology of Plautus* by Francesco Florido, who appoints himself the adversary of all the slanderers of the Latin tongue. An analysis of Florido's work will allow us to synthesize many of the implications of odious praise.

A further class of values is defined by the challenge they pose to humanism, and we can call these values, for brevity's sake, church values. Church values feature prominently in Lorenzo Valla's *Praise of Thomas Aquinas*, Giovanni Pico della Mirandola's letter to Ermolao Barbaro in praise of the scholastics, and Erasmus's *Praise of Folly*. In the case of the latter, the correspondence between Erasmus and Maarten van Dorp testifies to the resentment aroused by the *Moria* among professional theologians as well as the struggle Erasmus waged to identify his work with encomium rather than satire. These works, ostensibly works of praise, call into question some of the fundamental practices of church and university, and the controversy they generated testifies to the power of odious praise to undermine any stable system of values.

Needless to say, there are some values that transcend these corporate identities, values such as belief in god and adherence to the true religion, and to challenge these values is a very serious proposition. Here again, Isocrates's *Busiris* can come in handy. Rather than fall into the same trap as Polycrates, Isocrates directs his praise not at Busiris but at the venerable institutions of Egypt, and especially its religion, for which Busiris may be thought to deserve some residual credit. The irony of this praise is that the Egyptians represented, in the eyes of Isocrates's audience, the very paragons of superstition. So we can suspect some ulterior motive when Isocrates insists that the Egyptians are most to be praised and admired for their piety and cult of the gods (11.24). Why should gross superstition earn the praise of fourth-century rationalists? Because those who manage religious matters so that punishments and rewards seem more swift and sure than they really are confer a great boon on mortal life.[23] In other words, religion is a hoax and it works. Isocrates's sixteenth-century editor and commentator Hieronymus Wolf was quick to see through this reasoning and to spot the praise of superstition and imposture. He's trying to show the usefulness of religion, Wolf remarks in his commentary on 11.24, but he ought to distinguish between religion and superstition. If you can't tell the difference, you're an atheist.[24] Isocrates clearly makes Wolf nervous, because in the interim between Isocrates's era and his own, this argument had been adapted by Polybius, Cicero, Machiavelli, and a host of others to the praise of Roman religion and to the functional analysis of religion *tout court*. Isocrates's encomium and the reaction it provoked in the Renaissance remind us that no praise is more odious than the praise of religion. We will have ample opportunity to confirm this impression in the prose writings of Niccolò Machiavelli, Jean Bodin, and Michel de Montaigne.

This last and most insidious form of praise is also the most useful. In the hands of creative thinkers, odious praise becomes a tool of social thought and a technique for analyzing social institutions. It helps us to understand social dynamics without being inhibited by traditional value judgments. Ever versatile, odious praise fulfills a range of functions from rhetorical exercise to social science.

CHAPTER 1
Platonic Values

POLYCRATES AND THE POLITICS OF EPIDEICTIC

At the outset of the *Busiris*, Isocrates tells his contemporary Polycrates, "I have read some of the speeches you wrote."[1] We haven't. All of the many works attributed to Polycrates by sources of varying fidelity have been lost, including the two for which Isocrates takes him to task, the *Defense of Busiris* and the *Accusation of Socrates*. These two orations, unread for centuries, if not millennia, are notorious examples of sophistic epideictic. This is the genre that Isocrates both cultivates and disdains in his *Helen*, which was born out of emulation of Gorgias's *Helen*. In the beginning of his speech, Isocrates derides those compositions that praise beggars and exiles or bumblebees and salt. Above all, he deplores the relative facility of such paradoxes compared to praise of what is actually praiseworthy: "The greatest indication of this is that no one wanting to praise bumblebees and salt has ever been at a loss for words, but those who have attempted to discuss subjects that are commonly agreed to be good or noble or excelling in *arete* have all fallen short of the possibilities when they have spoken."[2] The term rendered as "commonly agreed to be good" is ὁμολογουμένων ἀγαθῶν, where the participial form ὁμολογουμένος represents the idea of consensus or the community of values shared by the speaker and his audience. This term will prove to be a key notion in epideictic theory throughout antiquity and a source of some controversy in modern rhetorical theory as well.[3] Isocrates seems to believe that praise has an antagonistic relation to consensus. Objects of ethical consensus resist praise, while the ethically dubious, or worthless, seem to attract praise.

Isocrates is eager to exemplify this intuition with his own speech on Helen. Since the endoxa (τῶν δόξαν ἐχόντων) are so much more of a challenge than paradoxical topics, he will rise to the challenge and praise Helen, as Gorgias did before him: "Therefore, among those who have desired to say something well, I praise especially the man who has written about Helen because he has recalled a woman of such quality, who was greatly superior in her birth, beauty, and reputation."[4] Would Isocrates have us believe that Helen was the object of consensus, one of the ὁμολογουμένων ἀγαθῶν that require supreme talent to praise? Gorgias himself thought she was universally decried, and so he set out to defy consensus.[5] In effect Isocrates conducts his praise by appealing to an imaginary consensus in defiance of a real consensus. He does the same in the *Busiris* when he talks about Alcibiades. Isocrates kindly admonishes Polycrates for the many flaws in the *Accusation of Socrates*, including the handling of Alcibiades: "And when you attempted to accuse Socrates, you gave him Alcibiades as a student as if you wanted to make that a point of praise. No one had noticed that Alcibiades had been taught by Socrates, although all would agree that he was a really outstanding Greek."[6] That must have been news to Athenians, who considered Alcibiades a really outstanding traitor. Yet Isocrates uses the verb of consensus, ὁμολογήσειαν, to confirm Alcibiades's stainless reputation. Once again, Isocrates alleges a fictional consensus in order to signal that epideictic disrupts consensus.

What we can learn from Isocrates and his reception of Polycrates is that consensus is political: it is always subject to negotiation and revision, often through epideictic rhetoric. Aristotle establishes in his *Rhetoric* the principle that amplification, more than example or enthymeme, is best suited to epideictic because epideictic appeals to consensus and therefore does not need to prove but only to magnify and adorn its subject matter (1368a26–29). The term he uses to designate the subjects of epideictic is τὰς πράξεις ὁμολογουμένας, or "actions that are agreed upon,"[7] perhaps recalling Isocrates's ὁμολογουμένων ἀγαθῶν. Yet Aristotle himself, especially in his discussion of enthymeme at the end of book 2, offers numerous examples of epideictic speeches that defy consensus, including some by Polycrates. Aristotle is our authority for Polycrates's authorship of a *Praise of Mice* and a *Praise of Thrasybulus*, the Athenian statesman and leader of the democratic faction that overthrew the Thirty Tyrants. In other words, Thrasybulus is a figure of civil war, not consensus, and his praise appeals to partisan spirit rather than to a community of values. Similarly, the *Accusation of Socrates* is likely to have taken a partisan stand and weakened any consensus about Socrates. Polycrates and his lost library raise the question of the relation between epideictic and politics: what are the politics of epideictic? Can a sophist be a democrat or just a sophist? Niall Livingstone dismisses the possibility "that the *Accusation of Socrates* was a serious political or philosophical document" because sophistic epideixis is a game.[8] By contrast, Michael Stokes suggests that Polycrates actually politicized the trial of Socrates by making Socrates guilty by association with Alcibiades, the traitor to Athenian democracy.[9] The pivotal figure for the politics of epideictic is thus Socrates, and the pivotal event his trial and condemnation.

In some respects, Socrates is the ultimate object of consensus. The whole history of philosophy is a tribute to Socrates. Yet the Athenians put him on trial, and his trial has provoked a long-lasting debate. There must be two sides to the question of Socrates, even if the rhetorical tradition has been loath to exploit the duality. We know that Polycrates spoke against Socrates and Plato spoke for him, and Libanius wrote a new apology in late antiquity as a sort of schoolroom exercise, but it wasn't until the Renaissance that Socrates realized his full epideictic potential, especially in the writings of Sperone Speroni, Girolamo Cardano, and Michel de Montaigne. It is this corpus that we will examine in this chapter, after pausing to take a leisurely tour through Plato's *Apology*. One of the key points of contention in Plato's portrayal of Socrates is the figure of the teacher, the σοφιστής, who teaches others how to speak. The trial of Socrates, as replayed through the centuries, is a trial of rhetoric, a trial of teaching, and a trial of speech.

THE TRIAL OF SOCRATES

Plato portrays Socrates in dialogue with most of the figures recognized by modern historiography as sophists, including Thrasymachus, Prodicus, Protagoras, Gorgias, Polus, Hippias, Euthydemus, Critias, and even Callicles (who may be Plato's invention), and Socrates offers his critical assessment of additional sophists including Evenus of Paros and Theodorus of Byzantium. Socrates's intermittent cordiality to his sophistic interlocutors cannot mask what Gisela Striker terms "Plato's devastating campaign to ruin their reputation."[10] Throughout his dialogues, Plato establishes a rigorous distinction between the sophist and the philosopher, restricting the traditionally wide semantic range of the Greek noun σοφιστής, encompassing poets, musicians, rhapsodes, diviners, seers, statesmen, religious leaders, and mythical figures,[11] to a narrow, pejorative meaning of antiphilosopher.

The dichotomy of sophist and philosopher receives its fullest theoretical expression in the dialogue *The Sophist*, while the early, Socratic dialogues give dramatic expression to this paradigmatic opposition. To appreciate this confrontation of philosophy and sophistic, we turn to a dialogue that is in fact a monologue, the *Apology of Socrates*, which is our leading source for the trial of Socrates in 399 BCE.

Socrates begins by assuring his audience of jurors that he has not learned rhetoric and will therefore, unlike his accusers, tell the truth. The dichotomy between truth and rhetoric will prove essential to the diffusion of Platonic values in later epochs. Apparently Socrates's accusers had warned the jury to beware of Socrates's command of rhetoric, calling him skilled at speaking, δεινὸς λέγειν (17b1), a charge that he indignantly repels. Plato's readers may have recognized in this phrase an echo of Sophocles's *Oedipus Rex*, where Oedipus calls Creon the same epithet, δεινὸς λέγειν, with a nuance of blame or irony.[12] In classical usage δεινός was often paired with σοφιστής, so that when Socrates disavows δεινότης, he also rejects sophistic. He promises the jury the whole truth without any fine speeches or well-ordered words and phrases. Instead he will merely say whatever comes into his head without any premeditation and without a written text that carries, for Plato, the stigma of falsehood.[13] Montaigne strikes the same Socratic pose in his essay on friendship, where he asks, what are his essays but haphazard compilations, "having no order, sequence, or proportion other than accidental" (135)?[14] Socrates assures the jury that they will hear from him things spoken by chance, εἰκῇ λεγόμενα (17c2), and this may remind us of the *Panathenaicus*, where Isocrates admits that he may sound like someone speaking εἰκῇ and off the top of his head (12.24). I retrieve this reference from Erasmus's *Adages*, where he explains the saying "to say whatever is on the tip of your tongue" or *Quicquid in linguam venerit* (ASD II-1:546). This is how Folly claims to speak at the beginning of the *Praise of Folly*, citing the adages.[15] So Socrates initiates the Platonic tradition of antirhetoric by using a topos of the unreliable orator in order to ingratiate himself with his audience.

Socrates then reformulates the legal charges against him in order to respond to the literary stereotype that had developed in Athens of Socrates the natural philosopher and clever speaker who teaches others what they should not learn. Above all, Socrates is eager to repudiate the charge of teaching, παιδεύειν (19d9), which he interprets to mean teaching for money. Not that he has anything against teachers, he adds rather gratuitously, such as Gorgias and Prodicus and Hippias. These are some of the leading sophists who came to Athens to make money from teaching, and especially from teaching ambitious youth how to speak effectively in public. Socrates is eager to segregate himself from professional teachers, who are tainted by their mercenary role and their instrumentalization of language. If he doesn't teach, it is natural for the jury to inquire about his occupation, his πρᾶγμα (20c5). He explains that since the oracle at Delphi declared him to be the wisest man, he felt it his sacred duty to undertake an investigation or ζήτησιν (21b8) and to examine his fellow citizens to see if he couldn't find anyone wiser than himself. Through aggressive interrogation, he wasn't able to find a wise man, but he annoyed just about everyone in Athens. It is this kind of civic harassment under the guise of piety that he construes as the philosophical life (28e5) and that he opposes to teaching, since he doesn't get paid. Though he goes around badgering his fellow Athenians, Socrates insists that he has always followed the guidance of his divine sign and stayed out of politics and public affairs (31c–d). Philosophy is apolitical and free of the taint of ambition and wage earning. These values will translate only imperfectly to Renaissance society, as we will see in Montaigne's essays.

Socrates does review the few highlights of his public career, which are meant to confirm his independence and inaptitude for public life. Naturally, he passes over his association with Alcibiades and Critias in discreet silence, but he does betray a clear anxiety over this compromising association when he insists, "I have never been anyone's teacher" (33a5). We know from Isocrates's *Busiris* that Polycrates reminded the Athenians that Alcibiades had been Socrates's student, and Xenophon answered this claim explicitly in the *Memorabilia* (1.2.24–26). Plato's Socrates actually concedes half the point when he says that he is not responsible for how his followers behave since he is not their teacher (33b4–6). Teaching is obviously a kind of guilt that stalks Socrates in court, and this is why Plato is so keen to portray Socrates in his other dialogues as the opponent of famous teachers, especially those who impart skills that confer social mobility, as does the skill of public speaking in a democratic society. Philosophy is meant to serve social stasis, while rhetoric is supposed to be more dynamic and more disruptive. Socrates wraps up his defense by appealing to those like Plato, whom he is supposed to have corrupted but who stand for him not against him. Finally, before the sentence and the verdict, he reminds the jury that he is too good to plead for mercy with anyone. Then, once the jury returns its verdict, there is a second phase to determine the penalty. The accuser Meletus proposes the death penalty, while Socrates proposes a sort of state pension as his reward for annoying everyone, before he finally offers to let his friends pay a fine for him, since it's not his money anyway. The jury is not impressed (and it must be said that ancient Athenian jurors were not as gullible as modern historians of philosophy), and they opt for the death penalty. After he is found guilty and sentenced to death, Socrates delivers a final address where he praises death and commends the jury for doing what is best for him, even if they did not mean to do so.

The praise of death at the end of the *Apology* is the properly epideictic or encomiastic section of a speech belonging to what is otherwise the forensic genre of apology. In his *Helen*, Isocrates criticizes Gorgias for confusing encomium with apology. Here is the passage immediately following the paradox that paradoxical encomium is easier than unparadoxical encomium:

> Therefore, among those who have desired to say something well, I praise especially the man who has written about Helen because he has recalled a woman of such quality, who was greatly superior in her birth, beauty, and reputation. However, a small point escaped him. He says that he has written an encomium about her, but he has actually spoken a defense (*apologia*) for what she did. His argument is not drawn from the same forms (*ideai*) nor is it about the same subject matter as an encomium. It is entirely the opposite. It is fitting to make a defense for those who have been accused of injustice, but one praises those who excel in some good.[16]

If one praises the good, that depends very much on what one's audience considers good. Socrates praises death to those who fear death, and his speech challenges their values while making Platonism more congenial to Christianity, which pretends to denigrate this life in favor of the next. Socrates is convinced that death will be good for him since throughout his trial his δαίμων or divine sign never discouraged him from goading the jury into convicting him and sentencing him to death. He reasons as follows: either death is a complete void such as eternal sleep, or the dead go to Hades, where the judges are fairer than in Athens. Either way, death is happier than life. Socrates is particularly attracted to the idea of spending eternity with the shades of famous dead men, foreshadowing modern celebrity culture. Best of all, he wouldn't even have to interrupt his career: "I could spend my time testing and examining people there, as I do here, as to who among them is wise, and who thinks he is, but is not" (41b5–7).[17] Under this scenario, it wouldn't be long before Socrates was kicked out of heaven, too, like *Julius exclusus e coelo*, but that's another dialogue. In closing, Socrates assures the jury that death cannot harm a good man (41d1), implying that the praise of death is simply the praise of what ought to be the consensus value of the good or τὸ ἀγαθόν. Yet his pursuit of the good has brought him to the brink of death, where few are eager to join him. The *Apology of Socrates* is a paradoxical encomium because its values are not persuasive: they are more easily admired than shared.

The *Apology* has had numerous apologists, but so have its targets: rhetoric and sophistic. Quintilian set himself the unenviable task of apologizing for both sides of the opposition. In book 2, chapter 15 of the *Institutio oratoria*, Quintilian asks, "what is rhetoric?" and he strives to neutralize the pejorative definitions offered by Plato before posing his own definition of rhetoric as "bene dicendi scientia" (2.15.38). He is particularly keen to cross-examine the *Gorgias* in order to show that the witness is actually testifying for rhetoric and not against it. Through selective citation, he manages to show that Plato viewed rhetoric as compatible with justice. "Otherwise," Quintilian remarks, "would he have written the Apology of Socrates and the praise of those who fell for their country? For those are certainly the works of an orator" (2.15.29).[18] The second work he has in mind is probably the funeral oration that Socrates improvises in the *Menexenus*. Quintilian's argument is clever, if primitive: the *Apology* is an oration, Plato wrote it, so he must have been in favor of oratory. Rather than reject Platonic values, Quintilian seeks to annex them to his own cause by insisting that Plato, contrary to appearances, endorses rhetoric simply by using rhetoric, often to denounce rhetoric. When he poses his next question, is rhetoric useful, he allows that it has been very useful for those who use the powers of speech to denounce speech making.[19] It is generally agreed that, though he names no names, Quintilian is thinking of Plato and especially of the *Gorgias*, which he has been at such pains to read against the grain in the previous chapter.[20] Quintilian represents no doubt a minor episode in the reception of Plato, but he does help guide to some extent the ambivalent response of Renaissance humanism to the legacy of Socrates.

A more important figure in the reception of Plato and Platonic values, perhaps the most important figure, is Aristotle. Aristotle shows himself most faithful to the spirit of Platonism in his treatment of sophistic in the *Sophistic Refutations* or *De sophisticis elenchis*. Aristotle begins his *Sophistic Refutations* by explaining that the title designates refutations that are apparent but not real, as if "sophistic" were a synonym for "false." Patiently, he explains that in the case of syllogisms and refutations, some are real and some are only apparent. Moreover, there are some people who prefer to appear wise rather than to be wise without appearing so. Here he adds a parenthetical definition of sophistic that would exert a powerful and enduring influence through its didactic concision: sophistic is a form of wisdom that is apparent but not real, and the sophist is a merchant, χρηματιστής, of apparent wisdom but not real wisdom.[21] The term χρηματιστής echoes a series of epithets that Plato uses in *The Sophist* to discredit the mercenary aims of the sophist: the sophist is a paid hunter, ἔμμισθος θηρευτής, a merchant, ἔμπορός, a retailer, κάπηλος, and a seller of his own goods, αὐτοπώλης (231D). Socrates in the *Protagoras* similarly describes the sophist as an ἔμπορός and κάπηλος (313d1). Following on these precedents, Aristotle helps to establish the indelible stereotype of the sophist as a mercenary impostor. He also invited a clever rejoinder in late antiquity from Flavius Philostratus of Lemnos, whose *Lives of the Sophists* from the early third century CE strive to rehabilitate the languishing fortunes of the sophists. Philostratus obviously has Aristotle's invidious distinction between real and apparent wisdom in mind in the introduction to his *Lives*, where he proposes a very peculiar classification of all sophists into three categories: ancient sophistic, second sophistic, and pseudo-sophistic, comprising well-spoken philosophers. This latter group, Philostratus explains, were not really sophists but appeared to be so: οὐκ ὄντες σοφισταί, δοκοῦντες δέ.[22] This is a neat reversal not only of Aristotle's phrase but also of his values, for now sophistic is genuine while philosophy is the impostor.[23] Those figures like Philostratus who are most sympathetic to the sophists and most skeptical of Platonic values are probably the least influential in the history of philosophy, but their point of view opens up some interesting possibilities for Renaissance rhetoric.

THE SOPHISTIC RENAISSANCE: SPERONE SPERONI AND GIROLAMO CARDANO

In the *Noctes Atticae* Aulus Gellius devotes a chapter of book 17 to the *infames materias* or unpraiseworthy subjects praised by sophists like Favorinus of Arles, a great favorite of Gellius. His examples are the praise of Thersites and the praise of the quartan fever, which returns every four days. This is the same epideictic tradition that Isocrates decries in his speech on Helen of Troy, but Gellius is less disdainful than Isocrates of those who exercise their wits by praising something that is generally devalued. Naturally,

Socrates is not counted as an *infamis materia*. Between Polycrates, the older contemporary of Isocrates, and Libanius, the contemporary of Emperor Julian who wrote a much belated refutation of the *Accusation of Socrates*, Socrates doesn't seem to have been of much interest to epideictic rhetoric. In this respect he was like Hercules: when a sophist proposed to deliver an encomium of Hercules before the Spartan king Antalcidas, the latter asked, "who blames him?"[24] Socrates must have seemed to be equally unsuited to praise or blame. This situation changed somewhat in the European Renaissance with the revival of sophistic epideictic. It was the sixteenth-century Italian humanist Sperone Speroni, taking his cue from the rhetorical reception of Plato in Quintilian, who discovered how to speak on both sides of the question of Socrates. Using the resources of sophistic rhetoric, Speroni reexamines and at times ridicules the values that Socrates represents in the philosophical tradition. Moreover, Speroni is the only author, up to now, to have proposed a poetics of odious praise. Speroni is best known to posterity for his literary dialogues published in Florence in 1542, especially the *Dialogo delle lingue*, which was imitated by Du Bellay in his *Deffence*, but the texts that interest us here are three of his numerous discourses, composed at uncertain dates and published posthumously: the discourses on encomiasts, against Socrates, and in defense of the sophists.[25]

We begin with the *Discorso dei lodatori*, which is an epideictic oration written against epideictic orators. What Speroni does here, essentially, is to update Isocrates's *Busiris* and to portray Renaissance Italian orators as so many heirs to Polycrates, who put themselves and their profession to shame. Unlike Isocrates, the speaker of the *Discorso* seems to include himself in his opprobrium, so we don't know what to make of his indignation. He starts out deploring that so many speakers praise vile and valueless things and many others commend things that are by nature odious so that their blame (both of the speakers and of their topics) shines out like the light of the sun.[26] And they do this, as far as Speroni can see, uniquely to show off the omnipotence of their wit and so they may seem superhuman, not understanding that in doing so, these *lodatori* blame themselves since merely speaking of such things, not to mention praising them, is a shame to whoever does so. This is the formula for odious praise, no longer the exclusive province of Busiris; the more we praise, the more we blame, creating a hopeless confusion of values. There is another class of *lodatori*, only slightly less vain than the first, who, by virtue of their lengthy panegyrics, only succeed in shaming those whom they think to honor. Once again, their praise turns to blame: "La qual cosa, se ben si stima, non è lodare; piuttosto è una maniera di vituperio di chi si crede che se ne debba onorare."[27] All these encomiasts are enrolled in the ranks of the sophists, who, since they are more interested in appearance than reality, are reputed to be the mere shadows of men. The notion that sophists "attendono anzi a parere che ad essere"[28] is a direct allusion to Aristotle's *Sophistic refutations*. Speroni reminds us that these sophists are the ones whom the great Plato in the person of Socrates scorned and rejected in his dialogues and against whom he warned his fellow citizens. Nowadays there remain some descendants of the ancient sophists, mere shadows of a shadow, and these are the ones he has been speaking of in his discourse. The *Discorso* then breaks off with a fairly incoherent phrase that seems to implicate the author himself. If these modern sophists only blame the way they praise, and the same orator with the same artifice accuses the same person he excuses, then blessed is he and worthy of much praise. Does he mean that whoever is blamed deserves praise, the way the subjects of odious praise really deserve blame? Moreover, the clause "e quale accusa tale egli soglia iscusare" applies to Speroni's treatment of Socrates, whom he praises here as "quel buon Socrate"[29] and blames elsewhere. So perhaps the honorific "il gran Platone" is actually vituperative. Every praise is poisoned. Speroni, more than any other modern author, enters fully into the spirit of ancient sophistic.

Among the *trattatelli* collected in volume 5 of the posthumous edition of Speroni's works are the brief speeches against Socrates and in defense of the sophists. The *Contra Socrate* begins by recalling the classical tradition that Socrates converted from natural philosophy to moral philosophy, a tradition epitomized by Cicero's claim in the *Tusculan Disputations* that it was Socrates who first brought philosophy down to earth.[30] This is in fact not the Platonic tradition of Socrates, as Speroni misinforms us, but is more in keeping with the Latin commonplace tradition, where Socrates is supposed to have said, "Quae supra nos, nihil ad nos" or what is above us is nothing to us.[31] In any event, Speroni agrees that Socrates brought philosophy down to earth, but he wishes he hadn't. It was a mistake. This is because there are two kinds of virtue: civic virtue and natural virtue. Civic virtue is merely the shadow of true virtue (just as we learned that the sophists were the shadows of men and their modern heirs the shadows of a shadow), for in civic terms, what is virtue in one place is vice elsewhere since the laws that define civic virtue vary from place to place. Natural virtue, by contrast, is the same everywhere and does not vary according to civic custom. So Socrates's mistake was to propagate a sort of moral relativism by adhering to civil virtue, not natural virtue, as we see in the *Crito*, where he prefers to die rather than to break the law (by escaping from prison while awaiting execution, as Crito exhorts him). Of course, moral relativism or the relativity of moral values is the great teaching or the great heresy of sophistic. So it appears that Socrates is to blame in so far as he's just another sophist. Now, if Socrates had considered virtue in the absolute sense, "as he appears to do when he speaks against the sophists,"[32] he would never have turned his back on natural philosophy and the inquiry into natural causes, which are necessary for natural virtue. Natural virtue, for Speroni, consists in the exercise of reason and the intellect, which entails self-knowledge according to the Delphic injunction *nosce teipsum*, which was supposed to be Socrates's specialty since, as he explains in the *Apology*, the oracle chose him as the wisest man because at least he knew that he was ignorant. The problem is that Socrates is inconsistent, and so he does not know himself. He is, by turns, all civil and legal or all metaphysical and abstract. He can't decide whether he's a sophist or an antisophist. "And this," in summation, "is what we can say against Socrates for the sophists."[33] But now Speroni is contradicting himself. He isn't speaking for the sophists; he's attacking Socrates for having turned from natural science to social science just like a sophist. Speroni puts his finger on the key attribute of odious praise when he says of Socrates, in an uncharacteristic departure from the vernacular, "non constaret sibi ipsi."[34] Odious praise is inherently unstable since it is constantly shifting and undermining its own position.

This feature becomes even more conspicuous in the last two sentences of the text, where Speroni unexpectedly reopens the trial of Socrates. He says that the judges may have acted unjustly since they put Socrates to death for the wrong reason. Apparently they should have put him to death not for impiety or corruption of youth or any civic reason, but for forsaking natural philosophy and metaphysics, or for being inconsistent, or for betraying the oracle. Or simply for not breaking out of prison when Crito told him to (they should have seen that coming). This is a grotesque parody of Platonism: "Death to Socrates but for Platonic reasons." It seems that Speroni is determined to outrage everyone. He has truly realized the potential of odious praise.

The last text by Speroni that we will discuss is his little treatise written ostensibly *In Defense of the Sophists*. Speroni defends the sophists by asserting that their adversary, Plato, was a greater sophist than any of them. This opening reminds me of Quintilian, who complains that Plato uses rhetoric against rhetoric. Both authors, Speroni and Quintilian, think that Plato can be read as an epideictic orator who disguises praise as blame. The first step in the defense is to define the sophist in relation to the wise man or *sapiens*, which we may recall is one of the opening moves of Folly in the *Praise of Folly*. There Folly announces that she is pleased to play the sophist, not the modern kind but one of the ancients who, to avoid the "infamous appellation of wise men," preferred to be called sophists.[35] This is the kind of insolent reversal of values that Speroni seems to admire. So he says that the sophist is not the wise man but rather resembles and imitates him as the portrait does the person portrayed. So far the sophist seems clearly inferior to the *sapiens*. Then he says that the sophist is to the wise philosopher as the good citizen is to the good man, perhaps because the good citizen (unlike Socrates) obeys civic conventions rather than some abstract notion of right. Then he adds that everything that Plato says of the sophist in his dialogue *The Sophist* is also true of the good citizen and indeed of human life and human existence. Now Speroni has endowed the sophist with genuine anthropological value as a model of the human condition. Indulging his own sophism, he adds that among Socrates's interlocutors there were good sophists and bad sophists, and Gorgias was a good sophist because of his use of sophistic rhetoric. Gorgias used rhetoric to get ahead in life and not to define the abstract nature of things. The sophists draw a distinction between the useful and the honorable (we may think of Montaigne's "De l'utile et de l'honneste," III, 1) because the citizens also make this distinction, and this helps the sophists to teach civic life and to account for the different values honored in different places. There is nothing contemptible about that (though there was in the *Contra Socrate*). Now he explains that Plato disputed sophistically (i.e., fallaciously) against the sophists because he had Socrates ask his interlocutors about the nature and essence of things when they had no use for such knowledge. Maybe if Socrates had known a practical skill like oratory, he adds maliciously, he wouldn't have been put to death. Then he adds cunningly that even if the knowledge of virtue is one and not many (as Socrates argues in the *Protagoras*), its use is variable and plural. So the Platonic value of knowledge has to compete with the sophistic value of use and is found wanting in practice.

Speroni's conclusion is particularly slippery. Who is truly wise, he asks, if not the one who knows his own ignorance, as Socrates used to boast?[36] In that case the philosopher is inferior to the sophist, for the philosopher loves wisdom, which he cannot attain, just as the suitors loved Penelope (and were slaughtered for their trouble). The sophist, by contrast, knows perfectly well that he can't have wisdom and so he settles for the reputation of wisdom. Sophists teach us how to live in the real world, like doctors, who cure us but don't restore us to perfect health or confer immortality. The medical analogy was a notorious favorite of Plato. Finally, we are reminded that Aristotle's *Poetics* defines the tragic hero as a mean between extremes, and we are to understand that the sophist is also a type of *mediocritas*. As an imitator, the sophist represents our alienation from being: "Sophist is our being, because it is not but looks like it is: it is not because the present being is an indivisible moment that rather was, and perhaps it will not be again, and only what is immortal truly is."[37] This is all very like the conclusion to the "Apologie de Raymond Sebond" (II, 12), "We have no communication with being,"[38] which Montaigne takes from Plutarch. Being is the attribute of divinity, while pretending is the lot of humanity. This is disarming precisely because it does not strike us as ironic. The sophist is now the tragic archetype of human existence. We are all shadows like the sophist, and Speroni is the shadow of a shadow. With his defense of the sophists, he has pronounced a speech of self-defense, the kind that Socrates did not know how to make.

Speroni is such a gifted student of the sophists that he has made an object of odium into a figure of tragic dignity. He has hopelessly confused the Platonic scale of values. We can see a similar process at work in the neo-Latin compositions of Girolamo Cardano, who, like Speroni, had a lot of free time for epideixis. Cardano is by no means a forgotten author, but his properly epideictic orations are rather neglected in favor of his numerous other eccentricities, more easily assimilated to the history of philosophy.[39] Like a modern Favorinus, Cardano cultivated the epideictic genre of paradoxical encomium, composing orations in praise of Nero and of the gout, and in dispraise of Socrates. We will examine two of these: the *Encomium Neronis* of 1562 and the *De Socratis studio* of 1566, which were probably intended as companion pieces.[40] If the Spartan king Antalcidas put a stop to an encomium of Hercules with the question "Who blames him?," no one in the Renaissance would have bothered to ask Cardano who blamed Nero. Nero was and remains a proverbial figure of the tyrant, as Cardano is pleased to acknowledge.[41] So his praise is necessarily an outrage to consensus values.[42] The *Praise of Nero* presents itself as a trial or courtroom ἀγών in which the speaker defends a widely vilified figure in the popular imagination, much like Gorgias in his *Praise of Helen*. As Nero's advocate, Cardano appeals the judgment of history and impugns the witnesses against Nero, primarily the Roman historians Tacitus and Suetonius. Moreover, the trial of Nero, he insists, is the trial of Rome, and it is easier to rule in favor of Nero than in favor of his accusers, the Romans, whose history is a mere catalogue of crimes. If Petrarch thought that all of history is the praise of Rome,[43] Cardano would reverse that judgment along with many others.[44] Within this rhetorical framework, Cardano also stages an ἀγών or competition between the two epideictic impulses of praise and blame, and that is the aspect of the text that interests me the most, although the text has many other claims to our attention, including its critique of Italian Renaissance social hierarchy.[45]

At the beginning of his encomium, Cardano cites what purports to be an apophthegm of the ancient Athenian philosopher Antisthenes (sometimes counted among the sophists). He reminds us of the golden saying or *aureum dictum Antisthenis*: "it is the same thing to be praised by the dishonest as to be blamed by the honest," and therefore it is the same to be blamed by the dishonest (as Nero was blamed by Tacitus or Suetonius) as to be praised by the honest, as he is now praised by Cardano.[46] So Nero's infamy is an honorable infamy, a praiseworthy blame. In fact, the classical tradition does not record this particular *mot doré*, but in his *Apophthegmata* Erasmus recounts the following anecdote about Antisthenes: when someone told him, "many praise you," he answered, "What did I do wrong?"[47] The source for this tradition is Plutarch's treatise Περὶ δυσωπίας, which Erasmus translated under the title *De vitiosa verecundia*, at the end of which Plutarch quotes a fragment from a lost work of Antisthenes in which Hercules teaches his sons never to be grateful to those who praise them.[48] Plutarch's commentary on this fragment asserts that whoever praises the bad or is blamed by the good must be a bad man.[49] This ingenuous claim assumes a clear distinction between the ethical categories of κακός and χρηστός, between good and bad, whereas the function of the paradoxical encomium is to demonstrate the instability and the reversibility of such fundamental value judgments. Any denunciation may just as well be an encomium, or whatever has been said against Nero can also be said for him.

One instance of this sophistic trick is the argument that Suetonius urges against Nero and that Cardano uses for him, namely that he never was willing or able to expand the frontiers of the Roman Empire. Obviously, Suetonius did not understand the duties of the best prince, which include maintaining the peace and prosperity of his realm and refraining from military adventures and wars of conquest. In effect, though Cardano does not put it in so many words, Nero respected the adage *Spartam nactus es* and lived up to the standards of Erasmian pacifism. It is at this point in his argument that Cardano invokes the name of Glaucon from Plato's *Republic*, saying that everyone knows the duties of the best prince even if there is no Glaucon or Polemarchos to confirm what he says.[50] The role of Glaucon in the *Republic* is to praise injustice so as to induce Socrates to praise justice. This is the role that Erasmus recognizes, in the dedicatory epistle to the *Praise of Folly*, as one of the founding models of the paradoxical encomium along with the praise of Busiris.[51] Glaucon and Socrates engage in an *agon* over justice just as Cardano challenges history or the historical record to an *agon* over Nero.

The remainder of the encomium unfolds as a sort of parody of Plutarch's parallel lives, where Cardano compares Nero and prefers him to a succession of Roman rulers such as Claudius, Titus, Tiberius, Julius Caesar, Vespasian, the Antonines, and Septimius Severus. This process culminates in a *syncrisis* of Nero and Cicero, which reveals Nero to be *Cicerone longe sapientior* or far wiser than Cicero.[52] In conclusion, Cardano observes that some malicious or misguided readers will say that he has only praised Nero in order to blame good men, like Cicero and the Roman historians.[53] In other words, he fears that his encomium will be understood as odious praise or praise meant to blame. This impression is due not to any bias on his part but rather to the fallacy of human judgment, which overestimates Cicero and underestimates Nero.[54] In this way, the speech concludes with the skeptical theme of the uncertainty or inadequacy of human judgment, which forms something of a refrain throughout. At one point the narrator exclaims, "Do you see these judgments? Do you see the errors of men?" and elsewhere, more plaintively, "O human judgment, O stupidity!"[55] In its skepticism toward human judgment, Cardano's encomium invites comparison with Montaigne's *Essays*, an invitation that I cannot refuse, and so I will quote from the essay entitled "De l'inconstance de nos actions," which is actually about the uncertainty of our judgments. When the great figures of the past, or the greatly reviled, behave virtuously under some circumstances and viciously under others, when they reveal now strength, now weakness, it is impossible to pass judgment on them. We can judge the action but not the actor: "the action is praiseworthy, not the man" (243).[56] This principle may clarify the meaning of Cardano's paradoxical encomium. Epideictic, which praises the man not the action, can only confirm the fallacy of human judgment.

Cardano further cultivates this genre in his dispraise of Socrates, entitled *De Socratis studio*. In this context, *studium* means devotion or favor, so Cardano will strive against the partisanship of the history of philosophy; he will contend with a widely prevailing cultural bias. Therefore, he declares *in exordio*, he has never run a greater risk of being contradicted and accused than he does now. Is he trying to kill Socrates all over again? Is he an impious ingrate? Worse yet, if he is persuasive and people agree with him, what hope will there be for the virtuous in the future? If mortals start to regard Socrates as the worst of men, overwhelmed by Cardano's irresistible eloquence, what's next: are they supposed to praise Nero?[57] This is a sly publicitary gesture toward the *Encomium Neronis* (published four years earlier with the same publisher), and it suggests that the two texts were meant as companion pieces. Referring to his speech as an *accusatio* or speech of prosecution, like Polycrates's *Accusation of Socrates*, he says that his intention is not as absurd or as useless as it may seem. Is he the only one to criticize Socrates? On the contrary, no wise or honest man has ever praised him.[58] In this way, Cardano acknowledges Socrates's long absence from the epideictic tradition, and he probably could not have known Speroni's earlier but unpublished *Contra Socrate*. Nevertheless, he takes the same point of departure as Speroni: Socrates diverted the course of philosophy from useful inquiry to the useless field of ethics and became, moreover, the enemy of all good disciplines.[59] Therefore, his accusation will serve as the vindication of learning and the liberal arts.

Cardano's first point is the completely gratuitous demonstration that lying is bad. Socrates denied the god's judgment that he was wise and always disclaimed wisdom. This was a lie, irony is no better than lying, and so on.[60] Next, he disparaged teaching and repeated the pernicious saying "Quae supra nos, nihil ad nos."[61] Socrates himself was a bad teacher since, having no formal education, he couldn't teach by example, and he discouraged others from learning what he didn't know, merely out of envy.[62] And yet he was hailed as the wisest of all men, and there are more people who would rather hear Christ defamed than Socrates, which merely reminds us of the deplorable fallacy of human judgment.[63] Now we are back in the atmosphere of the *Encomium Neronis*. In effect, odious praise is a powerful antidote to dogmatism. If we can't know whether to admire Socrates or abhor Nero, what can we know with certainty? What certain knowledge can withstand the corrosive impact of paradoxical reasoning? This may have been one of the most potent attractions of epideictic rhetoric in late sixteenth-century Europe. Apart from this skeptical insight, the text relies on a crushing accumulation of argument that is tiresome even in the swiftest summary. Cardano does put pressure on the weak point of the *Apology*, where Socrates claims never to have been anyone's teacher. The *De Socratis studio* marshals a long list of Socrates's disciples, culminating in the infamous Alcibiades, the name so carefully suppressed by Plato.[64] Finally, he identifies the lineage of Socrates, which leads, oddly, to Favorinus, the champion of paradox in Gellius and a sophist.[65] Was he thinking of Speroni's argument that Socrates is really a sophist? Actually the two authors are quite dissimilar: where Speroni sharpens the point, Cardano belabors it.

SOCRATES AND LYRIC LOVE POETRY

If Socrates was long absent from the epideictic tradition, his name is even more scarce in the lyric tradition. Yet there is one, perhaps justly, neglected revision of the trial of Socrates in a vernacular dialogue associated with Renaissance love poetry, Louise Labé's *Débat de folie et d'amour*, published with her poetic works in 1555 in Lyon.[66] This debate takes the form of a trial where Folly is accused of offending Love, and two Olympian orators, Apollo and Mercury, pronounce two forensic speeches, which are in fact epideictic orations. Apollo speaks in praise of Love, while Mercury reworks Erasmus's *Praise of Folly* to suit the author's parodic purposes. As critics have noticed, Labé's *Débat* takes inspiration from the traditions of Neoplatonism, Lucianism, and Erasmianism (which rather encompasses Lucianism, since Erasmus was one of the principal translators of Lucian's dialogues),[67] but in their haste they have missed some of the tell-tale traces of Plato's *Apology*. The work is divided into five discourses, of which the last and longest one stages the trial as a rhetorical *agon*, not so much between two rival conceptions of love as between two varieties of epideixis. In Isocratean terms, Apollo has the harder task, praising what others celebrate, while Mercury plays the sophist by neutralizing the invidious reputation of folly (and enhancing the invidious reputation of rhetoric). The first speaker, Apollo, is both prosecutor and encomiast, and similarly, Mercury's counterspeech is an apology as well as an encomium of Folly. Neither seems to respect the clear distinction between forensic and epideictic rhetoric that Isocrates urges against Gorgias. To defend his client, Mercury insists that whereas his opponent is a renowned student of oratory, he will speak the plain truth without any art or ornament: "Apollo, who for so long has heard lawyers plead their cases in Rome, has surely learned from them how to argue to his own advantage. But Folly, since she is always so open, doesn't want me to hide a thing. Rather, she wants me to speak to you using only simple, uncontrived words and no flowery rhetoric" (97).[68] This prologue echoes Socrates's opening address to the jury and annexes to Folly the Platonic value of unadorned truth. By the same token, Labé recognizes the disavowal of rhetoric as a rhetorical ploy. Moreover, Mercury insists that his client has forbidden him to appeal to the emotions of the jury; there will be no parading of distraught children and relatives in court to arouse the compassion of the jury. "Folly has forbidden me to make her appear pathetic, or to beg you to forgive her if there was fault on her part. She's likewise forbidden me to weep, or to throw myself at your feet, or to implore you with endearing glances such as have pleased you at times when coming from her, or to bring in her family, children, or friends to move you to pity" (101).[69] This seems to be not merely a reminiscence but more like a translation of the passage from the end of the first phase of the trial of Socrates, where the defendant refuses to appeal to the mercy of the jury: "Very well, gentlemen of the jury. This, and maybe other similar things, is what I have to say in my defence. Perhaps one of you might be angry as he recalls that when he himself stood trial on a less dangerous charge, he begged and implored the jury with many tears, that he brought his children and many of his friends and family into court to arouse as much pity as he could, but that I do none of these things, even though I may seem to be running the ultimate risk" (34b6–c7).[70] Socrates adds that he makes no such plea lest he be suspected of fear of death, which would be unbecoming someone with his reputation for wisdom. Folly and Socrates both have the same sense of decorum.

Then Mercury turns to Erasmus's *Praise of Folly* to explain the advantages of folly and the disadvantages of wisdom. Show me a wise man next to a fool, he says, and you will see who is more highly regarded. The wise man is too cautious and solitary, but the fool rushes into danger and accomplishes great things and becomes the subject of encomium: "he'll be admired, acclaimed, prized, and followed by everyone" (105).[71] Erasmus's Moria had explained that only the fool, undeterred by fear or shame, can acquire the prudence conferred by experience, from which wise men shrink away timidly.[72] Mercury then proceeds to enumerate the *commoditez* or benefits conferred by his client, just as Moria had boasted of all the advantages she brings to gods and men alike: "quantis commoditatibus deos simul et homines adficiam" (ASD IV-3:80). In particular, marriage seems to be the beneficiary of Folly: "How would the world go on if she didn't prevent people from knowing ahead of time all the problems and pitfalls of marriage? She stops us from seeing them, and she hides them so that the world continues to repopulate itself in the usual way. How long would any marriage last, if the foolishness of men or women permitted its flaws to be seen?" (105).[73] Similarly, Moria asks how marriage could ever last if she didn't teach the spouses how to deceive themselves and each other, in keeping with adage 750, *Connivere* or to overlook things.[74] The many echoes of Erasmus, combined with the occasional gestures toward Plato's *Apology* in Labé's *Débat*, may alert us to an overlooked feature of Erasmus's most famous work, namely the role of Socrates. Moria nominates Socrates as the prime example of the uselessness of philosophers, for though he was recognized by the oracle as the only wise man, as he reminds us in the *Apology*, whatever he undertook to do in public was met with universal derision.[75] The modern editor Clarence Miller dismisses this as "mere sophistry," but that is precisely the point. Socrates exercises the talents of sophistic epideixis, at least in the Renaissance.

SOCRATISM, LACONISM, AND HUMANISM IN THE ESSAYS OF MICHEL DE MONTAIGNE

The essay is usually not regarded as an epideictic genre, but its inventor, Michel de Montaigne, used it for epideictic purposes, that is to say, for reevaluating the normative values of his own culture. The author of the *Essays* presents himself as the new and improved Socrates who revives the Socratic method in order to challenge the new teachers, the humanists, who reprise the role played by the sophists in classical antiquity.[76] These tendencies can be found sporadically throughout the *Essays*, but it is easier to grasp them in the context of a few individual essays. Therefore, the following section examines in detail the essays "Du pedantisme" (I, 25) and "De la phisionomie" (III, 12) while tapping into the longest essay, the "Apologie de Raymond Sebond" (II, 12), which acts as a sort of reservoir of Montaigne's thoughts. In these essays, Montaigne speaks in praise of Sparta, of Socrates, and of ignorance, especially the ignorance of rhetoric. Like Plato according to Quintilian, the author of the *Essays* uses the powers of speech against the art of speech.

Essay I, 25 is ostensibly about teachers or *pedantes*, who, Montaigne remarks with insincere dismay, are usually the butt of comedy. The whole essay seems like a long diatribe against professional teachers and their need for money, inspired by resentment toward the social mobility made possible by humanist education. Platonic prejudice is alive and well in the European Renaissance. Yet what makes the essay so compelling is Montaigne's simultaneous affinity for Platonic bias and aptitude for sophistic reasoning. If, in Speroni's terms, Plato, in comparison with the sophists, was "maggior sofista di loro,"[77] Montaigne proves himself an even greater sophist than Plato. He treats his subject like the praise of Busiris, and he ends in a crescendo of paradox that seems to make Turks of his reactionary compatriots. Already, eighty-five years ago, in a festschrift for Paul Laumonier, Paul Porteau proposed to read "Du pedantisme" as a classic declamation in the tradition of Erasmus and Henricus Cornelius Agrippa.[78] His insight seems to me quite sound, and moreover his conclusion stresses the continuity between Socrates and Montaigne, a point that deserves elaboration.[79] Montaigne begins his essay with comedy the way Socrates begins his apology with the oracle: "I was often annoyed in my childhood to see a teacher always the butt in Italian comedies."[80] Just as Socrates wants to know why the oracle named him the wisest man, Montaigne wants to know why pedants are the butt of comedy, and he offers several explanations that he then rejects in the course of a neo-Socratic inquiry or *zetesis*. Each of these false starts leads on a detour, such as the consideration of the ancient philosophers who were the butt of comedy in their own day. Of course, the archetype of the philosopher "mocked by the comic license of their times" (98) is Socrates in Aristophanes's *Clouds*, which Plato makes the basis of the first accusation to which he responds in the *Apology*. The difference is that if the ancient philosophers were sometimes the target of ridicule, that was because they were above the common standard, while the modern pedants "are despised as being beneath the common fashion" and totally useless to society (99). So it is clear that Socrates has nothing in common with the pedants, except for the fact that both are the butt of comedy, as Montaigne reminds us maliciously.

Eventually, Montaigne suggests that the stigma against pedants derives from the flaw in their pedagogy: they train the memory while neglecting more important faculties such as "the understanding and the conscience" (100). The teachers never assimilate their own lessons but pass them on undigested to their students, which incidentally is what the author admits to doing in a late addition to his essay: "It is wonderful how appropriately this folly fits my case. Isn't it doing the same thing, what I do in most of this composition? I go about cadging from books here and there the sayings that please me, not to keep them, for I have no storehouses, but to transport them into this one, in which, to tell the truth, they are no more mine than in their original place" (100). So teaching is like writing: it involves imitation of a model that may or may not be properly assimilated. In effect, the pedants have been training a generation of parrots (a generation to which the essayist may belong) who cannot speak for themselves. Their instruction may impart knowledge or *savoir*, but it cannot impart wisdom or *sagesse* (101; I, 25, 138). Here Montaigne adds a Greek quotation that Villey identifies as "a verse from Euripides found in Stobaeus,"[81] where no one else has ever found it. Known as fragment 905 of Euripides, the verse "μισῶ σοφιστήν, ὅστις οὐκ αὑτῷ σοφός"[82] seems to carry the burden of Montaigne's essay: "I hate the sophist or the teacher," but for the perverse reason that "he is not wise for his own sake." Though not in Stobaeus, the verse appears in several of Montaigne's favorite authors, including Plutarch and Cicero, but he may well have found it in Erasmus's *Adages*. Adage 520, *Nequicquam sapit, qui sibi non sapit*, puts together several Greek and Latin testimonies to the same dubious principle that one ought to be wise for oneself, a moral from which Erasmus seems to distance himself through his last citation, from Suetonius, which is clearly censorious of self-interest.[83] Montaigne follows Erasmus by grouping together several concordant testimonies, added to the Exemplaire de Bordeaux (101; I, 25, 138 C), but he doesn't share Erasmus's distaste for what is simply the praise of selfishness. This strange paean to greed is the first of many epideictic moments that make the reader increasingly uneasy.

Montaigne shows his hand more clearly when, on the same page of the Exemplaire de Bordeaux, he quotes from Plato's *Meno*. "These schoolmasters, as Plato says of their cousins the Sophists, are of all men those who promise to be the most useful to men, and who, alone of all men, not only do not improve what is committed to them, as does a carpenter or a mason, but make it worse, and take pay for having made it worse" (101–2). So the *pedantes* or humanist pedagogues are the successors to the sophists, their "cousins," and Montaigne is the new Plato (or the new Socrates). However, in the dialogue from which Montaigne quotes, Socrates does not disparage the sophists but rather defends them against Anytus, who would later be one of the accusers at his trial. He asks if Anytus really thinks that the sophists are, "alone of those who claim the knowledge to benefit one, so different from the others that they not only do not benefit what one entrusts to them but on the contrary corrupt it, even though they obviously expect to make money from the process?" (91c–d).[84] Socrates can't believe it, since Protagoras has been a sophist for forty years and his reputation is as high as ever. Anytus hates the sophists but admits that he has never met any, and so he is obviously prejudiced (as if Plato were making fun of his own position). The *Meno* is important for Montaigne because it raises the question of whether virtue can be taught. Socrates maintains that virtue is knowledge and so it should be taught, but it isn't. Virtue is not διδακτόν. He famously reverses himself in the *Protagoras*, where he seems to conclude that virtue is διδακτόν, but the Athenians don't know how to teach it. This alternative concerns the distinction between faculties that are innate and so cannot be taught and those that are acquired or learned. Montaigne will return to this dichotomy at the end of "Du pedantisme" when he talks about the type of pedagogy that teaches its lesson "so that learning might be not merely a knowledge in their soul, but its character and habit; not an acquisition but a natural possession" (105). In effect, Montaigne seems to be revising the *Meno* and its impossible idea of teaching something that is not teachable. Moreover, the distinction between innate and acquired faculties relates to the complaint that the pedants cannot "incorporate"[85] their knowledge and make it their own. Their unassimilated knowledge is a double-edged sword: "Learning is a dangerous sword that will hamper and hurt its master, if it is in a weak hand that does not know how to use it" (103). The figure of the sword or *gladius* was a topos of the antirhetorical tradition popularized in neo-Latin by the foremost translator of Plato, Marsilio Ficino. In his argument to the *Gorgias*, which he translated under the subtitle *De rhetorica*, Ficino summarizes Plato's hostility to rhetoric: Plato detests the orator who, like Gorgias, prefers probability and opinion to truth and justice, because eloquence without wisdom is like a sharp sword in the hands of a madman.[86] So, when Montaigne repeats the topos of the *glaive* or *gladius*, he applies to his pedants the accusation that, according to the neo-Latin tradition, Plato uses against the sophists, who arm their students with a double-edged sword. What seems to be at stake in "Du pedantisme" is the dangerous prestige of humanism or neosophistic.

Given the dangers of humanist pedagogy, the essayist is neither surprised nor dismayed that the French set such little store by the humanities or "les lettres": "And so it is not so great a wonder as they claim that our ancestors took no great account of letters" (103). There is quite a bibliography to this claim of national neglect of letters, but we can concentrate on one particular testimony to France's reputation as an uncultivated country, drawn from the correspondence of Desiderius Erasmus.[87] In 1531, Erasmus wrote from Freiburg to Jacques Toussain, who had just been named *lecteur royal* in Greek at the Collège Royal, the predecessor of the Collège de France. He assures Toussain that France is more fortunate to have appointed the *lecteurs royaux* than if it had conquered all of Italy (thus demoting arms in relation to letters). His advice to the new professor: you have met your Sparta, now make the most of it.[88] This of course is a paraphrase of adage

1401, *Spartam nactus es, hanc orna*, which has several interesting implications here. First of all, France is Sparta, a land without letters, an enemy of learning. Secondly, adage 1401 is an antiwar adage, exhorting monarchs to be content with their inheritance and not to seek to expand their territories through conquest. It puts arms beneath letters. It is clear that Montaigne's approval of his country's neglect of letters engages with the humanist declamatory theme of arms versus letters, and he seems determined to reverse the values of Renaissance humanism. This same neglect may also be the answer to the question of why pedants are so mistreated on the comic stage. Given their lack of cultural prestige in France, the humanities have become the exclusive province of the professionals, doctors, lawyers, theologians, and teachers, whose base nature makes them unsuited for knowledge. These professionals have discredited learning and study with the stigma of the profit motive: "Our studies in France have almost no other aim but profit, except for those whom nature brought into the world for offices more noble than lucrative and who devote themselves to letters for such a short time . . . hence there ordinarily remain none to involve themselves completely in study but people of humble means, who seek a living in it" (104). This argument ought to sound familiar by now. When a new cultural class arises to threaten the established social order through instruction in the arts of speech, its representatives are denounced as merchants and salesmen in order to demean them according to a traditional scale of values. Yet this denunciation is itself a performance and is best performed by those trained in the arts of speech. It takes a sophist to write "Du pedantisme."

Montaigne is adamant that his pedants are inferior by nature to the feudal nobility to which he so tenuously belongs.[89] Social class is natural, not conventional: the nobles are "those whom nature brought into the world for offices more noble than lucrative." This is a typical subject of dispute among humanists: is noble birth a gift of nature or fortune? The humanist is trained to argue on both sides of the question, and Montaigne already has argued the other side, earlier in his essay, when he cited the view of the ancient philosophers who dismissed illustrious birth as "this gift of fortune" (98). Now he needs nobility to be innate rather than acquired. But is there any system of education that can transmit innate advantages, and if not, why go to school? Though they may be better off not going to school, the French can learn something from the ancient Persians and Spartans, who seem to have developed the same system of education. Both societies inculcate their principles by works and examples; they emphasize deeds over words, and moral qualities over verbal skills, so that their lesson becomes innate rather than acquired. They teach virtue, which can't be taught, and we're back in the dilemma of the *Meno* and the *Protagoras*. This educational utopia is opposed to the genuine and successful program of humanism, and this preference for the imaginary over the real might be in itself a Platonic value. A related Platonic value is laconism or the admiration of Sparta and of the brevity of speech for which Sparta was notorious. Montaigne finds it remarkable that the Spartans were so completely contemptuous of learning, and he systematically opposes the Spartans to the Athenians through a series of antitheses that favor Sparta in style and content. This is Montaigne's essay of laconism:

> A Athenes on aprenoit à bien dire, et icy, à bien faire; là, à se desmeler d'un argument sophistique, et à rabattre l'imposture des mots captieusement entrelassez; icy, à se desmeler des appats de la volupté, et à rabatre d'un grand courage les menasses de la fortune et de la mort; ceux-là s'embesongnoient apres les parolles; ceux-cy, apres les choses; là, c'estoit une continuelle exercitation de la langue; icy, une continuelle exercitation de l'ame. (I, 25,143)

> At Athens they learned to speak well, here to do well; there to disentangle themselves from a sophistical argument and to overthrow the imposture of words captiously interlaced, here to disentangle themselves from the lures of sensual pleasure, and with great courage to overthrow the threats of fortune and death; those men busied themselves with words, these with things; there it was a continual exercise of the tongue, here a continual exercise of the soul. (105)

Montaigne situates himself "here" in Sparta, where he remains estranged from the Athenian values of persuasion and fluency. Athens is the ancient model of cultural preeminence, and it is the subject of its own epideictic genre, the *panathenaicus*. Montaigne's praise of Sparta is the counterspeech to the humanist/sophist genre of *panathenaicus*.[90]

The first version of I, 25, published in 1580, ended with a couple of Spartan sayings or *apophthegmata laconica* collected by Plutarch, but Montaigne added a new conclusion on the Exemplaire de Bordeaux sometime before his death in 1592. In a Platonic mood, he recalls the scene from the *Hippias Maior* where Socrates makes fun of the sophist Hippias of Elis, the itinerant teacher whose tour of the provinces ran aground in Sparta, where he didn't make a cent. Spartan indifference to sophistic pedagogy strikes Montaigne as a happy precedent for French indifference to humanist pedagogy and comforts him in his role as the laconist of the modern era. If the Spartans were the champions of invincible illiteracy in the ancient world, cheered on by Socrates, who will Montaigne celebrate among modern nations? Who else but the Turks, "a people equally trained to esteem arms and despise letters" (106). Once the villains of Etienne de La Boétie's *Discours de la servitude volontaire*, which Montaigne refused to publish when he became the author's literary executor, the Turks are now the heroes of his own paean to ignorance. As a parting shot, he remembers the French invasion of Italy under Charles VIII, the ultimate triumph of arms over letters. Montaigne has made the weaker argument stronger, he has found the counterspeech to Renaissance humanism, and, oddly enough, he has left his readers in the position of the Athenians, who had to learn how to disentangle themselves from a sophistic argument ("à se desmeler d'un argument sophistique").

Montaigne reprises the role of Socrates in an essay from the third book, "De la phisionomie" (III, 12), where he improvises a new version of Plato's *Apology*. Montaigne structures his argument around a series of medical metaphors involving drugs and disease deployed against the backdrop of the plague that ravaged his region of France while he was writing the essay in 1585. Montaigne is as wary as ever of "science," and he borrows a key image from Plato's *Protagoras* in order to evoke the hazards of learning. In the dialogue Hippocrates comes to Socrates to announce that Protagoras has arrived in Athens and to ask Socrates to introduce him to the sophist so that he can become his student. Socrates agrees to accompany Hippocrates after first warning him of the potential danger of Protagoras's wares, the teachings that are his merchandise. "When you buy food and drink from the merchant you can take each item back home from the store in its own container and before you ingest it into your body you can lay it all out and call in an expert for consultation. . . . But you cannot carry teachings (μαθήματα) away in a separate container. You put down your money and take the teaching away in your soul by having learned it, and off you go, either helped or injured" (314a3–b4).[91] Montaigne renders Plato's μαθήματα as "les sciences":

> Car au reste, ce que nous avons achetté nous l'emportons au logis en quelque vaisseau; et là avons loy d'en examiner la valeur, combien et à quelle heure nous en prendrons. Mais les sciences, nous

ne les pouvons d'arrivée mettre en autre vaisseau qu'en nostre ame: nous les avallons en les achetant, et sortons du marché ou infects desjà ou amendez. Il y en a qui ne font que nous empescher et charger au lieu de nourrir, et telles encore qui, sous tiltre de nous guerir, nous empoisonnent. (III, 12, 1039 C)

For with other things, what we have bought we carry home in some vessel, and there we have a chance to examine its value and how much we shall take of it and when. But learning we can at the outset put into no other vessel than our mind; we swallow it as we buy it, and leave the market place already either infected or improved. There is some of it that only hampers and burdens us instead of feeding us, and also some which, under color of curing us, poisons us. (794)

The last sentence, "Il y en a . . . ," is not a translation but rather Montaigne's invention. The drug that poisons instead of cures is the φάρμακον, an idea developed at greatest length not in Plato but in Derrida's *Pharmacie de Platon*, but it goes back to the earliest era of Greek prose and indeed back to one of the founders of epideictic, Gorgias, who compares the persuasive power of speech to the power of drugs.[92] For Montaigne, knowledge is the fatal drug, the remedy that is worse than the disease. But this is only the prologue to the more urgent theme that civil war is the true φάρμακον.

Early in the essay, Montaigne informs us that the lines we have been reading were written during a resurgence of civil war in his home region of le Périgord. Referring to the wars as "these epidemics," he declares, "our medicine carries infection" (796). The military measures taken to cure sedition only make it worse. More explicitly, he asks, "But is there any disease in a government so bad that it is worth combating with so deadly a drug?" (797). Civil war is the poison drug, the *pharmakon*.[93] It is at this point of the argument, on the Exemplaire de Bordeaux, that Montaigne appeals to Plato's seventh letter, which describes a civil war, or rather power struggle, in Syracuse during the reign of the tyrant Dionysius II. "Plato likewise does not consent to have the repose of his country violated in order to cure it and does not accept an improvement that costs the blood and ruin of the citizens" (797). In his letter, Plato explicitly condemns revolution: "The same principle will be followed by a wise man in his behavior towards his own state; if he thinks anything amiss with its government, he will speak out, provided that his words are not going to be wasted or to bring him to his death, but he will not attempt to change the constitution of his native land by force. When reformation cannot be achieved without the infliction of exile and death on some people, he will simply keep quiet and pray for the welfare of himself and his country" (331D).[94] These are the sentiments that made Montaigne a Platonist before he had ever heard of Plato (797). They also characterize Erasmus's advice to the Lutherans at the beginning of the Protestant Reformation. In effect, Montaigne enlists Plato as an authority against the Reformation, which is the ultimate *pharmakon* in his view.[95]

As a moderate, the author is suspect to both sides of the civil war, and he has become the subject of shadowy accusations or "mute suspicions" (799). Like Socrates, when accused, he refuses to justify himself and offers "an ironic and mocking confession" (799), which is a good description of the *Apology*. Deserted by his friends, he decides to be self-sufficient, "to entrust myself and my need to myself" (799), which has already been identified as the lesson of Socrates's life.[96] In this way, his troubles become "utiles inconveniens," a good example of oxymoron in the *Essays*.[97] The calamity has tested his endurance or "patience" (802; III, 12, 1047 B), a quality he shares with Socrates and the local peasants. On top of all these useful troubles, the plague chased him from his home, and as he wandered for six months with his family, his region became a theater of Stoic resignation, without the benefit of formal instruction. In fact the peasants who dig their own graves and jump in without a complaint are the students of nature who benefit from ignorance (802–3). If you don't know how to die, Montaigne says, don't worry about it; nature will teach you when the time comes (804). This casual attitude to death leads straight to Socrates. In one of the characteristic paradoxes of the Essays, Montaigne says that it's time to hold a school of stupidity: "tenons d'ores en avant escolle de bestise" (III, 12, 1052 B).[98] Socrates will be our teacher, and his *prolusio* is the *Apology* in the truncated, vernacular version that Montaigne now offers us as a model of natural rhetoric.[99] It is instructive to consider what Montaigne retains from the trial of Socrates. At first he excerpted only a brief passage from the main section of the speech, where Socrates explains why he pursues the philosophical life even in the face of death (28B–29B). He doesn't fear death because he only fears things he knows are bad, and no one knows death. His courage is a kind of skepticism. To this laconic excerpt Montaigne added on the Exemplaire de Bordeaux several further excerpts, thus spoiling the Spartan brevity of the 1588 version. Within the original excerpt he embeds a passage from the final section, where Socrates speculates about the advantages of death (40c4–41a6). This is the praise of death, which Montaigne uses in the service of skepticism. He adds at the end of the original excerpt the last sentence of the dialogue: only the gods know who is better off, Socrates or his jury. Then Montaigne returns to an earlier part of the dialogue, the ἀντιτίμησις or alternative penalty, where Socrates proposes as a punishment that he be awarded a state pension at the Prytaneum (36d1–37a1). Montaigne liked this for its outrageousness, and Socrates admits that the jury may find him arrogant. Then Montaigne goes further back in the dialogue, to the conclusion of the defense speech, where Socrates refuses to make the customary appeal to mercy and where he also makes a perfunctory profession of faith (34b6–35d8). Montaigne makes this profession more emphatic. His Socrates trusts entirely to the gods (and not to oratory): "Je m'y fie du tout" (III, 12, 1054 C). That is the trial of Socrates for Montaigne.

This Socrates seems to speak for skepticism, against convention, and finally for a sort of pious resignation to fate that makes him a good Christian.[100] Yet, when the essayist comments on his new Apology, he emphasizes the rhetorical dimension. This is a model speech, adorned with truth and naïveté rather than with the tawdry figures of rhetoric. Montaigne approves of Socrates for having delivered his own speech rather than accepting the written text that the orator Lysias had prepared for him. How could he have done otherwise: how could "his rich and powerful nature have committed his defense to art, and, in its loftiest test, renounced truth and sincerity, the ornaments of his speech, to bedeck itself with the make-up of the figures and fictions of a memorized oration?" (807).[101] All this is perfectly consistent with Platonic values: speech over writing, spontaneity over premeditation, truth over rhetoric. Moreover, Socrates's supreme verbal effort is now "son plus haut essay," as if to identify the genre of the essay with natural, unpremeditated self-expression. The problem is that Montaigne is not only the new Socrates; he is also the new Lysias. He has written a speech for Socrates. He is a *logographos*, like Plato's bitterest rival, Isocrates. He is confident that his discourse represents the pure and primitive impression of nature, which is not the same thing as being natural.[102] He has created an *effet de nature* as the impressionists would try an *effet de neige*. Montaigne has used rhetoric to get the better of rhetoric, and he is rather proud of himself. In his leisurely manner, he has also reevaluated war, death, and plague (especially death, which is underrated), but primarily he has confirmed Quintilian's point. You can't speak against rhetoric.

CHAPTER 2
Ciceronian Values

CICERO AND THE PRAISE OF LATIN

Angelo Poliziano, in the very first chapter of his *Miscellaneorum centuria prima*, proclaims himself the champion of the Latins against the hubris of the Greeks, personified by his old philosophy professor John Argyropoulos, who had the temerity to disparage Cicero in his lectures on Aristotle, which Poliziano attended in his student days. Upon mature reflection, Poliziano considers it his duty, and the duty of all who profess Latin, to defend the glory of Cicero, even at the implausible risk of their life, for it is by means of such glory that the Latins stand firm against the Greeks.[1] For Latin humanists, Cicero is the source of their identity and the best bulwark against competing traditions such as Hellenism. Cicero fulfills this role in part because he had, in his philosophical dialogues, claimed for himself the role of champion of the Latins against the cultural supremacy of the Greeks.

Cicero was the self-conscious founder of Latin philosophical prose, and in that capacity he defended the parity of the Greek and Latin languages. He begins the *De finibus*, his ethical treatise on the *summum bonum* addressed to M. Iunius Brutus, by anticipating a series of objections to his work from those who refuse to read philosophy as well as those who cultivate philosophy, but only in Greek. To the latter, who may have read some bad Greek rendered into worse Latin by amateur Epicureans, Cicero affirms that it is the merest affectation to reject good ideas in good prose just because they aren't written in Greek (*De finibus* 1.8). In fact, he can never sufficiently express his amazement at this insolent disdain for native culture or "hoc tam insolens domesticarum rerum fastidium" (1.10). As he has often said, the Latin language is not only not poor, as is commonly thought, but is in fact richer than Greek.[2] To call Latin "locupletiorem quam Graecam" is a self-conscious paradox in the Hellenistic Age and one that Cicero repeats later in the *De finibus*. At the outset of book 3, Cicero resorts to the same turn of phrase, "as I have often said," to defend the Latin language as a medium for philosophical prose: "Moreover, we have often declared, and this under some protest not from Greeks only but also from persons who would rather be considered Greeks than Romans, that in fullness of vocabulary we are not merely not surpassed by the Greeks but are actually their superiors."[3] Here, Cicero responds to a class of Roman snobs "who would rather be considered Greeks than Romans." His quarrel involves a sort of imported ethnocentrism, and in this regard his praise of Latin will resonate more deeply and more widely in the Renaissance than it ever could in antiquity. In the Renaissance, collective identity will be determined by Ciceronian values and especially by the value assigned to the use of the Latin language.

The context of this odious praise of Latin at the beginning of book 3 of the *De finibus* is the need for neologism in philosophical prose. If the Greeks can get away with so many neologisms in their language, which is reputed to be richer than others or *uberiorem*, why can't Cicero claim the same license in Latin, which is just beginning to treat of philosophy (3.5)? And yet this reputation is false, and so Cicero takes a detour through his praise of Latin. Elsewhere, Cicero frequently weighs his options of transliterating Greek words, such as *sorites*, or inventing new ones in Latin, such as *acervalem* (*De divinatione* 2.11). More generally, in his self-appointed role of founder of philosophical prose in the *patrius sermo*, Cicero closely examines the lexical capacities of the Latin language, comparing what can be said in Latin to what can be said in Greek. This topic comes up in the *Tusculan Disputations*, where he compares the nuances of meaning conveyed by the words *labor* and *dolor* before remarking that Greek has only one word to render these two concepts, πόνος. Cicero can't resist the temptation to gloat: "O Greece, you are sometimes deficient in the words of which you think you have such a plentiful supply!"[4] This noble exclamation, as Poliziano would have it,[5] defines a sort of red line for Renaissance humanists, many of whom, regardless of nationality, take offense at hearing anyone call Greece "poor in words" or *verborum inops*. Humanists are conscious of a composite debt to antiquity, both to Greece and Rome, and so they cannot ignore the tensions within this dual legacy.

However, in antiquity Cicero's boast seems to have passed fairly unremarked, while the author earned broad renown for his emancipation of the Latin language from Greek tutelage. Characteristic is the tribute rendered to Cicero as the preeminent defender of Latin by Seneca Rhetor in his *Suasoriae*. Suasoria 7 takes up the invidious question of whether Cicero should have burned his books if Marc Anthony had promised him immunity from proscription for doing so. No one argues in the affirmative, according to Seneca; everyone cares more for Cicero's books than for Cicero.[6] To burn his books would have been an injury to the Roman people, whose language Cicero exalted to first place, so that Rome could so far surpass insolent Greece in eloquence as it had in fortune.[7] Though no one misses him, Cicero became the benefactor of the Roman people by challenging the cultural chauvinism of "insolent Greece." In so doing, he founded a new cultural chauvinism that would flourish in the Renaissance under his name, Ciceronianism. This role as the founder of national linguistic pride makes of Cicero and his legacy one of the most productive topics of Renaissance rhetoric.

ANGELO POLIZIANO AND THE PRAISE OF CICERO

The first chapter of Angelo Poliziano's *Miscellaneorum centuria prima* bears the title "Defensus a calumnia Cicero super enarrata vi novi apud Aristotelem vocabuli, quod est Endelechia," which can be translated as "Cicero defended against calumny concerning the commentary of a new word in Aristotle, which is *Endelechia*." This new word in fact appears in book 1 of the *Tusculan Disputations*, where Cicero reports that Aristotle calls the soul by the new name of ἐνδελέχεια as if to say a continuous and perennial motion (1.22). This passage earned Cicero the hostility or, as Poliziano would have it, the calumny of the Byzantine émigré John Argyropoulos, who taught philosophy at the University of Florence when Poliziano was a student there. In Poliziano's account, Argyropoulos was so incensed by Cicero's apostrophe "O verborum inops . . . Graecia," also from the *Tusculan Disputations*, that he dared to assert (what the ears can hardly bear to hear) that Cicero was ignorant not only of philosophy but also (please god) of Greek literature.[8] His main argument for such an outrageous affront to Latin dignity was Cicero's use of ἐνδελέχεια in *TD* 1.22. There is no one, Argyropoulos claimed, even slightly conversant with Aristotle who does not know that Aristotle's term is ἐντελέχεια (with a τ), and furthermore, the meaning is not what Cicero thought, continuous and perennial motion, but rather a certain perfection or consummation, in other words the fulfillment of a *telos*.[9] Poliziano is not the only or even the earliest witness to this quarrel over the Aristotelian definition of the soul, but his commentary is for our purposes the most important intervention in the debate, for he explicitly portrays himself as the champion of the Latins against the hubris of the Greeks. In this way, he means to reenact the role of Cicero in the *De finibus*, but whereas Cicero took his stand against the philhellenism of the Romans, who disdained their own language, Poliziano claims to stand up to the itinerant ethnocentrism of the Byzantine émigrés. And he does so by praising Cicero, as if the praise of Cicero and the praise of Latin were one and the same thing.

This conflation is evident when Poliziano complains of how Argyropoulos and others of his "nation" try to exclude the Latins from the heritage of ancient Greece (which seems rather incompatible with the primary role of the Byzantines as university professors and language teachers in Italy).[10] Here is Han Lamers's English translation of Poliziano's reproach: "It is almost inexpressible in words how unwilling this nation is to allow us, Latin men, to participate in its language and its learning. They think that we possess the scrapings of Hellenism, its slices and its skin: they the fruit, the whole, and the core."[11] As Remigio Sabbadini remarked, what really seems to matter to Poliziano in this controversy is the question of nationality, and Cicero embodies the Latin nation.[12] That is why his defense of Cicero is a kind of patriotism. Or at least it appears so. While Poliziano's defense of Cicero has elicited a variety of responses from the Renaissance to the present, most often regarding the proper understanding of Aristotelian psychology or doctrine of the soul, most readers take his Latin chauvinism and his encomiastic intent at face value. I am rather more inclined to understand this initial chapter from the *Miscellanea* as a paradoxical encomium, a performance of sophistic rhetoric. In this sense, the chapter puts into question the values it claims to represent, not only Ciceronian values but also the Platonic values it is generally thought to endorse.

My interpretation hinges on the passage where Poliziano maintains that Argyropoulos, as a Greek, resented that noble exclamation "O verborum inops . . . ," which Cicero pronounced perhaps no more eloquently than truly or "non eloquentius fortasse, quam verius."[13] Presumably we are meant to understand that Cicero spoke both eloquently and truly, and that Greece really was poor in words, but the assertion "non eloquentius quam verius" is perfectly reversible, just like the *argumenta reciproca* that Aulus

Gellius discusses in the *Noctes Atticae* and that he illustrates with the quarrel of Protagoras and his disciple Euathlus. Euathlus hired the sophist Protagoras to teach him rhetoric under the condition that he pay his teacher any price as soon as he won a case in court. The student made good progress in his studies but never pleaded a case in court, no doubt to avoid paying his tuition. So Protagoras decided to sue Euathlus, telling him that whatever happened, he'd get his money since either the court would find in his favor or Euathlus would win the case and have to pay up under the terms of their agreement. Euathlus was such a quick study that he answered, "in either event I shall not have to pay what you demand, whether judgment be pronounced for or against me. For if the jurors decide in my favour, according to their verdict nothing will be due you, because I have won; but if they give judgment against me, by the terms of our contract, I shall owe you nothing, because I have not won a case" (*Noctes Atticae* 5.10).[14] So this type of reversible argument is a venerable sophistic trick.

Moreover, the formula *non eloquentius quam verius* revives the Platonic attack on the sophists, as those slippery adversaries who would rather win the argument than tell the truth. If the sophists are known as those who speak *eloquentius quam verius*, then Cicero must not be a sophist: whether he speaks well and truly or ineptly and falsely, he doesn't subordinate one term to the other. Of course, if the sophists prefer eloquence to truth, Socrates favors truth over eloquence. Cicero, in Poliziano's formula, assigns equal value to rhetoric and philosophy, to truth and eloquence. In this sense he rejects the hierarchy of Platonic values, and his example even insinuates a parity between Socrates and the sophists, none of whom could balance truth and eloquence. Moreover, Poliziano's defense of Cicero tends to obscure the truth and to hold in suspense the question of the true Aristotelian usage, ἐνδελέχεια or ἐντελέχεια. Like an ancient Greek sophist, Poliziano will demonstrate that any question can be debated *in utramque partem*.

To defend the honor of the Latins and repudiate the calumny of the Greeks, Poliziano must show that Cicero is ignorant neither of philosophy nor of Greek. On the first point he will muster authorities, including patristic and even scholastic authorities, whom he generally holds in little esteem, to counter the authority of Argyropoulos. Then he must show that the criticism of Cicero only increases his praise, rather than decreases it.[15] In other words, what is said against Cicero can be said for him; the accusation, of confusing two Greek terms, returns against the accuser. This tactic, I suggest, is a classic instance of making the weaker argument stronger, a tactic that Aristotle associates with Protagoras in the *Rhetoric* (1402a24). Cicero's reading ἐνδελέχεια is the weaker argument, going against all the extant manuscripts, and therefore Poliziano will defend it to demonstrate his own credentials as a Renaissance sophist.

What allows Poliziano to make the weaker argument stronger in this controversy is that neither argument is inherently superior. Of the two readings, entelechy and endelechy, Poliziano suggests that either one is plausible. To Cicero's detractors, he asks, on what basis do you maintain that Aristotle wrote ἐντελέχεια instead of ἐνδελέχεια, since both are neologisms and both can mean "the soul"? Nor does Aristotle say that his neologism means perfection rather than continuous motion. At least that's what the ancient Neoplatonists thought, and why should we begrudge Cicero the same license, as long as he can defend his position?[16] Eugenio Garin has pointed out the fallacy of this argument,[17] but the function is clear enough: he wants to keep the question of Aristotelian psychology, and Ciceronian authority, in suspense. To do so, he next rehearses the legend of the transmission of the *corpus aristotelicum* based on the testimony of Strabo and Plutarch. Wrapping up his summary of the precarious transmission of Aristotle's works, he says there is no reason why we should doubt but that, on the validity of Cicero's reading, either there is equal weight on either side or else Cicero is right.[18] The expression "libera in utramque partem suspicio" expresses Poliziano's own rhetorical objective of ἰσοσθένεια or equal force of opposing arguments, a technique that Montaigne will cultivate in his essays. If someone has to be right, Cicero is certainly a better authority on antiquity than any modern. After all, who's to say that Cicero couldn't have seen the matrix or the original of Aristotle's manuscripts, which were published in Cicero's lifetime before they were hopelessly corrupted?[19] This is the phrase that has retained the attention of modern scholarship, because here Poliziano seems miraculously to intuit Cicero's access to Aristotle's exoteric works, his early philosophical dialogues produced under the influence of Platonism, or what Ettore Bignone calls "the lost Aristotle."[20] What I would like to point out is that Poliziano's argument is hypothetical: "Quid autem prohibet?" He doesn't affirm anything.

Poliziano also points out that Cicero adapted his reading of Aristotle to Plato's view in the *Phaedrus* on the eternal motion of the soul.[21] Once again the Neoplatonists testify in Cicero's favor by arguing that Aristotle and Plato agree with each other, and Pico della Mirandola has worked tirelessly to demonstrate the concord of Plato and Aristotle, especially "in quadam suarum disputationum praefatione," which may mean his *Oration on the Dignity of Man* or else the preface to his *De ente et uno*, as Garin conjectures.[22] In either event, Pico's authority, which weighs heavily with Poliziano, seems to endorse Cicero's reading. Thus what people hold against Cicero, his definition of the soul and his conflation of Aristotle and Plato, should really be alleged in his favor. His weakness is his strength. Where all this is leading is to what Poliziano calls the *diverticulum* (more commonly, but still uncommon, *deverticulum*): a detour or a turning point, or perhaps, from Tacitus, a place of ill repute where Cicero's reputation hangs in the balance. The place where Cicero was most exposed to calumny is the place where he has triumphed most broadly.[23] With a sophistic mastery of *kairos*, Poliziano has shifted the balance at the crucial moment from *calumnia* to *praestantia* or from blame to praise. Though ostensibly written to vindicate the glory of Cicero against overbearing Hellenes, this whole first chapter of the *Miscellaneorum centuria prima* is a sophistic exercise and, as such, a homage to the Greeks, or at least to some of them. The revival of sophistic is rather an affront to Platonic values.

ERASMUS AND THE CRITIQUE OF CICERONIANISM

If we return to the progenitor of odious praise, *illaudatus Busiris*, we can say, by analogy, that Poliziano undertakes the praise of *illaudatus Cicero*, or, more precisely, *illaudata latinitas*, in a self-conscious sequel to the work of Cicero himself. In both cases, both Cicero and Poliziano, this praise can be seen, from the viewpoint of Greek ethnocentrism, as a praise of barbarity or *laus barbarorum*. In respect to the very specific question of the relative lexical richness of classical languages, Poliziano and Cicero undertake a praise of poverty or *laus inopiae* when they prefer their own medium of expression to Greek. They praise what others blame in order to affirm a collective identity, and this identity allows them in turn to ostracize others. The next phase of this process within Renaissance humanism involves Desiderius Erasmus and his *Dialogus Ciceronianus*, which rejects the new ethnocentrism of the Roman humanists and their superstitiously exclusive imitation of Ciceronian style. To the Roman idol of Cicero, Erasmus prefers, in a brazen paradox, *illaudatus Christus*. The Ciceronians are reputed to banish all Christian terminology from their lexicon and to hate the very name of Christ,[24] so that Erasmus must come to what might otherwise seem the superfluous defense of the Son of God. Where Poliziano considers it his duty as a Latin patriot to defend the glory of Cicero, Erasmus, as he explains at the end of the *Ciceronianus*, writes in order "to celebrate the glory of Christ" (CWE 28:447). Erasmus rejects Ciceronianism as a pagan anachronism, but he cannot do so without calling into question some of the fundamental values of the European Renaissance.

Though a champion of Cicero, Poliziano was never a Ciceronian in the pejorative sense intended by Erasmus. In fact, at roughly the same time he was compiling his *Miscellanea*, he conducted a famous debate with Paolo Cortesi in which he advocated eclectic imitation and opposed the exclusive cultivation of Ciceronian style. Before his death in 1494, Poliziano prepared his correspondence for publication in twelve books, and he placed at the end of book 8 his exchange of letters with Cortesi on imitation. Both authors shared a common identity as Latin humanists, but they disagreed about style. In an undated letter thought to be from the 1480s,[25] Poliziano regrets to inform his correspondent that he was unimpressed by the latter's epistolary eloquence, which he sampled at Cortesi's own invitation. Poliziano does not share the other man's evident conviction that we must reproduce Cicero's traits, his *lineamenta*, in our own Latin composition. Rather than seek to ape or to parrot another's style, Poliziano thinks, we should strive to express ourselves, but only after long study, when we are finally ready to trust to our own forces or, as the saying goes, to swim without cork.[26] We can run faster when we're not following in another's footsteps. This sententious advice, borrowed from classical models, made such an impression on Erasmus that he couldn't help imitating it in his own dialogue.

In answer, Cortesi disclaims any superstitious devotion to Cicero but does insist on the necessity of imitation, for the following reasons. Eloquence is in decline and you cannot speak well unless you choose a model to imitate, just as foreigners who do not speak the language cannot traverse alien territory without a native guide. "First, about my opinion I shall willingly confess that, when I saw the pursuit of eloquence lying so long deserted, public speaking so neglected and our people lacking a kind of native voice, I often and openly asserted that nothing in these times could be said with elegance and variety except by those who set out a model for themselves to imitate, just as travelers ignorant of the local language have difficulty traversing foreign lands without a guide."[27] By this logic, the Latins have become, through the lapse of time, foreigners in their own land, in need of a guide in the modern sense of *Cicerone*. Ciceronianism is thus an admission of estrangement or alienation from an original identity. Cortesi's stance is hardly chauvinistic; it is rather elegiac. The ancients knew the proper method of imitation, he adds, but that knowledge has been lost.

Responding to Poliziano's provocation, Cortesi assures him that he does not want to resemble his model as an ape does a man but rather as the son resembles his father, "ut filium parentis" (8). Erasmus will remember this formula all the more so since Cortesi singles out Cicero as the "fons perennis" (12) or perennial source of Latin eloquence. In the *Ciceronianus*, Erasmus will reassign this role of *fons* to the heart or mind or innermost self of the speaker, whose speech is like a river flowing from the source.[28] Finally, Cortesi cannot admit Poliziano's ideal of independent self-expression, since the writer who goes out of the beaten path, or "de praescripto egredi" (4) in Poliziano's terms, ends up like one who wanders aimlessly (14), reminding us of the travelers traversing a foreign land without a guide. The Poliziano-Cortesi correspondence, first published in the 1498 *Politiani opera omnia*, sets the terms, especially the figurative terms, for the discussion of imitation in Erasmus's later dialogue.

Yet Cortesi's interpretation of Ciceronianism is strangely inoffensive and tentative. We need Cicero because we are lost. This is not at all the attitude proclaimed by those Ciceronians with whom Erasmus came in direct conflict in the course of his career, especially in the 1520s as he was simultaneously embroiled in his controversy with Martin Luther. We hear the first rumors of this clash between Erasmus and his Ciceronian adversaries in a letter dated August 31, 1524, where Erasmus answers various criticisms proffered by Angelo Colocci and the members of the Roman Academy.[29] Apparently, the academicians have their doubts about both his style and his religious orthodoxy, and it is this pairing that will prove crucial to the argument of the *Ciceronianus*.[30] It is here, in this epistle addressed to Haio Herman, that Erasmus accuses the Ciceronians of hating the very name of Christ.[31] In effect, Erasmus casts his adversaries as pagan idolaters, while they portray him as an apostate both in style and in faith. In closing, Erasmus congratulates his correspondent for making progress in the study of Greek but cautions him not to linger too long on such studies but rather to take up philosophy. For the humanities lead to paganism, especially if we linger too long in their study, like the Italians.[32] This is quite an extraordinary claim for a champion of the *bonae litterae* to make and all the more unexpected for its ironic echo of a phrase from Erasmus's 1512 treatise on education *De ratione studii*. There he warns the student not to grow old in the study of dialectic: "Nor again should he rest at that point and (to quote Gellius) pass into old age by the rocks of the Sirens" (CWE 24:671). Whereas before the rocks of the Sirens stood for scholastic philosophy, now in 1524 they designate good letters, and all because of the Ciceronians. Their ineptly aggressive promotion of Ciceronian values has provoked from the leading northern humanist a denigration of the humanities.[33]

The correspondence offers further signs of growing animosity. In a letter from May 1526, after some perfunctory condolences for the untimely death of Christophe de Longueil, Erasmus confides to Andrea Alciati that a new sect has arisen of Ciceronians, who seem no less active in Italy than the Lutherans are in the North (as if both were threats to Christian unity). For the first time, but not the last, he predicts that, if Cicero were to come back to life, he would mock this new gang of Ciceronians.[34] The next month he again complains of the "nova secta Ciceronianorum, quae non minus incruduit quam Lutheranorum."[35] Clearly, Erasmus wants to discredit the Ciceronians, many employed at the Roman Curia, as sectarians and enemies of church unity. Also in June, a Flemish scholar then residing in Italy, Leonard Casembroot, writes to say he has heard from Froben that Erasmus is planning to reveal to the world the "φίλαυτα iudicia" or self-infatuation of certain Italians who will not grant anyone besides Cicero a reputation for speaking.[36] Moreover, this opinion has turned many famous men against Erasmus, especially Lazzaro Bonamico, that new Aristarchus, not to say *Erasmiomastix*.[37] This letter is not only a sort of advance notice of the *Ciceronianus* but also a reminder of the evolution of the controversy since the fifteenth century. Poliziano in the *Miscellanea* called Argyropoulos *Ciceromastix* for attacking Cicero and defaming the Latins, who rise up boldly to defend their champion. Now Erasmus's partisan, a fellow northerner who styles himself *Flandrus*, calls the Ciceronian Lazzaro Bonamico *Erasmiomastix* for defaming Erasmus, the champion of the non-Italians or the transalpine humanists (whose common language is still Latin). In effect, just as Greek cultural chauvinism provoked the counterreaction of Ciceronianism among the Latins, now Ciceronianism calls forth Erasmianism as a counterideology with its own partisans.

This dynamic is clearly on display in a letter of March 1527 written from Spain by Pedro Juan Olivar under very particular circumstances. Olivar reports on the early phase of the Conference of Valladolid, which was convened by the Spanish Inquisition in order to deliberate on suspect passages in Erasmus's work and to determine whether his books should be banned in Spain.[38] Olivar reports dismissively that there are twenty-one articles brought against Erasmus by the Spanish friars, and he outlines the principal actors in this *tragoedia*, especially the faithful Erasmians. Then, without transition, he passes on to certain Italian expatriates in Spain who criticize Erasmus's style and call him a barbarian.[39] They prefer Giovanni

Pontano to Erasmus and, please god, consider Christophe de Longueil to be the most eloquent of all the northerners.[40] Olivar trusts that this news will not deter Erasmus from persevering in the service of Christian philosophy. Olivar is a valuable informant on the many jealousies and rivalries that contributed to the *Ciceronianus*. More importantly, his letter confirms the seamless connection, at this stage of European history and of Erasmus's career, between religious orthodoxy and stylistic orthodoxy. The Spanish monks and clerics challenge Erasmus's Catholic orthodoxy, while the expatriate Italians (Castiglione, Navagero, and Tagliacarne are the three named in the letter) challenge his Ciceronian orthodoxy. For one group he is *hereticus*, while for the other he is *barbarus*. Clearly Ciceronianism has something to do with the authoritarian Catholic reaction to dissent, which has a lot to do with anxiety over Lutheranism. Erasmus repudiated Luther but would not make common cause with the guardians of Catholic orthodoxy. He preferred a similar nonconformism in matters of style. Erasmus's independent stance appeals to his correspondent as an instance of "philosophia Christiana,"[41] which naturally suggests Erasmus's *philosophia Christi* or philosophy of Christ, but which I would translate here as Christian humanism, to distinguish it both from scholasticism and from Ciceronianism. His means of expression is therefore Christian humanist Latin, which is neither scholastic Latin nor Ciceronian Latin, but an intermediary style that the *Ciceronianus* will call "medium quiddam inter Scotos et Ciceronis simias" (ASD I-2:642), echoing Poliziano's scornful usage of *simia* to designate the slavish imitator.[42]

In October 1527, when the Conference of Valladolid had already disbanded without reaching a verdict, Erasmus wrote to a young Spanish Hellenist named Francisco de Vergara a long letter containing, in the words of Pierre Mesnard, a complete outline of what would soon become the *Ciceronianus*.[43] Erasmus portrays himself here as an aging gladiator eager to retire from combat but condemned to die in the arena.[44] Once he fought the scholastics on behalf of humane letters, but now a new type of enemy has come out of hiding. These enemies would banish the name of Christ from all good literature, as if nothing could be elegant that was not pagan. They praise Pontano to the skies (we know who they are from Olivar's letter) and cannot endure Augustine or Jerome. For his part, Erasmus prefers one Christian ode to a boatload of Pontano's verses, however elegant and erudite they may be. Such people think it is more shameful not to be Ciceronian than not to be Christian, and this hubris marks an estrangement from the most basic identity of a Christian.[45] Moreover, Ciceronianism violates the rhetorical principle of decorum, or suiting one's words to the present circumstances, which Erasmus here terms "apposite dicere."[46] Times have changed completely since the age of Cicero, and nothing has changed more than religion. Superstitious devotees of Cicero are pagans living in a Christian land. In this context we might recall, though there is no proof that Erasmus did, Paolo Cortesi's metaphor of Latin authors as *peregrini* or foreign travelers in need of a guide. In Christian tradition, life on earth is a kind of exile and the Christian is a *peregrinus* passing through an alien land on his way to salvation.[47] The Ciceronian has hired the wrong guide to lead him home.

Finally, in March 1528, the *respublica litterarum* was able to peruse the first edition of Erasmus's dialogue *Ciceronianus*. The *dramatis personae* are Bulephorus, Hypologus, and Nosoponus. Nosoponus is afflicted with a malady designated by the neologism *Zelodulea* (ASD I-2:606): he is too eager for the servitude of Ciceronian imitation. If Nosoponus is the patient, his interlocutors assume the role of doctors or medical consultants, and their speech will be his cure. The therapeutic value of speech emerges in the course of the dialogue as a major theme with evangelical resonances. Bulephorus confides to Nosoponus that he was once afflicted with the very same malady until he was cured by the *logos* or speech.[48] Erasmus had already evoked this principle in adage 2100, *To a sick spirit speech is a physician* (CWE 34:223), and now he will try to enact this proverbial wisdom in the long course of his healing dialogue. Preliminary to any treatment, the patient must display his symptoms, that is to say, he must explain his Ciceronian mania. The first symptom is a hopeless confusion of the sacred and the profane. According to Nosoponus, "A sacred vocation like this requires a heart not only pure from all sin but free from all care, just like the esoteric disciplines of magic, astrology, and so-called alchemy. . . . This is the main reason I've decided to remain a bachelor, though I'm well aware what a holy state matrimony is" (CWE 28:352). The word rendered here as "bachelor" is *coelebs* (ASD I-2:613), which means celibate or monk. In effect, Ciceronianism is a parody of monasticism, and Nosoponus has taken vows of verbal poverty and celibacy. Monasticism was a prime target of humanist satire, in Erasmus's *Enchiridion*, Rabelais's *Gargantua*, and elsewhere, because it involves a denial of individuality.[49] The counterideal is the recognition of individual self-expression, which comes to the fore in the course of the dialogue. Another symptom is complete abstention from spontaneity: the Ciceronian never speaks extempore (which does not stop Nosoponus from engaging in such a long dialogue against his own principles). As Nosoponus says, quoting Erasmus's adages, he is not ashamed "to smell of the lamp,"[50] since he has no use for spontaneity and no aptitude for public speaking. Implicitly, he is of no use to society.

It doesn't take long to diagnose the illness, but it does to propose the cure. Erasmus devotes most of his dialogue to elaborating a healthy doctrine of imitation based on the rhetorical principle of decorum. Decorum requires us to suit our speech to present circumstances, and no circumstance further alienates us from Cicero than our religion. "Shall we as Christians," asks Bulephorus, "before other Christians, discuss these topics in exactly the same way as the pagan Cicero did before pagans?" (CWE 28:387). We cannot speak appositely, appropriately, decorously, if we speak like an ancient pagan from an inaccessibly remote era. The principle of decorum, what George Pigman calls "historical decorum,"[51] also entails confessional decorum in the sense of suiting one's speech to one's religion. For Bulephorus, the exclusive cultivation of Ciceronian diction is symptomatic of a larger and more insidious problem, which he identifies as paganism: "It's paganism, believe me, Nosoponus, sheer paganism, that makes our ears and minds accept such an idea. The fact is we're Christians only in name. . . . We have Jesus on our lips, but it's Jupiter Optimus Maximus and Romulus that we have in our hearts" (CWE 28:394). Bulephorus's tirade against paganism veers toward an attack on the Renaissance and on all the cherished motifs of Renaissance art and literature. He even derides Erasmian adages, to which he prefers biblical sayings and figures of speech.[52] The critique of paganism envelops the enthusiasm for ancient statues, funerary inscriptions, coins, and all the other antiquarian pursuits characteristic of Renaissance humanism (ASD I-2:646–47). Bulephorus is similarly impatient with the use of classical mythological motifs in modern painting such as Danaë, Ganymede, and Bacchus (ASD I-2:647). In effect, Erasmus challenges not only Ciceronian values but more globally the values of Renaissance humanism that he himself espoused and promoted. Ciceronianism and the personal antagonism of Ciceronians, as reported in his correspondence, have provoked a sort of identity crisis in the author of the *Ciceronianus*, who feels estranged from the very idea of Renaissance. Émile Telle has found an interesting expression of this same ambivalence in a letter of 1517 to Wolfgang Capito.[53] In a letter that proclaims the advent of a new golden age, Erasmus cannot conceal "one misgiving in my mind: that under cover of the reborn literature of antiquity paganism may try to rear its ugly head" (CWE 4:266). Ten years later, the tensions inherent in Renaissance humanism and its conflicting value systems have grown even more acute.

To the critique of paganism, Nosoponus replies that Bulephorus is not being helpful, as if the author suddenly realized that he had gone too far. Bulephorus assures him that he is still determined to help him achieve Ciceronian eloquence, as long as we understand by such a term not superficial imitation but adherence to the primordial rule of decorum or *apte dicere* (ASD I-2:647). It is here that Erasmus develops the rhetorical ideal of self-expression, based on the conviction that speech must reflect the individuality of the speaker. As Bulephorus puts it, each one of us has a unique *ingenium*, and our speech has to be true to our self.

> Habent singula mortalium ingenia suum quiddam ac genuinum, quae res tantam habet vim, ut ad hoc aut illud dicendi genus natura compositus, frustra nitatur ad diversum. Nulli enim bene cessit θεομαχία, quemadmodum Graeci solent dicere. (ASD I-2:647–48)

> Every one of us has his own personal inborn characteristics, and these have such force that it is useless for a person fitted by nature for one style of speaking to strive to achieve a different one. As the Greeks say, no one ever succeeded in battling with the gods. (CWE 28:396–97)

It is interesting that, in order to formulate the principle of self-expression, he resorts to a proverb and one related to the pagan myth of θεομαχία or the battle of the gods and the giants.[54] Here the struggle is between the speaker's inalienable nature and an arbitrarily chosen model such as Cicero, which impedes self-expression. It is futile to go against our own nature and copy a model for which we have no personal affinity. The dilemma of the Ciceronian is that his goal is to reproduce Cicero in his entirety, but when Nosoponus asks where Cicero exists in entirety, Bulephorus answers, "Nowhere except in himself" (CWE 28:399). Only Cicero can be a Ciceronian.

To convey his doctrine of imitation, Erasmus has recourse to the crucial metaphor of the mirror. Bulephorus chides Nosoponus: "if you want to express the whole Cicero you cannot express yourself, and if you do not express yourself your speech will be a lying mirror" (CWE 28:399). He returns to this metaphor at the end of the dialogue, where he invokes the natural relationship between speech and self: "Not to reiterate that your ambition conflicts with nature herself, who intended speech to be the mirror of the mind. Minds differ far more than voices and physical features do, and the mirror will lie unless it reflects the true born image of the mind" (CWE 28:440). Or again, "Speech reveals the features of the mind much as a mirror reflects the face, and to change the natural image into something different is surely the same as appearing in public wearing a mask" (CWE 28:441). This natural image, what Erasmus calls "nativam mentis imaginem" (ASD I-2:703) or "nativa specie" (ASD I-2:704), is something like the personal voice of the speaker, our personality. Accordingly, Jacques Chomarat recognizes Erasmus as one of the founders of the notion of personality.[55]

More than the treatment of decorum or the ideal of self-expression, the aspect of the *Ciceronianus* that had the greatest impact on its audience was the long catalogue of humanist pretenders to the title of Ciceronian. Erasmus develops this lengthy exercise in literary criticism ostensibly in order to fulfill the therapeutic goals of the dialogue and to cure Nosoponus of his illness by showing that there is no shame in being refused the name of Ciceronian since no one has deserved the title since Cicero. Beginning with the question "whom will you offer me as a Ciceronian apart from Cicero himself?" (CWE 28:408), Bulephorus and Nosoponus will spend the next forty or so pages systematically disqualifying any and all claimants to what Chomarat calls "the honorific and infamous title of Ciceronian."[56] Erasmus's catalogue of writers is inspired to some extent by the catalogue of orators in Cicero's *Brutus* and is thus a Ciceronian exercise in its own right. Passing over the ancients with a strange alacrity, the list focuses on the moderns arranged by nation, beginning with the Italians and proceeding through the Byzantine émigrés, then more Italians, culminating in the author's archenemy Alberto Pio da Carpi, then the French, the English, among whom Thomas More gets short shrift, the Scots, the Danes, the Dutch, where Erasmus lists himself as a mere πολυγραφός (ASD I-2:681) or prolific scribbler, the Germans, the Hungarians, the Poles, and finally the Spaniards. As Émile Telle points out, for Erasmus's contemporaries it was just as bad to be included on the list as to be omitted.[57] In effect, in his catalogue of failed Ciceronians, Erasmus found the perfect formula for odious praise where silence was just as exasperating as all the backhanded compliments he offered his fellow humanists. The most controversial passage in this list regards the humanist printer Josse Bade, whom Nosoponus would sooner admit to this contest of praise, "in hoc laudis certamen" (ASD I-2:672), than Guillaume Budé himself, the preeminent French Renaissance humanist. This may have been a gratuitous slight on a brilliant friend and rival, but it reminds us that the title of Ciceronian is really a dispraise, whether it is granted or denied. That is Erasmus's genius, not his negligence.

FRANCESCO FLORIDO AND THE DEFENSE OF LATIN

The torrent of indignation released by the publication of the *Ciceronianus* shows what a bitter dose of odious praise Erasmus administered to his readers. It is this furious reaction, surveyed by Betty Knott in the introduction to her translation (CWE 28:330–34), that confirms the crucial role of language and style in the formation of collective identity. Erasmus's adversaries felt their own identity threatened by the critique of Ciceronianism. Moreover, Erasmus's own motive in writing this polemic may have been to retaliate against those who denigrated his Latin style and thus undermined his identity and credentials as a humanist. Language is a key terrain in the contest of values, but so far all the contestants in this arena are using the same language, which they recognize as the natural and universal means of communication. When vernacular humanists enter the fray, they will provoke even more antagonism, both from those who identify with a national tradition and from those who identify as Latins. This we will see in the case of Joachim Du Bellay, but before we examine his offensive defense of French, there is one more defense of Latin that we need to take into account, and that is by the Bolognese humanist Francesco Florido. Florido is unique in the sense that he was both a Ciceronian and an Erasmian.[58] He defended Erasmus's reputation against Etienne Dolet's slanderous dialogue *De imitatione ciceroniana* in his own miscellany entitled *Succisivae lectiones* published in 1540. Under the rubric *Qui auctores sint legendi, quive imitandi* or "Which authors are to be read and which ones imitated," Florido advocates eclectic imitation and repudiates Dolet's exclusive devotion to Cicero as an outrageous slight on the wealth and variety of the Latin tradition.[59] In other words, the praise of Cicero is felt to be a dispraise of everyone else. This logic informs the principal work by Florido that we examine here, the *Apologia in Marci Actii Plauti aliorumque poetarum et linguae latinae calumniatores*, first published in 1537 in Lyon and reissued with significant, Ciceronian revisions in 1540 in Basel.[60] Earlier, Florido had published a brief apology of Plautus, which he then expanded into an apology of the Latin language against all its detractors. Curiously, the *Apologia* does not address the turmoil provoked by Erasmus's *Dialogus Ciceronianus* but instead looks back to a much earlier phase of the controversy over imitation and of the vindication of the Latin language. What emerges in the course of the work as the prime motive and stimulus of Florido's linguistic patriotism is an epigram by the Greek émigré Michele Marullo or Michael Marullus, which was first printed circa

1490 and republished by Pietro Crinito in his humanist miscellany *Commentarii de honesta disciplina* of 1504.

Among the vast and importunate horde of *linguae latinae calumniatores*, Marullus distinguishes himself with his epigram in praise of Latin poets, which appeared in his first book of epigrams under the innocuous title *De poetis latinis*. In his poem, Marullus nominates the leading representatives of the principal genres of classical Latin poetry through the conceit that "Love is beholden to Tibullus, Mars to Virgil, comedy to Terence, etc."

> Amor Tibullo, Mars tibi, Maro, debet,
> Terentio soccus levis
> Cothurnus olim nemini satis multum,
> Horatio satyra et chelys,
> Natura magni versibus Lucretii
> Lepore Musaeo illitis,
> Epigramma cultum, teste Rhallo, adhuc nulli,
> Docto Catullo syllabae:
> Hos siquis inter caeteros locat vates,
> Onerat quam honorat verius.[61]

Love is indebted to Tibullus; Mars to you, Vergil; the loose-fitting shoe to Terence. The buskin for some time now does not owe very much to anyone; to Horace the satire and lyre are indebted; Nature is indebted to the verses, daubed by the charm of the Muses, of great Lucretius. The polished epigram still owes nothing to anyone, according to Rhallus; the hendecasyllable is beholden to Catullus. If anyone wishes to place these poets among the others, it would be more of an onus than an honor.[62]

This restrictive, idiosyncratic canon of Latin literature may well have seemed invidious if not odious to its original audience, partly because two of the titles remain vacant, tragedy and epigram, while only six poets are named: Tibullus, Virgil, Terence, Horace, Lucretius, and Catullus. The poet seems moreover to reserve to himself, on the authority of a fellow Byzantine exile, Cabacius Rhallus, the category of epigram, as if it were beyond the native capacity of the Latins. In closing, he suggests that to rank these six among other contenders would be rather a burden than an honor to them, "onerat quam honorat verius" (v. 10). In other words, it would be odious praise. As an apologist of Plautus, Florido is naturally incensed by this favoritism toward Terence, but more generally he cannot endure the arbitrary restriction of the Latin canon. In the case of elegiac poetry, the exclusive preference granted to Tibullus seems intolerable when there are worthy rivals such as Propertius and Ovid. In fact, nothing could be more odious than this favoritism: "Quamvis autem nihil sit odiosius, quam de aequalibus statuere velle" (43). Parodying Marullo's own turn of phrase, he declares that the faculty of judgment owes but little to Marullo.[63] He is particularly irate at the impudence of a Byzantine, a mere *Graeculus* (40) who presumes to judge the Latins, thus mobilizing the ethnocentrism of his own Latin readership. Here we sense that Marullo is the successor to Argyropoulos, whose censure of Cicero called Poliziano into the fray (all the more so since Marullo directed many of his epigrams against Poliziano).[64]

What annoys Florido even more than this odious epigram is Pietro Crinito's enthusiasm for it in book 23, chapter 7 of the *De honesta disciplina*, which not only reprints the offending poem but also reports approvingly a conversation in which Marullus systematically disqualifies the Silver Latin poets Ovid, Statius, Silius Italicus, Valerius Flaccus, and Lucan.[65] The notion that there is only one age of Latin poetry, analogous to the idea that there is only one model of Latin prose, impoverishes the Latin tradition and discredits subsequent phases of literary history. According to Crinito, Marullo had the nerve to say that there were more versifiers than poets among the Romans (a charge that Du Bellay will turn against the French in his *Deffence*) before offering his own take on the Latin canon. Rather than recoil in horror at this blasphemy, Crinito endorses Marullo's judgment.[66] This is the last straw for Florido. Declaring Crinito completely devoid of judgment, "omnis prorsus iudicii expertem" (40), he warns that the *De honesta disciplina* is so potent that it can make a fool insane and can render the unlearned supremely unlearned (41). After deconstructing Marullo's epigram verse by verse, the *Apologia* returns to Crinito and proclaims, "Whoever takes Crinito, supremely eager for self-praise, to be other than Aesop's jackdaw, then such a one can doubtless do or say nothing that is not against Minerva's will" (53).[67] Here Florido combines two Erasmian adages, *Aesopicus graculus* and *invita Minerva*, to accuse Marullo's partisan of plagiarism and vanity, like the crow in borrowed feathers.[68] The second adage, applied to any reader inclined to favor Crinito, can mean simply to be mistaken or, more provocatively, to go against one's nature, which is what the Ciceronian does according to Bulephorus. So this proverbial invective can be seen as a nod to Erasmus and the *Ciceronianus*.

Marullo's epigram, which praises the best Latin poets, is a characteristic case of odious praise. Praise turns to blame when it demotes through omission and exclusion. Praise can never satisfy and it rarely means to satisfy. This may be why Florido calls Marullo "poetarum irrisor" (52) for his sparing praise. And yet Florido is constrained to acknowledge that Marullo is quite innocuous compared to a new menace, a new class of detractors unnoticed by the earlier writers surveyed here: the champions of the vernacular. The turn of events may have rendered the question of the Latin canon moot: there are now those who, unlike Marullo, would set aside all Latin authors "tamquam exteros supervacaneosque" (54) as so many foreigners and superfluous figures.[69] The nativism inherent in Ciceronian values, the nativism that rallies Latins against Greeks, leads naturally to the vernacular. This linguistic nativism is the most potent challenge to the collective identity of the Latin humanists. Florido will rise to the challenge with a catalogue of all the leading humanists from Petrarch to his own time, meant to put the partisans of the vernacular to shame. One problem with such a ploy is that many of these figures wrote in the vernacular, but Florido insists that they owe their true fame to Latin, an argument easily reversed by Du Bellay in the *Deffence*.[70] The most obvious model for this census of Latinists is Erasmus's own catalogue of Ciceronians. As we know, Erasmus predictably offended all of Europe when he tried to list the major Latin prose writers of his era, for no one could abide to see his name either on or off the list. No one really cared about Florido's opinions, but he certainly saw the potential, let us say the Erasmian potential, of such a list. Curiously, he begins with Giovanni Pontano, whose celebrity proved so annoying to Erasmus, but to whom Florido grants unreserved praise as "omnium summum ac principem" (63), just the sort of encomium that infuriated Erasmus. In fact, of all Pontano's works, he singles out for praise the dialogue *Actius*, which is precisely the text that Olivar criticized in his debate with the Ciceronians, which he reported in his letter to Erasmus discussed above.[71] Florido may well have had this letter in mind when he began his catalogue of humanists. The only fault one can find with Pontano is that he was a little too fond of neologisms (64). For his part, Florido repudiates neologisms, a position clearly at odds with Cicero, who framed his defense of Latin in the *De finibus* with an explanation of the need for neologism in philosophical prose. It may be that Florido sees neologism as a confession of weakness or linguistic poverty, and he feels it more important to deny this weakness than to agree with Cicero.

The rest of Florido's catalogue, ostensibly written in praise of the Latins, is not sparing in criticism. Whereas the trio of Byzantines George of Trebizond, John Argyropoulos, and Cardinal Bessarion are hailed as "viros numquam satis laudatos" (67), which I will take at face value, Theodorus Gaza and Ermolao Barbaro are taken to task for their own penchant for neologism (65). Lorenzo Valla has no fault, except for his own gift for calumny, and Poliziano is even better than Pliny, but Niccolò Perotti is classed with the commentators and compilers who make children hate Latin authors and who oppress young minds with their confused hodge-podge of information: "et invisos pueris Latinos autores faciunt, et indigesta quadam farragine iuveniles animos opprimunt" (69). Filippo Beroaldo was a man of wide and varied learning, but he discredited himself through his criticism of Servius, who was as far superior to Beroaldo as Cicero himself to Asinius Pollio (72). Cristoforo Landino traduced Virgil's *Aeneid* with his tedious allegorical reading, and he even translated Livy and Pliny into Italian "non sine manifesto crimine" (73). There is a fine eulogy for Florido's patron Alberto Pio da Carpi, which might compensate for his poor showing in the *Ciceronianus*, and some even better tributes to the living. Guillaume Budé is the most learned man alive, and Erasmus seems somehow to defy praise: "Erasmus of Rotterdam is a new dawn and the greatest glory of literature, but if I wanted to praise him, I'm afraid everyone would call me crazy, since he wrote so many and such learned works that among the ancients, he not only equaled many but left them far behind."[72] Florido's fear that his praise of Erasmus might seem insane recalls one of the *Apophthegmata laconica* compiled by Erasmus: "A sophist was about to give a reading from a book, and Antalcidas asked him what it was about. When told that it was in praise of Hercules, he said, 'But who speaks ill of him?' He thought it was pointless to waste effort on eulogizing someone whom everyone was unanimous in praising" (CWE 37:72–73). This anecdote reminds us that we only praise what others blame: praise is never consensual or uncontroversial. But Erasmus, unlike his hero Hercules, was plenty controversial, and Florido still pretends reluctance to praise him, since his merits are so obvious. A few lines further, Florido salutes Sadoleto, Alciati, and a few others as above all praise, "omnique laude maiores" (77). Florido is nothing if not sensitive to the problems and the limits of praise. He suggests that the highest praise may be to withhold praise.

JOACHIM DU BELLAY AND THE DEFENSE OF THE VERNACULAR

Florido closes his work with the claim that if the partisans of the vernacular would just leave everyone alone, Latin would soon be restored to pristine condition and become common to all, even innkeepers.[73] This seems like extravagantly wishful thinking, as if a classical language could reinvent itself as a vernacular, and yet this may be Florido's parody of Erasmus's idea of making Latin into a modern means of mass communication. Erasmus complained that the Ciceronians, with their pagan usage, rendered Latin unsuitable for everyday use in a Christian society. It didn't seem to occur to him that the vernacular was the common language of everyday speech. The charge of anachronism that Erasmus brings against Ciceronian Latin can be brought against his own Latin or any Latin in the postclassical world. Florido and Erasmus seem to share the same blind spot: the only language "omnibus vel cauponibus communis" is the vernacular. This insight did not escape the Ciceronian Etienne Dolet, who, in the midst of his bitter quarrel with Florido over Erasmus's *Ciceronianus*, took the time to compose a work in the vernacular in defense of the vernacular, *La maniere de bien traduire d'une langue en aultre*. In his dedicatory epistle to Guillaume Du Bellay, he points out that the Greeks and Romans always wrote in their own vernacular, and the French need to cultivate their own language so that foreigners will no longer call them barbarians.[74] Here Dolet recognizes a new kind of cultural chauvinism, vernacular chauvinism (usually of the Italians toward the French), and a new basis of collective identity, the national vernacular. His brief treatise of 1540 can serve as a sort of prologue to the more famous and indeed infamous treatise of Joachim Du Bellay, *La Deffence et Illustration de la Langue Françoyse* from 1549 or later.[75]

In 1908, Pierre Villey recognized that Du Bellay's *Deffence* included long passages adapted if not simply translated from Sperone Speroni's *Dialogo delle lingue*, which was first published in 1542 and translated into French in 1551 by Claude Gruget.[76] Villey also keenly noted that Gruget himself recognized Du Bellay's use of Speroni and, so far from objecting to such plagiarism, applauded his compatriot's intuition of Speroni's utility for the French. Speroni reenacts a conversation supposedly held in Bologna in 1530 between the following interlocutors: Lazzaro Bonamico, staunch Ciceronian and one of Florido's champions of the Latin language;[77] Pietro Bembo, author of the *Prose della volgar lingua* and here a lapsed

Ciceronian; an anonymous courtier who defends a position close to Castiglione's in the *Libro del cortegiano*; and a self-effacing student, who has no opinion of his own but reports an earlier debate between Janus Lascaris and Pietro Pomponazzi on the capacity of the vernacular to serve as a medium of philosophy. These six speakers, designated as Bembo, Lazaro, Cortegiano, Scolare, Lascari, and Peretto (for Pomponazzi), conduct a cordial if aggressive debate on the mutual or exclusive merits of Greek, Latin, and the vernacular that constitutes a worthy intervention in the Italian Renaissance "questione della lingua." They also conduct an exercise in epideictic rhetoric. Bembo begins the dialogue by inviting Lazaro to praise the Latin language, to which he agrees under the condition that he also be allowed to blame the vernacular, which Bembo accepts under the further condition that he should defend what the other attacks.[78] The argument between Lascari and Peretto begins as a praise of Greek that turns to the dispraise of language study itself. It is this epideictic dimension that must have struck Du Bellay as laden with potential for his own odious praise of French. For his part, Du Bellay does not adhere to any of the positions defended in Speroni's dialogue (positions expressed in the vernacular regardless of their ideological orientation). Lazaro defends the exclusive imitation of Ciceronian Latin and the inaptitude of the vernacular to immortalize its authors, Bembo advocates exclusive imitation of trecento Tuscan to a cinquecento audience, the courtier favors his own native Roman dialect and says that if he's going to study a foreign language it won't be Tuscan, Lascari defends the preeminence of Greek and contests the validity of the vernacular as a medium of philosophy, and Peretto says every language is capable of philosophy and we shouldn't waste our time on language study. In a self-conscious paradox, he says such study is worthy "not of envy but of odium, not of effort but disdain, not to be learned but to be scorned."[79] Here Peretto neatly reverses humanist values, turning praise to blame. It is not their individual positions that recommend Speroni's speakers to Du Bellay's attention but rather their collective engagement with epideixis.

Du Bellay's own ambition is to found a new French poetry based on the imitation but not translation of classical models rather than French models. To do so he has to defend the vernacular while disparaging French literary tradition. As Helene Harth points out in the introduction to her translation of Speroni,[80] Du Bellay's real quarrel is not with the Latin humanists and partisans of the ancient languages, but rather with earlier French poets, whom he wants to consign to oblivion so that French literary history can begin anew with his own poetry and the poetry of his colleagues in the Pléiade. In this sense, the key chapters of his work are the survey of French poets (II, 2) and the review of poetic genres (II, 4), neither of which owes anything to Speroni. By contrast, he borrows liberally from his Italian model in order to develop arguments on the aptitude and development of the vernacular that are not really germane to his polemical purpose and that are not disputed by his French poetic rivals. Du Bellay's point is that the French language has not realized its potential because French authors have not studied enough. They are content to produce facile verses and to echo each other rather than to draw on the sacred sources of Greek and Latin verse. The French ought to be more like the Italians and imitate the ancients. This argument is poorly calculated to endear its author either to his contemporaries or to literary historians unwilling to evacuate several centuries of vernacular poetry.[81] When the Lyonnais humanist Barthélemy Aneau read the *Deffence* and the accompanying sonnet cycle *L'Olive* and authored a rebuttal under the pseudonym *Quintil Horatian*, he suggested that Du Bellay got his title wrong: he should have called it *Offense and Denigration*, not *Defense and Illustration of the French Language*.[82] In other words, the *Deffence* was received as odious praise. More specifically, Quintil easily sees through Du Bellay's ruse in his chapter on French poets, where he claims to report anonymous criticism brought against some recent French poets (unnamed by Du Bellay but usually identified as the fashionable poets of the 1540s Clément Marot, Antoine Héroët, Mellin de Saint-Gelais, and Maurice Scève) so that he can defend them. Quintil tells him, "the anonymous critic is you."[83] He understands that the *Deffence* is trying to disguise blame as praise. Moreover, when Du Bellay sums up his covert criticism by dismissing the crowd of minor French poets who follow in the footsteps of the "five or six best," Quintil's note resonates with our genealogy of Ciceronian values: "that's a fine way to defend and enrich the French language, to only admit five or six good poets, when there are five dozen worthy candidates, or at least a round dozen."[84] France can boast more than five or six poets, and to nominate so few is to discredit all the rest. This may remind us of Marullo's controversial epigram *De poetis latinis*. Like Marullo, Du Bellay reduces the poetic canon to such strict limits that he seems to hate the national tradition he purports to defend. Quintil plays Florido to Du Bellay's Marullo and tries to vindicate the true dimensions of French poetic tradition. But this new fight is over the vernacular canon, which is something that neither Florido nor Marullo would have recognized as an object of contention or even of cognition.

While the debate has shifted from Latin to the vernacular, the Ciceronian antecedents of the debate are still important to the debaters. Cicero had the temerity to say in Latin that Latin was not only not poor but even richer than Greek: "Latinam linguam non modo non inopem, ut vulgo putarent, sed locupletiorem etiam esse quam Graecam" (*De finibus* 1.10). This he maintained even to the displeasure of would-be Greeks or "eorum etiam qui se Graecos magis quam nostros haberi volunt" (*De finibus* 3.5). In the *Deffence*, Du Bellay purports to challenge the same imported ethnocentrism, as he announces at the very end of book 1: "Let those who may think I am too great an admirer of my own language consult the first book of the *Ends of Goods and Evils*, written by that father of Latin eloquence Cicero, who at the beginning of the said book, among other things, answers those who despise things written in Latin and prefer to read Greek. The conclusion of the argument is that he judges the Latin language not only not poor, as the Romans then thought, but even richer than Greek."[85] Apparently, Du Bellay sees himself as the heir to Cicero: each defends the validity and the potential of the vernacular against the prestige of a classical language. Each must also be conscious of advancing a paradox: my language is not only not inferior but even superior to what everyone else considers superior. The difference is that Du Bellay does not have the same stomach for paradox as Cicero, and so he retreats, leaving Ciceronian values to hang in the balance. He cannot praise French as highly as Cicero praised Latin, because French does not yet have any Ciceros or Virgils of its own.[86] So French is not "non modo non inops sed locupletior etiam": it remains poorer than Latin and, moreover, than Italian, its most overbearing rival. As long as Du Bellay seeks to revolutionize French poetry, he cannot stand as the spokesman of French tradition. He cannot identify unproblematically with the French language. This dilemma emerges most patently in the chapter on French poets, where Du Bellay eventually realizes that he is not living up to the promise of his title, since he has such a low opinion of the leading poets of the vernacular that he undertook to praise and to defend.[87] Nevertheless, he hopes we will not find it strange (or foreign) if we just consider that he has no better way to defend French than to attribute its poverty not to its own intrinsic defects but rather to the negligence of past writers.[88] So French is a poor language after all. It is "non modo non locupletior sed etiam inops," to reverse Cicero's terms. This conclusion to the chapter "Des Poëtes Francoys" (II, 2) provokes from Quintil a long tirade where he classes Du Bellay among "les Grecaniseurs, Latiniseurs et Italianiseurs en Françoys: lesquels à bon droit on appelle peregrineurs" (102). Du Bellay is a foreigner in his own language: the more he praises French, the less French he seems.

In effect, Du Bellay's work and its reception, what Henri Chamard calls the attack and defense of the *Deffence*,[89] revive the invidious legacy of Busiris, the patron of odious praise. Du Bellay makes the same impression on Quintil as Polycrates did on Isocrates. He refutes the accusations brought against the French language in such a way as to confirm them; his praise is an outrage to national feeling. The more he defends French, the worse it appears. He makes of French and the native literary tradition a new Busiris: *illaudata Gallia*. Du Bellay cannot fit any of the collective identities defended from Cicero to Poliziano to Erasmus to Florido to Quintil. He is neither a Latin patriot nor a Christian patriot nor a French patriot. He values a vernacular, supranational identity, and in his subsequent poetry, both neo-Latin and French, he will develop the theme of exile and estrangement from home.[90] One way for him to negotiate his new identity is through odious praise.

CHAPTER 3
Church Values

LORENZO VALLA AND THE PRAISE OF THOMAS AQUINAS

Odious praise can be judged by the controversy it causes. When Lorenzo Valla pronounced his encomium of Thomas Aquinas to an audience of Dominican friars in Rome, the cardinal of Rouen thought he was insane.[1] When Pico took up the defense of the philosophers against Ermolao Barbaro, Barbaro was delighted and the philosophers offended. When Erasmus composed his declamation in praise of folly, the theologians were incensed. In that respect, odious praise is a kind of reception theory that evaluates a text in relation to the reactions it provokes in order to confirm its generic pertinence. For each of these three epideictic performances, by Valla, Pico, and Erasmus, we will look not only at the rhetorical techniques deployed by their authors but also at the traces they left in contemporary correspondence and historiography, traces that their authors were eager to publicize. In order to provoke a lasting reaction, these authors have to challenge some of the key institutional values of their contemporary society, not to reform society but to relativize its values. One of their prime targets is the value of theology as a system of knowledge and as a professional competence. All three authors react against the hegemony of scholastic theology and its peculiar deformation of the Latin language. In order to undermine the prestige of scholasticism, they exploit the most insidious resources of odious praise.

Valla delivered his speech in praise of Thomas Aquinas on March 7, 1457, to an audience gathered in the church of Santa Maria sopra Minerva to celebrate the feast of Saint Thomas. The liturgy of the occasion is presumed to have informed the structure and content of the speech, according to Salvatore Camporeale.[2] While Camporeale strives to show how appropriate Valla's rhetoric is to the occasion, I would rather focus on how impertinent a speech it is for the occasion, and how well calculated it is to undermine the shared values of its audience. Valla begins as if he were writing an *ars rhetorica* by offering a few preliminary remarks on the conventions of public oratory. It was the custom, he observes, among the ancient Greeks and Romans, when delivering a speech in court or in a public forum ("vel ad iudices vel ad populum"), to begin with an invocation of the gods.[3] Eventually this custom lapsed, either because of incredulity or because of the prejudice that prayer is somehow effeminate, an attitude exemplified by a citation from Sallust's *Bellum Catilinae*. Valla means to revive this neglected custom, not in order to paganize but rather to show that Christians are not inferior to pagans in their religious devotion. Therefore, he will begin his praise of Saint Thomas by reciting the Ave Maria. All of this leisurely, metacritical prologue seems strangely irrelevant to the ostensible subject of the oration and to its clerical audience.

Next he reminds us, and this may be a reflection of the liturgy, that the church recognizes two kinds of saints, the martyrs and the confessors. The martyrs are generally ranked higher than the confessors, but, if you think about it, etymologically speaking, both categories are the same. They both bear witness to their faith. The Latin *confiteor* is the same as the Greek μαρτυρέω. So there's no reason why the confessors cannot be just as good as and even better than the martyrs. As if aware of his audience's growing impatience, he asks, "So, what's the point?" "Quorsum autem haec?"[4] The point is that Thomas Aquinas, though a mere confessor, was just as good as martyrs like Peter of Verona and Thomas Becket. Plus his name was better, because Thomas means, in Hebrew, twin or abyss, and he was an abyss of knowledge, "abyssus quaedam scientiae."[5] It is interesting to consider whether Rabelais could have seen this speech, first printed in 1886, before he wrote the letter to Pantagruel where Gargantua lays out an ambitious plan of study for his son, which he summarizes as follows: "Somme que je voye un abysme de science."[6] Is the giant raising his son and heir to be a Thomist? True to his name, Thomas Aquinas achieved the twin goals of knowledge and virtue to such a degree that Valla does not hesitate to rank him among the highest orders of angels, the cherubim and the seraphim. This may be an allusion to the *Celestial Hierarchies* of the pseudo-Dionysius, whose pseudonymity emerges as a critical topic later in the encomium. The labored etymologies here seem frankly parodic, and again pre-Rabelaisian, since, as we all know, the name Pantagruel also has a double etymology.[7]

Valla interrupts himself at this point to acknowledge a hypothetical objection to the hyperbole of ranking Thomas as high as the angels. What more could he say of Saint Paul or of Saint John the evangelist? Though he thinks that all those who are imbued with knowledge of divine matters have something in common with cherubim, he grants that the objection is valid.[8] This concession may not have pleased the audience, especially since he then begs their forgiveness if he is somewhat sparing in his praise of Thomas, whose praises are so well known to the assembled members of the Dominican Order that they are rather to be abbreviated than elaborated.[9] So he will expedite the praise, the better to linger on the blame.

Since Thomas was a twin sun of virtue and knowledge, Valla will talk first about his virtues and then his *scientia*, which is where he lays an ambush for his unsuspecting audience, who unaccountably commissioned this speech in the first place. Following a well-established epideictic topos, Valla informs us that the birth of Saint Thomas was preceded by signs and portents sent by god.[10] In just the same way, god sent *signa et vaticinia* to announce the coming of Saint Dominic. Valla won't say whose prophecies were greater, lest there appear to be a competition between Dominic and Thomas or, as it were, between father and son. They were of equal merit and equal majesty, neither to be preferred to the other, both adorned with all virtues and famous for infinite miracles. If Dominic founded the house, Thomas laid the pavement, if Dominic built the walls, Thomas did the frescoes, if Dominic was the column, Thomas was the *specimen* or "shining example" in Baker's translation.[11] *Bref*, one wrote the best of all monastic rules, and the other composed the most and most excellent books.[12] But, says Valla, anticipating another objection of his own contrivance, it's better to have written books than a rule, but why? Surely Thomas didn't send more people to heaven with his books than Dominic with his rule (especially if neither sent anyone there).[13] Having thus insinuated a doubt about Thomas and dissipated his praise through comparison, the speaker concludes that Thomas and Dominic are no more different from each other than Lucifer is from Hesperus, meaning the star, presumably, and not the devil.

Excusing the simplicity of his praise on the basis of the dignity of the occasion, an odd pretext, Valla now turns to the second phase of his encomium, where he will praise Thomas for his *scientia* and say to whom he holds the saint superior and to whom he considers him equal (while throwing in as a bonus all those to whom he is inferior). The encomiast is not unaware that others who have pronounced the encomium of Thomas in the same place and on the same occasion have not scrupled to prefer Thomas to all the other doctors of the church. For his part, Valla has plenty of scruples. His predecessors in this task argued that Thomas was the greatest doctor of the church because he was the first to apply to the proof of theology the disciplines of logic, metaphysics, and all of philosophy, of which prior theologians had only a superficial knowledge.[14] While quite happy to acknowledge that Thomas did indeed import philosophy into theology, Valla is not sure whether this is more a topos of praise or of blame. In effect, he will make the stronger argument weaker and convert praise to blame by suggesting that Thomas may have ruined theology by contaminating it with dialectic. To show that those disciplines which the scholastics admire the most are not worth knowing for the proper study of theology, Valla will appeal not to argument but to authority, the authority of the patristic tradition. The Greek and Latin fathers never speak of metaphysics or the *modos significandi* that so preoccupy the scholastics, designated as *recentes theologi* or *novi theologi*.[15] The patristics follow the authority of Paul, who seems to equate philosophy with vain deceit in his epistle to the Colossians.[16] So Valla's encomium establishes a genealogy of Christian theology that leads from Paul to the patristic writers to the humanists, bypassing the medieval doctors.

Speaking to the members of the Dominican Order, Valla rejects their values in favor of humanist values based largely on grammatical criteria. Patristic Latin is correct while scholastic Latin is barbarous.[17] The patristics used only the Latin vocabulary they could find in the classical authors whom they revered and never employed scholastic neologisms such as "ens, entitas, quidditas, identitas, reale, essentiale, etc."[18] They respected their identity both as Christians and Latins, but their style was pre-Christian. This leaves Valla in something of a bind, the bind in which Erasmus would enclose the Ciceronians, and so he nominates Paul as the model not only of wisdom but also of style. Paul's theology is the true method of theology and the true law of speech and writing.[19] Of course, Paul didn't write in Latin, and as Erasmus points out, his Greek is a little provincial, but the *Encomium Thomae* elides these questions in part because Paul's Latin is Jerome's Latin, which is exempt from any scholastic blemishes. When it comes to rankings, therefore, Thomas cannot rank above the patristics, who are the true heirs to Paul and, oddly, to Pauline Latin. But is Thomas at least their equal? Here Valla hedges but readily admits Thomas's superiority to medieval doctors like Anselm, Bernard, Bede, Isidore, Albert the Great, Bonaventure, Duns Scotus, and all the rest of their conceited company, who think themselves so great that they cannot endure to be compared to the ancients.[20] He is even willing to rank Thomas above Lactantius and Boethius, but only in theology (not in style). At the very limit, "licet invitus," he might put Thomas before Saint Hilary of Poitiers, one of the most eloquent of the Latin fathers. Isn't this good enough for him, he asks indignantly. "An ne hoc quidem Thomae satis est?"[21] What kind of an ingrate is this saint, he asks the audience, who may have been expecting a somewhat more gracious treatment of their patron. It is a stroke of epideictic genius to convert a typical topos of praise into an accusation of ingratitude.

Valla draws the encomiastic line at the four greatest Latin fathers, Augustine, Ambrose, Jerome, and Gregory the Great. These four can only be compared to the four preeminent Greek fathers, Basil, Chrysostom, Gregory Nazianzen, and Dionysius the Areopagite.[22] Gregory the Great is paired with Dionysius because he is the first to have read the Areopagite's works (which thus could not have been written by the character in Acts 17:34). Thomas will rank fifth among the Latins, as John Damascene does among the Greeks, all the more appropriately since Damascene dabbled in logic and metaphysics (thus initiating the decadence of the patristic tradition). Inspired by the symmetry of this professional hierarchy, Valla adds a final flourish to his dubious tribute to Saint Thomas: he imagines a heavenly choir composed of his five princely pairs of theologians accompanying in song the twenty-four elders of the book of Revelation, who are seated around the throne of the lord. Each pair performs on an allegorically appropriate musical instrument, and which instrument is better suited to Thomas than the cymbals? For the cymbals are a twin instrument, and Thomas, the twin, took equal delight "in singing to the double sound of theology and philosophy," which for Valla is a sign of a bad ear.[23] It is not clear if he is counting on his readers and hearers recalling Paul's use of the *cymbalum tinniens* to characterize spiritual gifts without love in 1 Cor 13:1, but there is a broader connotation of dissonance associated with cymbals. We have it on Pliny's authority that Tiberius called the grammarian Apion "cymbalum mundi" for his noisy, endless disputations, and this is precisely the discredit that Valla seeks to attach to scholastic practices. After this touching image of Thomas raising a racket in heaven, the encomiast concludes with a prayer to god to grant that all mortal men may achieve salvation, the same goal that Thomas has reached.

Perhaps the most telling feature of this surprising oration is that the orator should use such a formal and solemn occasion to discredit the scholastic tradition and its contamination of theology with philosophy. And he does so precisely because this amalgamation of theology and philosophy is an established epideictic topos among his predecessors in the praise of Thomas. In other words, Valla wants his oration to stand out against the tradition of praise and against the values conveyed by that tradition. His praise is a betrayal of the tradition he is supposed to honor, a trap for those lured by the comforting routine of praise. He gives his audience an unwelcome lesson in praise, in theology, and in Latin. The subsequent Renaissance tradition of odious praise will be remarkably loyal to this model, if not always generous in recognition of Valla's priority.

We can find a prolongation or, chronologically, an anticipation of these themes in the prefaces that Valla wrote for the six books of his *Elegantiae* and especially the very polemical preface to book 4. This preface is ostensibly a defense of rhetoric against clerical critics of secular learning. The author identifies his critics as holier-than-thou and claims that they are the ones primarily responsible for the loss of Latin literature.[24] In the course of the preface, these critics emerge more distinctly as the scholastic theologians and philosophers who wanted to preserve their university appointments against their upstart rivals the humanists. If you scorn eloquence, Valla asks his interlocutors, whose works shall we read besides your own, which lack all power and beauty?[25] So Valla is arguing with writers who lack eloquence, who divorce wisdom from eloquence in violation of the Ciceronian ideal.[26] He is writing on behalf of a profession or a social class that values eloquence in competition with a rival class that depreciates eloquence in the name of religion or piety. But why, he asks, should eloquence be considered in any way inferior to philosophy, disingenuously adding that he has no intention of making a comparison between philosophy and rhetoric, thus alerting us that his theme is precisely such a comparison of philosophy and rhetoric.[27] Many have shown, he remarks, that philosophy is incompatible with Christianity and that all heresies derive from philosophy. In this way, he makes explicit what remained implicit in the praise of Thomas, namely that the scholastics are in fact the enemies of religion when they import philosophy into the discipline of theology, where it doesn't belong. For its part, rhetoric, so far from detracting from religion, is of great service and ornament to divine matters.[28] Here he appeals to the same patristic tradition that we saw in the *Encomium Thomae*: starting with Jerome, all the Greek and Latin fathers dressed up the gems of divine speech with the silver and gold of rhetoric.[29] In short, whoever ignores eloquence is unworthy to speak of theology, which is a sentiment or a provocation that Erasmus would endorse eagerly in his epistolary battle with Maarten van Dorp in the wake of the *Praise of Folly*.

In this way, Valla neatly inverts the value system asserted by his adversaries. While they repudiate rhetoric, he insists that not only is rhetoric not to blame, but not studying rhetoric is to blame.[30] This clever, chiastic formula shows how odious praise seeks to invert the scale of values by simply displacing the negation *non*. What they negate, we assert, and what they assert, we negate. Moreover, Valla appeals to an ostensibly universal scale of values when he adds that whoever writes about theology without elegance is impudent, and whoever does so on purpose is insane.[31] Presumably, *pudor* and *sanitas* are universal values, and Valla would place his adversaries beyond the limits of society defined by such values. In closing, he praises the patristic writers, "veteres illi theologi," who resemble the bees that gather their honey from the flowers of the field (according to a well-known figure for eclectic imitation), while the scholastics, the *recentes*, are like the ants who hoard up in their stores what they have stolen from others. Valla is confident that most readers will prefer, like him, to act the part of the bee rather than the ant, or at least he expects the *iuvenes* to share his preference, even if the *senes* are beyond hope.[32] Oddly, it is the *iuvenes* who prefer the *veteres*, while the *senes* cling to the *recentes*. Humanism simultaneously values youth and tradition against age and modernity. It is a new traditionalism that appeals to the young, while the older you get, the more recent, and more corrupt, your taste in theology becomes. This temporal scheme will endure in humanism until Francis Bacon expresses the conviction that the ancients were mere children while maturity belongs to modernity, announcing yet another reversal of values.[33]

GIOVANNI PICO DELLA MIRANDOLA AND THE PRAISE OF SCHOLASTICISM

In May of 1494, Angelo Poliziano wrote to Bernardo Ricci, secretary to the Florentine ambassador to Milan, to acknowledge receipt of the latter's love poetry and to respond to some disturbing rumors that Ricci had reported concerning their friend Giovanni Pico della Mirandola.[34] Apparently, Pico had many envious detractors in Milan who depreciated his style, though they didn't dare to impugn his learning. Therefore, Ricci had asked Poliziano to send him some letter or other short text of Pico to vindicate the latter's competence as a Latin stylist and also to vindicate Poliziano's well-known admiration for Pico. Therefore, Poliziano announces, he is sending Ricci a copy of a letter that Pico had sent to Ermolao Barbaro in defense of the scholastic philosophers, designated as "barbaros philosophos," and the reply by Barbaro, so that Ricci could compare the two authors' style of writing. Moreover, Poliziano wants Ricci to understand that Pico, accustomed to treat of weightier and more recondite matters, had only invested the minimum of time and effort in this correspondence, which thus allows but a superficial appreciation of Pico's genius, in keeping with the adage *Leonem ex unguibus aestimare* or *To know a lion by his claws*.[35] And yet, for all its haste and extemporality, the letter is a veritable manual of rhetoric, embodying all the virtues admired by rhetorical humanism, designated by the Latin terms *Latinitas, nitor, concinnitas, color, venustas, ornatus*, and so on, right up to *mira maiestas*.[36] Still Pico cannot gain the reputation of eloquence, but Poliziano is confident that time will right this wrong. In the meantime, he trusts that Ricci will enjoy the letter, even though it destroys eloquence, for it destroys it so eloquently that it restores what it destroys. For nothing can destroy eloquence but eloquence itself, and even it can't, granted that it can do what it can't do.[37] Thus ends the letter with an unintelligible flourish of paradox. When Poliziano prepared his correspondence for publication, he included at the outset of book 9 a sequence of four letters: his own to Ricci, Barbaro's original missive to Pico, and the two letters he had already copied for Ricci.[38] In this way, Pico's letter, which can be read in any number of contradictory ways, first appeared and circulated widely in the form in which Poliziano chose to present it, namely as a flamboyant demonstration of the preeminence of eloquence, which, when turned against itself, fortifies itself.

Poliziano's editorial commentary orients our reading of the letter as an exercise in odious praise or paradoxical encomium, and this reading is supported by the original reception of the text and its circumstances of composition. The Venetian humanist Ermolao Barbaro had written to Pico on April 5, 1485, to reciprocate the young man's praise and to comment on his course of study. He is particularly pleased by Pico's progress in the study of Greek and exhorts him to continue this study, admonishing him that no one has ever written anything important in Latin who didn't also know Greek. For, he adds, he won't count as Latin authors those Germans and Teutons who, though they might be learned, are commonly called "dull, rude, uncultured, barbarians."[39] Evidently, Barbaro didn't see any need to further identify "Germanos istos et Teutonas," whom Pico readily identifies in his reply dated June 3, 1485, as the scholastic philosophers in whose study he has wasted his precious youth.[40] He names Thomas Aquinas, Duns Scotus, Averroes, and Albert the Great, and his letter alludes to or cites many others from the same tradition. If any of these contentious bores could come back to life, they would surely have something to say for themselves, and so Pico imagines a speech in self-defense delivered by the scholastics against the humanists. This is the famous epideictic performance known to posterity as *De genere dicendi philosophorum* (On the style of the philosophers). Some historians of philosophy have interpreted Pico's letter as a genuine defense of philosophy against rhetoric, ignoring Poliziano's packaging of the text. This is the attitude of Eugenio Garin in his seminal if schematic work *L'umanesimo italiano*, which hails Pico's text as "a true and proper manifesto against the degeneration of rhetoric" and "an eloquent defense of pure thought and of the dignity of research."[41] Others have been most attentive to the alternations of Pico's own style, from scholastic to humanistic, depending on the genre he cultivates.[42] Still others are sensitive to a consistent hostility to the scholastics in Pico's work.[43] Martelli hedges his bets by saying the letter is like Proteus; it can't be pinned down.[44] A more properly rhetorical reading of the text can show how Pico uses the techniques of epideictic rhetoric to undermine a system of values.

Pico's imaginary philosopher begins by positing that philosophy is as far removed from rhetoric as truth is from falsehood. For what else is rhetoric, he asks, than the art of lying, while philosophy is occupied in knowing and demonstrating to others the truth.[45] That is why we read the Holy Scriptures, written rustically not elegantly, for nothing is less suited to the search for truth than rhetoric.[46] Here Pico puts his finger on a crucial point of contention in the debate between scholasticism and humanism: who will have the professional competence to interpret the Bible? We have already seen Valla's assertion that you can't do theology if you don't know rhetoric, and throughout his career Erasmus would insist on the role of rhetoric in Bible studies. What is at stake in this debate is not the value of the Bible, which both sides recognize, but the privilege of expounding its meaning, either through the methodology of philosophy as taught in the universities or through the knowledge of rhetoric and the ancient languages. Pico exacerbates this professional rivalry by praising philosophy in such a way that his immediate audience understands him to exalt the power of rhetoric and to challenge the institutions of church and university that he purports to uphold. The rest of the letter follows the same course, where the speaker praises the unadorned truth of philosophy with all the adornments put at his disposal by rhetoric. When he says that philosophers are interested in what they say, not how they say it, he makes sure that we notice how he says it: "Quaerimus nos quidnam scribamus, non quaerimus quomodo; immo quomodo quaerimus, ut scilicet sine pompa et flore ulla orationis . . ."[47] The construction of the phrase contradicts the argument by drawing our attention to *quomodo*, that is, to the manner rather than the matter of the speech. Martelli has analyzed other passages of the letter to reveal the figures of rhetoric in which Pico's speaker luxuriates.[48] The most subversive element of the letter may be its consistent appeal to the Bible, as if the Bible were a work of scholastic philosophy. What is more moving and more persuasive, asks the imaginary philosopher, than reading Holy Scripture?[49] Fine, answers the humanist, but you didn't write it, and you can't even read it without a translation. Pico insinuates that the scholastics claim the Bible for their side as if it were written in their language (and thus had to be explained in their language), but the humanists, especially Valla and Erasmus in their annotations on the New Testament, show that it isn't. The question is still unresolved for Pico and his generation, who didn't know Valla's *Collatio*, and this irresolution adds to the protean quality of the letter.[50]

At the end of his speech, the philosopher grants the humanist a concession: eloquence and wisdom belong together and should be reunited. But both sides are to blame: if philosophers have separated wisdom from eloquence, their rivals, designated as "historici, rhetores, poetae," have done the same.[51] For Hanna Gray, this is the whole point of Pico's letter, to rehabilitate an ideal unity betrayed by both sides.[52] This is a plausible reading and consistent with Pico's reputation as *comes concordiae* and spokesman of syncretism. We can test it against the end of the letter. The letter ends with what is known as the palinode, the final section where Pico addresses Barbaro ostensibly in his own voice: "Well, dear Ermolao, the above is perhaps what those philosophers might present in defense of their barbarism."[53] Speaking for himself, Pico does not agree with his fictitious speaker, and in fact he has written his letter as an exercise in infamous praise: "Sed exercui me libenter in hac materia tamquam infami, ut qui quartanam laudant."[54] The expression "in hac materia tamquam infami" and the example of the praise of quartan fever lead us back to Aulus Gellius and book 17 of the *Attic Nights*, where chapter 12 treats of infamous subjects, "De materiis infamibus." The first example Gellius can think of is the praise of the quartan fever by the sophist Favorinus of Arles, who wrote "exercendi gratia," like Pico. In this way, Pico's letter inscribes itself in the tradition of the sophists, who praise what others blame. At the same time, Pico claims to have vented his sincere indignation at certain *grammatistae* (second-rate humanists?) who, as long as they know a couple of etymologies, lord it over the philosophers and reject what they don't understand, as a dog rejects Phalernian wine.[55] This is supposed to be Pico's true voice, but it's too late to look for the true voice in this kind of exercise.[56] And what does he mean by "a couple of etymological discoveries"?[57] Could he be thinking of Poliziano and his pair of *entelechia* and *endelechia* and his not yet published argument in defense of the Latins against the Greeks and Cicero against Argyropoulos? Is he making fun of his own champion? His parting words are in praise of Barbaro, who realizes the elusive ideal of wise eloquence: "it is not easy to say what praises are yours to boast, who among philosophers are the most eloquent, among the eloquent the most philosophical."[58] This may be the proof of Gray's argument, but it may also be just another exercise in infamous praise by an avowed student of sophistic. Is anyone safe from his praise? All values seem to be endangered by odious praise, which leaves no solid ground beneath it.

Barbaro wrote back to Pico to recognize his generosity in answering a mere letter with a whole volume and to testify to his pleasure at receiving such an elegant and erudite work. He is especially gratified to see that they are both on the same side, even if Pico pretends to speak for the other side. "Consequently you give yourself the appearance of an enemy who champions the enemy, of an ally standing against an ally, of yourself opposing yourself. This gives me the most exquisite pleasure, because under the guise of defending you utterly kill off those you defend."[59] This is an interesting turn of phrase, "yourself opposing yourself," which suggests that odious praise allows the speaker to duplicate himself and to stand at once on both sides of an issue, in a literal rendering of "in utramque partem" argumentation. For Barbaro, this can only be an illusion, since he is convinced that Pico has really slaughtered those whom he pretends to defend. First of all, he has shown that the enemies of eloquence must rely on others' eloquence to defend themselves. Moreover, Barbaro can testify to the impact that Pico's letter has made on friend and foe alike: "I am informed by friends of mine in Padua that your defense—which is already being given the title of Concerning Scythians and Teutons, in other words, Laudation of Typhon and the Furies—has mightily annoyed the majority of those you defend, while in other groups your deed is differently interpreted. So at least in our circles, with whom you quarrel in word but agree at heart, the thing you did is to everybody most gratifying."[60] Here we have some empirical evidence of odious praise, to which Barbaro adds his testimony that to the humanists it was "most gratifying." So where praise offends, blame ingratiates, but it still leaves everyone a little perplexed, "aliis aliter factum tuum interpretantibus," which is a good way to summarize the bibliography on Pico's letter. Barbaro responds to the challenge of Pico's text with a counterspeech delivered by a Paduan Aristotelian, "that apelike Paduan,"[61] who repudiates Pico's offensive defense of the philosophers. Barbaro brings to his task a humanist command of adages, remarking, for instance, that Pico defends the philosophers as if he were crying at his mother-in-law's grave.[62] He also teaches Pico a lesson in decorum, since his bad guy speaks badly. But Barbaro's univocal performance is no match for Pico's equivocality, his fusion of two voices in one. The enduring appeal of Pico's letter is the confusion it causes with its ambivalent praise that seems to undermine everyone's confidence in their own values, whether or not they admit it.[63]

Before we leave the Pico-Barbaro debate on the *genus dicendi philosophorum*, we can acknowledge an instance of reception that has been somewhat neglected heretofore and that can help to elicit the rhetorical significance of the debate. In 1531, Josse Bade published in Paris an edition of Quintilian's *Institutio oratoria* with commentary by Petrus Mosellanus, and this edition was reissued throughout the decade, sometimes in combination with the commentary of Joachim Camerarius. What interests me is Mosellanus's commentary on *Institutio* 2.16.1, where Quintilian raises the question of whether rhetoric is useful and is constrained to admit that it can be very useful to its enemies, who use the powers of speech, *orandi viribus*, to denounce rhetoric. Following Cicero's lead, Quintilian most likely has in mind Plato's assault on rhetoric in the *Gorgias*, whereby he showed himself to be a consummate orator (*De oratore* 1.47). At the lemma *orandi viribus*, Mosellanus has the following annotation: "Thus for the sake of sharpening his wit Pico della Mirandola devotes nearly a whole volume to defending the barbarians and attacking eloquence, and for that he relies on the power of eloquence. Ermolao Barbaro answered him copiously in his defense [of eloquence]."[64] So Mosellanus has updated the topic of using rhetoric against rhetoric with a nearly contemporary reference to humanist culture. What the *Gorgias* was for antiquity, the Pico-Barbaro debate is for modernity: a reminder that whatever is said against rhetoric can also be said for rhetoric as long as it is well said. When Mosellanus says "exercendi ingenii gratia," he may have in mind an adjacent passage of the *Institutio* where Quintilian addresses the Platonic question of whether rhetoric is an art. For Quintilian, rhetoric is assuredly an art, and those who say otherwise do so merely to practice their skill, like Polycrates and his infamous praise of Busiris.[65] Now we are back to the origins of odious praise and Isocrates's testimony to the sophist Polycrates. Mosellanus's commentary on Quintilian helps to confirm Pico's place in the tradition of odious praise.

DESIDERIUS ERASMUS AND THE PRAISE OF CHRISTIAN FOLLY

In 1511, Erasmus published his *Moriae Encomium* or *Praise of Folly* with a dedicatory epistle to his friend Thomas More. He presents the work to More as a sort of memento of their friendship, and he insists that he was inspired by More's name to compose an encomium of Moria. He foresees that there will be no lack of detractors (he's too good a detractor himself to ignore that possibility), who will bring two principal complaints against his work. First, they will say that the work is too frivolous for a theologian, and next they will say it is too mordant, too satirical for a Christian. As for the first count, Erasmus appeals to a long list of literary precedents, including Homer's Βατραχομυομαχία, Virgil's *Culex*, Ovid's *Nux* (on which Erasmus wrote a commentary), the praise of Busiris by Polycrates and Isocrates, Favorinus's praise of the quartan fever, and so on up to a certain Grunnius Corocotta, who wrote a last will and testament of a pig, according to Jerome's commentary on Isaiah. This is a very serviceable bibliography of odious praise from the beginning to the end of antiquity, and Erasmus's work inscribes itself as a modern revival of this ancient tradition. If every other walk of life has its relaxations, why not studies too, especially if trifles lead to serious reflection.[66] Frivolous matters treated seriously can yield more profit than the pretentious speeches of certain writers. For instance, some authors write a long premeditated speech in praise of rhetoric or philosophy, some write panegyrics for princes, and some issue a call for a new crusade. These are supposed to be examples of frivolous treatment of serious subjects, to which Erasmus prefers his trifling topic, folly. As the author of a *Panegyricus*, Erasmus ought to know what he is talking about, but who does he have in mind by "someone [who] delivers a laborious patchwork speech in praise of rhetoric or philosophy" (CWE 2:163)?[67] This sounds suspiciously like the Pico-Barbaro correspondence in praise and dispraise of philosophers along with Poliziano's editorial intervention in praise of rhetoric. Erasmus has chosen a sneaky way to acknowledge this modern precedent after proudly listing all his ancient precedents.

As for the second anticipated charge, of mordancy or cruel satire, he appeals to a sort of poetic license that has always been granted to moderate social criticism. As long as he doesn't name names, besides his own, he's not attacking so much as he is teaching and admonishing. Moreover, his satire is equal opportunity: he doesn't leave anyone out, and the reader can tell that he is more interested in pleasure than biting. Finally, if there is someone who is still not placated by all his excuses, let that person remember that it is an honor to be criticized by Folly, who always speaks in character.[68] The problem is that Folly does not always speak in character. There are times when Erasmus betrays the principle of "decorum personae," and this feature endows the work with the sort of destabilizing equivocality that fascinates readers of Pico's letter. Folly can step out of character to espouse values that seem very congenial to Erasmus and Erasmianism, and these are the moments that incensed his critics.

Our own reading can be guided by the very first documented reception of the text, the letter sent by Maarten van Dorp to Erasmus from Louvain in September 1514. Dorp writes to warn Erasmus that his Moria has offended the faculty of theology at the University of Louvain, which is a formidable adversary. He reports the most prevalent reaction: even if you tell the truth, isn't it crazy to take such pains just to make yourself odious?[69] Two things in particular have caused a scandal: the acrimonious satire on the order of theologians and the final section of the work, which focuses on Christ and life in heaven ("de Christo vitaque beata").[70] Consequently, these are the parts of the work that deserve our attention, since they were read as odious praise. The structure of the Moria has attracted the ingenuity of many critics, who have proposed elaborate schemas to explain the elusive organization of the text. One of the best-known and most thorough schemes is that proposed by Jacques Chomarat in his chapter on declamation from his *Grammaire et rhétorique chez Érasme*.[71] Chomarat recognizes, after the preliminary sections, four major parts of the argumentation followed by a brief epilogue. The satire of the theologians occupies section 6 of part 3, while the passage that Dorp's colleagues found most scandalous goes from the fourth to the sixth and final subsection of part 4. In Miller's critical edition for ASD, these occupy pages 144 to 158 and 186 to 194. To these we will add sections 2 and 3 of part 4, where Folly plays the theologian and cites the Bible and especially Saint Paul in her own favor (ASD IV-3:178–86).

In Chomarat's division, part 3 of Erasmus's work surveys the folly of those professions that are most renowned for wisdom and that have seized, as it were, the famous golden bough (ASD IV-3:138). Among these the theologians tend to monopolize Folly's attention, though she wonders if it wouldn't be prudent to pass them over in silence rather than stir up such a hornet's nest, according to the adage *movere Camarinam*, and end up being denounced for heresy (ASD IV-3:144–46). No group is less willing to acknowledge Folly's patronage, and yet none is more loyal to her attendant *philautia* or self-love than the theologians. They derive a great deal of their self-pride from their own incomprehensible vocabulary and their own futile disputes about uselessly subtle questions. She is thinking particularly of the scholastics, for she warns that you will sooner escape from the labyrinth than from the snares of the "Realists, Nominalists, Thomists, Albertists, Ockhamists, Scotists," and the rest (ASD IV-3:148–50). So subtle is their reasoning that this new race of theologians completely overshadows the apostles and the church fathers. Paul knew how to keep faith, but he didn't know how to define it. The apostles baptized the faithful, but they couldn't tell you the four causes, formal, material, efficient, and final, of baptism. They had Christ but they didn't have Aristotle. The scholastics are willing to make some allowances for the apostles, but they have no patience for the patristic writers, like Chrysostom, Basil, and Jerome, who relied more on morality than on syllogisms in their own disputes with pagans and heretics (ASD IV-3:154). Like all her followers, the theologians are quite happy to be fools, since they regard themselves as the sole support of the church, which would collapse without their syllogisms, and they are convinced that no one can be a Christian without their approval. Admittedly, Folly does find it amusing that they speak so barbarously, "quam maxime barbare spurceque loquantur" (ASD IV-3:158). In this way, Erasmus revives Valla's polemic against the scholastic theologians while adding his own emphasis on their alienation from the apostles. This is the section of the encomium that proved professionally odious to Dorp's colleagues.

Another section calculated to give offense comes at the outset of what Chomarat identifies as the fourth part of the speech, where Folly performs a parody of the characteristic gesture of theology, to distort the meaning of Scripture. She says that she will cite literary testimony in her favor, and after a paragraph of testimony taken mainly from Horace, she turns to biblical testimony, begging the pardon of theologians for trespassing on their territory.[72] Assuming the persona of the theologian ("dum theologum ago," ASD IV-3:179), she invokes not the nine Muses but the spirit of Duns Scotus to guide her on the thorny path of interpretation. Seeing as she has always kept such close company with the theologians, she reminds us, she must have learned some of their tricks. After a preliminary foray through Ecclesiastes, Folly turns to Saint Paul, who tells the Corinthians, "I am talking like a madman" in the Revised Standard Edition or, in Folly's version, "ut insipiens dico" (ASD IV-3:182), departing from the Vulgate "minus sapiens dico" (2 Cor 11:23). This is an ambivalent passage because of the comparative form that Paul uses when preferring himself to false or rival apostles: "ministri Christi sunt minus sapiens dico plus ego." Does *plus* go with *minister* or *minus sapiens*? Folly naturally presents Paul as competing for the championship of *stultitia* among the apostles. This flagrant misreading prompted Erasmus to add in 1514 a long digression on theological hermeneutic license that is the most important change he made to the text after the initial 1511 edition. First Folly anticipates the objections of the *graeculi* or humanists, whose acknowledged leader is her own disciple Erasmus, who understand Paul to claim to be a better minister of the gospel than the other apostles, not a bigger fool (ASD IV-3:182). The correct reading is all the same to Folly, who can appeal to more standard authorities like Nicolas de Lyra, whose name reminds us of the adage *Asinus ad lyram*, not to mention *delirium*. But why should she appeal to authorities when it is a well-known privilege of theologians to distort the meaning of Scripture (ASD IV-3:182–83)? After all, Paul himself set the example when he misread the inscription on the altar to the unknown god in Acts 17:23. This type of distortion, which Erasmus always renders with the verb *torqueo*, may be the only continuity between Paul and the scholastics. From here, Folly turns to other examples of misreading that seem to have in common their relevance to the soon to be inflamed question of the treatment of heretics. For instance, what does Christ mean in Luke when he tells his disciples to sell their belongings and buy a sword (ASD IV-3:184)? Even Folly knows he means the *gladium spiritus* or the spiritual arm of the gospel, but that's not how Nicolas de Lyra read it, who understood *gladium* literally as an instrument of violent repression. More provocatively, Folly says she recently attended a theological meeting, as she often does, where the question of religious persecution was raised in relation to Paul's epistle to Titus 3:10. Paul cautioned his readers to avoid the heretic, *devita*, whereas one of the disputants in this recent meeting, that is, recent in 1514, called for heretics to be killed, reading the verb *devita* as the prepositional phrase *de vita*.[73] So persecution goes together with misreading, and the humanist polemic against the theologians is related to the larger question of how to maintain concord in the church. Here as elsewhere, Erasmus espouses a value system based on peace and concord, not authority and repression.

Finally, Folly gets tired of citing witnesses on her behalf and says that there's no point in belaboring the obvious, for even Christ boasts of being a fool (ASD IV-3:186). We know from Dorp that this final section of her speech, "de Christo vitaque beata," alarmed the faculty of theology at Louvain, and they must have had good reason for their anxiety. Their alarm may have something to do with Erasmus's faltering principle of "decorum personae," announced in the dedicatory epistle to Thomas More. The transition is gradual. First Folly reminds us that Christ in the Gospels always exalts the humble and humiliates the proud, and he gives thanks that god has hidden his mysteries from the wise and revealed them to children, that is, to fools. Moreover, Christ calls his followers his "flock" and calls himself their "shepherd," and the sheep is the dumbest animal, according to Aristotle. So far, so good: that is the typical sophism that we expect from Folly. However, what are we to think when she says that Christ became a fool when he assumed human form, just as he became sin to redeem our sins (ASD IV-3:188)? Is this a sophism or a Christian mystery? Moreover, Christ chose to redeem our sins through the folly of the cross or *stulticiam crucis* (ASD IV-3:188), which is an important image in the Pauline epistles and one that implies that folly can in fact be a Christian value. When she says that the whole Christian religion has more to do with folly than with wisdom (ASD IV-3:189), is she being ironic or profound? Finally she turns to the *vita beata*, much to the scandal of Dorp's colleagues. With a carefully worded preamble, to which Erasmus will later draw his critics' attention, Folly promises to show that Christian salvation is nothing other than a certain kind of insanity and folly.[74] The demonstration hinges on the Platonic dichotomy of body and spirit. What will that life in heaven be, she asks, to which all pious minds aspire? Won't the spirit absorb the body, and then the spirit will be absorbed by the supreme mind so that the whole man will be outside himself, according to the principle of *ecstasis* or ecstasy?[75] Folly too seems to have stepped outside herself. Now she is speaking not as the patron of vanity and arrogance and self-deceit, but as a Christian mystic or a Neoplatonic visionary. Is it still an honor to be criticized by Folly? In conclusion, she remarks that while perfect felicity is only possible in the next life, in this life a privileged few experience a foretaste of future felicity when they take leave of their senses and experience a kind of dementia. This is what Folly modestly calls her contribution, "Moriae pars" (ASD IV-3:193), though later editions have the variant reading "Mariae pars." In his answer to Dorp, where he defends this final section on Christian folly, Erasmus asserts that he has done everything to respect

Christian piety, even at the expense of rhetorical decorum, by making Folly speak out of character.[76] So Erasmus acknowledges what his audience sensed: he has dropped his pretext of "decoro personae serviendum" and laid bare a devastating anti-intellectual, antirationalist critique of hyperrationalist theology, a critique that can't be dismissed as typical foolishness. This is the part that proved ideologically odious to many readers.

In his letter of September 1514, Dorp had referred plaintively to the real context of hostility to Erasmus's work: the clash of disciplines between humanism and scholasticism. He implores Erasmus to empathize with his critics (something unprecedented in academic disputes): "But those who condemn you and your work are only human; they do it from weakness and not wickedness—unless you think nothing but the humanities, not even philosophy or sacred study, can make a good man."[77] In his own reply, epistle 337, Erasmus seizes on this point to promote, in a brutally sectarian way worthy of his adversaries, the humanities over the scholastic disciplines of philosophy and theology. In this long epistolary diatribe against the university theologians, Erasmus lays bare the stakes of the dispute. Theologians hate the humanities because, if good letters revive and the world grows wise (under the tutelage of the humanists), then the theologians will appear to know nothing, who heretofore appeared omniscient.[78] More bluntly: theologians are afraid of good letters and fear for their tyranny.[79] What is at stake is cultural hegemony in Europe at a time of transition, a time when Europe is making a language turn that threatens to leave the scholastics behind.[80] The *Encomium* exacerbates this bitter clash of values because it threatens the vulnerable prestige of an entire cultural class.

CHAPTER 4

Religion and the Limits of Praise

ISOCRATES AND THE PRAISE OF SUPERSTITION

Like many modern statesmen, the legendary Egyptian king Busiris, while prone to atrocity, was a friend of religion. It's known as cultivating your base. Isocrates makes Egyptian religion the centerpiece of his unlikely encomium of Busiris: "It is especially worthwhile to praise and admire the piety of the Egyptians and their service to the gods" (11.24).[1] Isocrates's appraisal of Egyptian religion, and especially his regard for Busiris's institution of animal worship, strike some observers as insincere,[2] while others find them plainly alarming. Especially provocative is Isocrates's enthusiasm for the religious deception practiced by Egypt's rulers from the time of Busiris: "But those who have been such effective leaders in religious matters that the rewards and punishments of the gods appear greater than they really are, these people benefit human life most. Indeed, by instilling in us a fear of the gods from the beginning, they cause us not to act like beasts toward one another" (11.24–25). Isocrates admires Egyptian religion for its effectiveness as an instrument of social control, which is precisely what provoked the Renaissance commentator Hieronymus Wolf, whose great edition, translation, and commentary on the letters and speeches of Isocrates appeared in 1570. Wolf begins his commentary on the central section of Isocrates's *Busiris* under the rubric "de utilitate religionis," and he gets right to the point.

> He treats the commonplace of the utility of religion, and in such a way that his treatment pertains more to superstition than to

true piety. People who can't see the difference between the two are guilty of a gross error and fall into extreme impiety, holding that everything which is said about divine providence, the immortality of the soul, and rewards of the pious and punishment of the impious is a lie. Therefore, opinions like this have to be read judiciously, and the true, revealed cult of god has to be kept a mile apart from the superstitions of the pagans.[3]

Wolf is wary of Isocrates because his praise of the Egyptians draws no distinction between religion and superstition, and this confusion tends to encourage rampant irreligion. It's all very well to analyze someone else's religion in terms of utility, but what happens if people start thinking about their own in those terms? If we start to understand our religion as a social institution, we'll no longer believe in it.

These fears seem all the more founded when Wolf turns from paragraph 24 of the *Busiris* to the beginning of paragraph 25, "Indeed, by instilling in us a fear of the gods from the beginning, they cause us not to act like beasts toward one another."[4] Wolf explains that acting like beasts means performing acts of open violence, like lions and bears, or stealthy fraud, like foxes and snakes. Unfortunately, the whole world is now full of such beasts, he exclaims. The reason for this emotional outburst in a learned commentary is Wolf's apprehension that the common people, who are wont to go from one extreme to the other, have converted from mass superstition (i.e., Roman Catholicism) to rampant Epicureanism and religious indifference, so that religion is completely neglected.[5] This of course is the "everything is going to hell" topos, one of the few constants of human civilization, but Wolf is nevertheless an important witness to a rise in secular values, what he labels a "conversion." It is interesting to speculate what this conversion may have to do with the impious potential that Wolf recognizes in the praise of superstition. For the praise of superstition didn't end with Isocrates but rather enjoyed quite a Renaissance in Wolf's day and may have encouraged a new way of looking at religion as a social institution rather than a revealed truth. Odious praise is a precursor of social science.

To judge by Wolf's nervous reaction, Isocrates's *Busiris* is not like other examples of odious praise. The other examples we have seen are entertaining, surprising, even perplexing, but rarely alarming. Wolf senses in Isocrates's praise a transgression, and not because of Busiris's legendary crimes. It is the treatment of religion that goes too far, that transgresses the limits of praise.

In other cases, odious praise challenges some professional, national, or linguistic identity, some partisan identity that does not implicate humanity in general. Theism or belief in god is supposed to be a constituent element of human identity, an innate idea common to all peoples, according to Cicero (*De natura deorum* 2.12). The praise of superstition then challenges an otherwise unchallenged value, a value that is not meant to be reversed by insidious reasoning or verbal effrontery. Odious praise deals in paradox, and paradox reveals the fallacy of consensus. No *doxa*, no opinion is common to all peoples. Every opinion is local, except for theism. For the believer, religion is not laudable, it's true; and it certainly is not laudable for being false. When Isocrates praises Egyptian religion, he disrupts the ultimate consensus. So the praise of religion is the last frontier of odious praise.

In his commentary, where he recognizes the utility of religion as a commonplace, Wolf mentions other authors who treat the same commonplace. First he mentions the Sisyphus fragment attributed to Euripides by Plutarch in the *De placitis philosophorum*, Wolf's source, but more likely by the sophist Critias, identified as the author by Sextus Empiricus.[6] This verse fragment of a lost play about Sisyphus credits a wise man with inventing the fear of the gods in order to deter clandestine crime.[7] Then Wolf says that Livy is of the same opinion talking about Numa Pompilius and his political use of religion in early Rome. Then he cites Statius's *Thebaid*, where Capaneus exclaims, "Primus in orbe deos fecit timor" or "in the beginning fear created the gods."[8] So this is the reading list of ancient authorities on the political uses of religion, but Wolf is noticeably reticent about their modern successors. After Isocrates, Critias, Livy, and Statius, where does our reading list lead? For the Renaissance, I nominate two obvious candidates, Niccolò Machiavelli and Jean Bodin, and a sleeper, Michel de Montaigne. We will take them in chronological order, after returning to an ancient author unaccountably omitted by Wolf.

SUPERSTITION IN ROME: POLYBIUS, MACHIAVELLI, AND INNOCENT GENTILLET

Book 6 of Polybius's *Histories* contains the famous account of the Roman constitution, diagnosed as a mixed constitution, and of the Roman military system that enabled Rome's rise to world empire. To highlight the merits of the Roman constitution, Polybius compares it to the Carthaginian constitution, and this comparison culminates in a highly provocative assessment of Roman religion. In effect, Polybius treats the Romans the way Isocrates treats the Egyptians. First of all, he says that Rome excels over other peoples most of all in its conception of the gods or ἐν τῇ περὶ θεῶν διαλήψει (6.56.6).[9] We may recall that Isocrates admired the Egyptians especially for their piety and "service to the gods" or τὴν περὶ τοὺς θεοὺς θεραπείαν (11.24). Polybius adds that what holds Rome together is what other people blame, namely superstition (6.56.7). So here we have an unabashed praise of superstition. In fact, Roman religion is so theatrical, so sensationalized that it can hardly be exaggerated, and Polybius recognizes that his readers may be amazed at this (6.56.8). Presumably the Greeks were amazed by Roman gullibility, but they might also have been surprised by Polybius's eagerness to praise what others blame. This praise of religion is a self-conscious challenge to Hellenic values and will become, in the course of time, an involuntary challenge to Christian values. Polybius explains to his skeptical audience that it is all very well to dispense with superstition in some utopia of wise men, but in real life the people or the πλῆθός is governed by passions and impulses and so can only be controlled by "invisible fears" and suchlike "tragedy" (6.56.10–11). The ancients knew what they were doing, Polybius assures us, when they propagated the fear of the gods (echoes of the Sisyphus fragment); it is the moderns (i.e., us readers) who are wrong to look down on superstition (6.56.12). Curiously, Polybius acknowledges the same decline of religious belief in his own time that Wolf did in his; both are concerned with a kind of decadence. So the praise of religion is a sort of nostalgia that challenges the self-confidence of the present. To sum up, because of their gross superstition, the Romans actually honor their oaths, unlike the Greeks (6.56.13–15). Isocrates says nearly the same about the Egyptians: "The Egyptians are so holy and solemn about these matters that oaths sworn in their sanctuaries are more credible than those sworn by others" (11.25). When Wolf read "by others" or παρὰ τοῖς ἄλλοις, he immediately understood the Greeks, adding that Isocrates was bound to admit what everyone knows, that the Greeks never keep their word.[10]

What is remarkable about Polybius is his ability to stand outside of religion and to appreciate the role of religious belief without sharing that belief. Religion is in effect an article of the Roman constitution. It is an institution that developed over time in order to ensure the stability and coherence of an expansionist state. When the Renaissance got its hands on Polybius, readers, especially those interested in political theory, reacted with a mixture of fascination and repulsion to such frank atheism. One of the keenest readers seems to have been Machiavelli, but it is still not clear how he could have read Polybius. The *editio princeps* of book 6 dates to 1549, but Janus Lascaris published a condensed version already in 1529. Dionisotti speculated that Machiavelli knew Polybius by word of mouth, perhaps through discussions in the Orti Oricellari.[11] In any event, Machiavelli didn't read Greek and there was not yet any translation in print when he wrote his *Discorsi*, which nevertheless presuppose a knowledge of book 6 of the *Histories*. Indeed, in the estimation of Gennaro Sasso, Machiavelli is the first Western writer to make a systematic use of book 6 of Polybius's *Histories*, in his *Discorsi* I, 2.[12] Sasso has in mind the theory of ἀνακύκλωσις, or the cycle of constitutions, which Machiavelli adapted from Polybius (6.9.10), and Sasso has treated this theme so extensively and tenaciously that I'm not sure there is anything left to say. Instead, I would rather look at the series of chapters from book 1 of the *Discorsi* (I, 11–15), where Machiavelli analyzes the function of Roman religion in a Polybian spirit superimposed on a narrative derived from Livy.[13] These chapters sponsor what is known as the functional analysis of religion.[14]

Chapters 11 to 15 of book 1 of the *Discorsi* constitute a praise of Roman religion motivated by what might strike us as an unseemly sincerity and even fervor on the part of an ostensibly Christian author. Chapter 11 celebrates Numa Pompilius and his foundation of Roman religion, which Machiavelli regards as a more important contribution to Rome's greatness than the foundation of the senate and the military by Romulus.[15] Numa's triumph was to instill in his undisciplined subjects the fear of the gods that made them obey the senate and the optimates throughout the course of the Roman Republic. So it is the political function of religion that counts, not its spiritual function and certainly not its doctrinal content. Numa stands at the head of a long tradition, for every legislator who seeks to change the customs of his people must resort to god. That's what Lycurgus did in Sparta, Solon in Athens, and so on.[16] Montaigne will complete the list in his essay "De la gloire," where he sums up the whole tradition as follows: "And every polity has a god at its head" (477). Moreover, Machiavelli regards religion as the motor of the rise and fall of states, which rise with the observance and fall with the neglect of religion.[17] So religion is an organic factor in the life cycle of republics and not simply, as Sasso points out,[18] a trick that the ruling class plays on the people. This is a more reverential approach to odious praise than we have seen elsewhere.

In closing, chapter 11 returns to the theme of the *Proemio* and the importance of studying Roman history in order to imitate it. Numa set an example by using a sort of salutary imposture to establish a system of belief that endured long after him, and we should not despair of following his example. Admittedly, it was easier for him since he was dealing with simple, primitive people, but Savonarola was able to convince the cynical Florentines that he spoke with god and to command their belief. So it's still possible to imitate the past, because, as we read in the preface, human nature hasn't changed. Yet, if religion sustained the Roman Republic for several hundred years, it didn't work so well in Florence, and Savonarola would have been horrified to learn that he was imitating Numa. Machiavelli's example seems best calculated to contradict his own theory and to leave us wondering what lessons we can retain from antiquity.

Chapter 12 maintains that the state can only remain uncorrupted as long as religion is uncorrupted. To gauge whether religion is corrupted, we have to identify the foundations of religion and see how far a given people has strayed from those foundations. Pagan religion was founded on two practices, oracles and divination, and everything else was subsidiary. As long as the oracles flourished in the ancient world, the pagan state remained strong, but once the oracles were discredited and their political manipulation was discovered, religious belief declined and the people became unruly.[19] This explanation seems somewhat tangential to Roman history, since the obvious examples of oracles speaking "a modo de' potenti" involve Macedonian rulers. For instance, we learn from Cicero's *De divinatione* (2.118) that King Philip "corrupted" the Pythian oracle (long before the rise of Rome), and this may be what Machiavelli had in mind. So he drops oracles and stresses the role of miracles in promoting religion. For example, when the Romans sacked Veii, the soldiers entering the temple of Juno thought they heard the goddess speak to them. The military leaders fostered this false miracle, because miracles encourage credulity, and credulity strengthens obedience. Roman religion achieved the perfect match of cunning with credulity. By contrast, Christianity has grown completely alienated from its foundations and so Christendom has grown weak and impotent. Machiavelli does not hesitate to blame Italy's ruin on the church, and this for two reasons. First, the rampant immorality of the papal curia has extinguished religious devotion in Italy. Second, the church's territorial ambitions have prevented the unification of Italy, and only a unified state can survive. Clearly, Machiavelli's theory does not allow for an ecclesiastical state, and this is probably because an ecclesiastical state instills in its subjects a contempt for religion.

In the following chapters, 13 to 15, Machiavelli turns to Livy's history for some specific examples of how the Romans used religion to promote civic order and military discipline. Chapter 13 treats the expediency of religion in internal politics and more bluntly in class conflict between the nobility and the plebs. In one case, when the people created tribunes from their own class, the nobles exploited various portents and omens to induce the people to reverse their choice and appoint tribunes from the nobility. On another occasion, the nobles brought out the Sibylline Books and used their oracles to deter the people from following their tribunes. Always, the ruling class used the sanctity of oaths to keep the people in line. Basically, the senate manipulated the credulity of the people in order to defeat the tribunes and maintain a monopoly on political power. For Machiavelli, this is a credit to religion. As long as religion is effective, no one cares if it's true. Chapter 14 deals with the special class of Roman augurs known as *pullarii*, who took the auspices from the sacred birds before each battle to determine whether or not the army should fight. In fact, Roman military commanders relied on strategy rather than augury to engage with the enemy, but the good generals, like Lucius Papirius Cursor, can go to battle when the time is right while seeming to respect the auspices, while the bad ones, like Appius Pulcher, make no pretense of respecting the auspices. What counts is prudence on the part of the generals and confidence on the part of the soldiers. Meanwhile, the augur is out of luck since he's a casualty of military prudence. John Najemy has a good reading of Papirius and the chickens that stresses the distinction between those who interpret religion and those who believe in it.[20] Roman religion seems to work precisely because the authorities don't believe in it and the people don't understand it. Finally, chapter 15 shows us how the Samnites use religion as a last resort in their battle with the Romans, led by Papirius, that master of psychology. Since both sides mobilize superstition, what can this prove? Do the winners vindicate religion or do the losers discredit it? This example seems to warn against exemplarity: "tout exemple cloche," says Montaigne in his essay on experience (III, 13, 1070). To recapitulate, the Romans use religion to enforce the law and maintain order in the city. In war, religion is used to enforce military discipline. In no case does religion fulfill a spiritual function. The division of labor between those who use religion and those who believe in it points to a problem that Jean Bodin will intuit in his *Methodus*: if religion keeps the people in line, what will keep their rulers in line? Those who use religion cannot use it on themselves. So either religion has to be a coercive force for everyone, or it has to be supplemented by some independent force or *virtù* in order to maintain the integrity of the system. In this way, the praise of religion offers a very lucid critique of what it praises.

Though studied obsessively and annexed to nearly every discipline, Machiavelli is rarely understand in terms of epideictic rhetoric, and yet he guides us to this context himself.[21] Chapter 10 of book 1 of the *Discorsi* can be seen as a sort of prologue to the following chapters on religion. Here Machiavelli extols history as the arbiter of praise and blame. Most people are perfectly able to distinguish between what is laudable and what is blameworthy, but they still are lured by false values to imitate those who deserve more blame than praise. The problem, apparently, is that they don't read history, for if they did, they would rather emulate the virtuous than the vicious and be enrolled among the *laudati* rather than the *vituperati*.[22] As an indelible record of praise and blame, history shows us what to imitate and what to avoid, and at the top of the scale of praise are the founders of religion, who are, among all subjects of encomium, worthy of superlative praise.[23] Machiavelli's analysis of Roman religion will thus reveal what to imitate and what to avoid in statecraft by a judicious assignment of praise and blame. Of course, he tends to praise what conventional Christian morality blames: deceit, coercion, imposture, but his analysis is still epideictic.[24] He praises efficacy and success, and he blames imprudent candor. Above all he tends to discredit truth as a meaningful criterion of praise or blame, and this is his legacy.

The reception of Machiavelli in the sixteenth century can vindicate to some extent the epideictic reading of his work. In 1576, the Protestant jurist Innocent Gentillet authored the *Discours sur les moyens de bien gouverner et maintenir en bonne paix un royaume ou autre principauté*, which has come to be known as the *Anti-Machiavel*. This work reduces the *Prince* and the *Discourses* to a series of numbered maxims that Gentillet fears have led France to its ruin and that he means to rebut with countermaxims of good government. The bloated and polemical preface blames every one of France's calamities on Machiavelli and implores the princes of the realm to restore the old-fashioned principles of government that prevailed in France before the invasion of this insidious foreign doctrine. Gentillet seems particularly incensed that Machiavelli presumes to talk about the art of war when he never fought in one (much like Gentillet himself), and he retrieves from the classical commonplace tradition an anecdote that seems to him quite apt to his purposes. In brief, Machiavelli telling other people how to wage war is like the philosopher Phormio lecturing to Hannibal *de re militari*:

"Herein it falls out to Machiavelli as it did once to the philosopher Phormio; who one day reading in the Peripatetic school of Greece, and seeing arrive and enter there Hannibal of Carthage (who was brought thither by some of his friends, to hear the eloquence of the philosopher), he began to speak and dispute with much babbling of the laws of war and the duty of a good captain, before this most famous captain, who had forgotten more than ever that proud philosopher knew or had learned."[25] In book 2 of Cicero's dialogue *De oratore*, the speaker Catulus expresses his impatience with those who purport to teach the art of rhetoric. "I don't need some Greek doctor to tell me my job," he protests, "when he's never been to the forum before."[26] This reminds him of Phormio lecturing to Hannibal about war. People who teach the art of speech are like Phormio: they teach others what they have never learned from experience.[27] So in this version, Phormio is the figure of the *rhetor* or theorist who presumes to instruct the *orator* or practitioner. The anecdote opposes theory and practice, Greek and Roman, teaching and doing. It seems like a synopsis of Montaigne's essay "Du pedantisme." Phormio is one of those useless teachers of whom Montaigne says, "They know the theory of all things; *you* find someone who will put it in practice" (102). When Gentillet transposes this anecdote to Machiavelli, he appeals to a similar indignation against rhetoric and sophistic and idle theorizing. Now Machiavelli is the *rhetor*. Even worse, his rhetoric is the rhetoric of blame, and Gentillet even provides a bibliography of Machiavelli's calumnies against the kings and people of France.[28] Gentillet conceives of his own work as a defense of the French against these foreign slanders and a rectification of Machiavelli's twisted principles. Responding to the challenge of *Discorsi* I, 10, Gentillet's *Discours* will praise what Machiavelli blames (the French) and blame what he praises (treachery, tyranny, and atheism).

Gentillet responds to Machiavelli's chapters on Roman religion in book 2 of his *Discours*, rearranging the material according to his own impenetrable logic and training his indignation above all on Machiavelli's dismissal of the criterion of truth in the assessment of religion. Each maxim in Gentillet's work consists of a paraphrase of Machiavelli's argument in large type and then an hysterical rebuttal in different typography. Ordinarily, the paraphrases are quite intelligent and on their own might serve to propagate Machiavellianism, just as some patristic writings conserve the anti-Christian arguments they are supposed to refute. Under the title "A Prince ought to sustain and confirm that which is false in religion" (135),[29] maxim 2 of book 2 recalls the ways in which Rome's military and political leaders exploited popular belief in portents and prophecies in order to ensure discipline and obedience. In the margin, beneath the title, we learn that maxim 2 targets *Discorsi* I, 12, 13, and 14. What particularly incenses Gentillet is the business about false miracles in I, 12. How can you advocate falsehood in religion, he asks, when religion is what ties us to god, who is truth itself? Of course, for Machiavelli, religion is what ties us to each other, and therefore it falls within the scope of sociology, not theology. Incredibly, in order to rebut Machiavelli's functional analysis of Roman religion, Gentillet feels compelled to offer his version of natural theology, so that he can prove the veracity of the Christian religion by natural reason.[30] We may wonder why he feels so defensive about his religion that he thinks he needs to prove it. What is it about Machiavelli's interpretation of Roman religion that makes him so insecure? Machiavelli is interested in how the Romans used religion to achieve their political aims, and he appreciates the role of deceit in religion. For him, religion is a method, not a doctrine. What distinguishes between religions is not their truth but their effectiveness (which may be inversely proportional to their truth). If Gentillet is a believer, Machiavelli is an interpreter, and the two roles are mutually exclusive. Above all, Machiavelli challenges Gentillet's confessional identity as a Calvinist. Western Christianity splintered into several confessions through the fanatical assertion of an exclusive truth, often by means of martyrdom. If we evacuate the criterion of truth and replace it with expediency, what becomes of confessional identity? Is it expedient to be persecuted for the truth? Machiavelli's ideas are a supreme provocation in the age of confessionalization.

There is a subsidiary point that needs to be developed in regard to maxim 2. Gentillet's natural theology appeals, naturally, to non-Christian authorities, all of whom recognize divine providence. Well, almost all. The notorious exception is Epicurus, father of atheism and patron of "Machiavelli and the Machiavellians, who are well enough known to be very Epicurean in their lives" (138).[31] This is a commonplace association, endorsed even by authors like Bodin who were suspected of atheism themselves, but it doesn't make sense. Epicurus taught that the gods are indifferent to human affairs and therefore we cannot gain an advantage from prayer or sacrifice. Religion is completely disinterested because it can't do anything. Machiavelli praises Roman religion because it is effective, it works. If, as Wolf suspected in his commentary on Isocrates, the atheist is the one who praises the expediency of religion, then Epicurus is a true believer because for him, religion is totally inexpedient.

Gentillet returns to *Discorsi* I, 12 in maxim 5 of book 2, which takes issue with Machiavelli's emphasis on the decline of oracles in the ancient world. For Machiavelli, paganism was founded on oracles, and so when oracles declined or were discredited, religious feeling declined and social order deteriorated. For Gentillet, however, the decline of paganism meant the rise of Christianity and the consequent improvement of morals. Gentillet is interested in the role of Christianity in universal history, and for him, the conversion from paganism to Christianity represents progress, not decline. But Machiavelli is interested in a process that he considers common to all religions: when paganism neglected its foundations, it declined. When Christianity neglected its foundations, it too declined. The content of religion is irrelevant, since all religions undergo the same pseudobiological process. Most importantly, for Machiavelli, when a religion becomes alienated from its foundations, the people grow incredulous and social discipline implodes. Farewell to "buoni ordini." In this theory, incredulity (which Machiavelli is supposed to personify) is the threat that must be avoided or postponed. Naturally, Gentillet asks, if that's so, then why are you an atheist? How can an atheist advocate credulity?[32] Here Gentillet puts his finger on a key issue. In order to analyze how religion works, you can't believe in it. Atheism is not a system of belief; it is a way of looking at systems of belief. Whoever explains religion is an atheist. Before the development of the social sciences as university disciplines, this explanation is the task of epideictic.

SUPERSTITION IN FRANCE: JEAN BODIN

Jean Bodin is a superstitious fanatic, a prescient and trenchant political thinker, a retrograde Aristotelian, and, naturally, an atheist. He's hard to classify.[33] So it's no very welcome contribution to scholarship to volunteer another classification: Bodin the epideictic orator. Bodin published his masterpiece *Les six livres de la République* in 1576, the same year that Gentillet published his cruelly obtuse rebuttal of Machiavelli. The preface to the *République*, addressed to Guy du Faur de Pibrac, similarly attacks Machiavelli and with similar obtuseness or else with Machiavellian cunning. Either is possible. Bodin insists that Machiavelli identified impiety as one of the twin pillars of the state even though everyone knows that religion is the foundation of the state: "Machiavelli, who laid down as the twin foundations of Commonweals impiety and injustice, and condemned religion as hostile to the state. However Polybius, tutor and lieutenant of Scipio Africanus, and deemed the wisest statesman of his time, even though he was an outright atheist nevertheless recommends religion above everything else as the principal ground in all Commonweals. . . . He states that the Romans never had anything of greater force than religion."[34] For Bodin to appeal to Polybius in order to defend the political utility of religion against Machiavelli is rather provocative. Perhaps Bodin knows that he is going to advocate a Machiavellian position and so he feels obliged first to repudiate Machiavelli, thus setting an example for future disciples. Turning to the second supposed pillar of the Machiavellian republic, injustice, Bodin compares Machiavelli to the Academic philosopher Carneades, who in 156 BCE went on an embassy from Athens to Rome, where he delivered, on consecutive days, two opposing speeches for and against justice. This is a notorious instance of epideictic rhetoric, and by situating Machiavelli in the lineage of Carneades, Bodin shows that he appreciates the rhetorical dimension of the *Discorsi*. In fact, he appreciates it so much that he will pronounce his own epideictic oration in the great chapter on religious tolerance from book 4 of the *République* (IV, 7).[35]

Book 4, chapter 7 of the *République* begins with an axiom: faction and sedition are bad for every kind of republic.[36] To say otherwise, to praise them, is a mere paradox, as if one were to praise the quartan fever like the sophist Favorinus of Arles (635). This axiom is a self-conscious rejoinder to the notorious thesis of the *Discorsi* that Rome owed its greatness to the conflicts between the patricians and the people. In book 1, chapter 4 of the *Discorsi*, Machiavelli speaks in praise of what he calls "i tumulti" or the civil discords and upheavals of early Republican Rome that led to the establishment of the tribunes of the people. Moreover, he is conscious of advancing a paradox and of praising what others blame in his appreciation of tumult.[37] This thesis proved to be, as its author anticipated, quite provocative. Gentillet, for one, was not amused. Maxim 31 of part 3 responds to *Discorsi* I, 4 and to its praise of tumult, suggesting that Machiavelli's argument resembles the logic of a certain philosopher, mentioned in Aulus Gellius's *Attic Nights*, who praised the quartan fever.[38] The philosopher, whose name Gentillet doesn't remember, is correctly identified by Bodin as Favorinus. In other words, both Bodin and Gentillet recognize Machiavelli's praise of tumult as a paradoxical encomium in the tradition of sophistic rhetoric, and both ostensibly repudiate this tradition.

However, if we return to book 4, chapter 7 of the *République*, we can see that Bodin emulates Machiavelli's rhetorical performance, not in praise of civil discord, which he disparages, but in praise of superstition. The topic of faction and sedition in the republic leads to the question of how to deal with religious discord or "les guerres touchant le faict de la Religion," which have spread throughout Europe in Bodin's lifetime.[39] Bodin's first principle is that the state should never tolerate any debates about religion, for to debate a religious belief is to weaken it and encourage disbelief. As if to illustrate his point, Bodin mentions some ancient philosophers who questioned the *endoxa* or received beliefs of their society: Anaxagoras maintained that snow is black, Favorinus said that fever is good for you, and Carneades praised injustice.[40] All these epideictic performances merit scorn, but it is even worse to question religious beliefs. After all, even notorious atheists like Polybius recognize that religion is the foundation of the state. In this way, the chapter on civil war echoes the preface while insinuating a critique of the widespread policy of secular authorities in the European Renaissance to organize colloquies or debates in a vain attempt to pacify religious tensions.

Far better, in Bodin's estimation, is the policy that we would call, but that he does not call, religious tolerance. Modestly refraining from identifying the true religion (and thus subscribing to a sort of Machiavellian neutrality), Bodin says that if the prince wants to unite his subjects under one confession, he should not resort to force. Rather than persecute the minority, he should take a page out of the book of Emperor Theodosius the Great, who confronted the Arian heresy: "Yet would not this good emperour either force or punish the Arrians, although that hee deadly hated them, but graunted unto them both the Arrians and the Catholikes their churches, and suffered them in everie towne to have two bishops, of either religion one: and albeit that hee commaunded certaine edicts to bee published against the Arrians, yet was hee well contented to have the same holden in suspence, and not put into execution" (537).[41] So Theodosius granted the Arians freedom of conscience and freedom of cult, and he even suspended certain edicts of persecution that he formerly issued against them. These are precisely the concessions that French Protestants were trying to negotiate with the Valois monarchs during the French Wars of Religion. The business about the edicts is particularly important because it relates to Bodin's famous theory of sovereignty: the sovereign has the right to make and unmake the law when it is convenient to the state. The French king might find it convenient to end the war and legalize Protestantism.

If he doesn't like ancient history, the prince can simply emulate the Ottoman Empire, where, according to a commonplace of Renaissance thought, the subjects of the empire enjoy absolute freedom of conscience.[42] The praise of the Turks to a European audience is itself a subgenre of paradoxical encomium. In Bodin's view, the prince should never force the conscience of his subjects, for intolerance is likely to breed atheism: if you deny people their own religion, they won't want any religion, and society will descend into utter lawlessness. This striking argument first appears in the 1579, Lyon edition, where Bodin adds, just as the worst tyranny in the world is preferable to anarchy, so the most powerful superstition is less harmful than atheism. Admittedly, it is not a particularly ringing praise of superstition to say that it is not nearly as detestable as atheism.[43] In this version, the Republic could probably do without either superstition or atheism.

However, when Bodin rewrote his work in Latin in 1586, he expanded the chapter on civil discord to incorporate a more extensive discussion of the function of superstition in society. It is quite clear upon inspection that Bodin composed the Latin version of book 4, chapter 7 of the Republic while he was working on his interconfessional dialogue *Colloquium Heptaplomeres*, which remained in manuscript at his death. In any event, the Latin text of IV, 7, echoing the vernacular, says that just as there is no form of government worse than anarchy, so there is no plague more harmful to the state than atheism, adding that people are wrong to equate polytheism with atheism since, as the Latin text remarks in a passage that has no precedent in the vernacular version, superstition, of whatever sort it may be, keeps people in check and holds them to their duties whereas impiety or atheism cancels all fear of wrong doing.[44] What atheism and anarchy have in common is the fact that they both breed impunity, while superstition, which in this respect seems indistinguishable from religion, fosters a salutary fear of punishment. This is the same argument deployed by one of the speakers of the *Colloquium Heptaplomeres*, the Roman Catholic Coronaeus, in the context of a defense of religious tolerance initiated by another speaker, the nonsectarian Senamus.[45] Coronaeus rephrases the argument more concisely later in the dialogue when he says that superstition of any sort is more "tolerable" than atheism, because the atheist fears nothing but a witness or a judge.[46] Atheism is like the ring of Gyges: it allows you to hide from your own conscience. By contrast, the superstitious man is convinced that he is always under surveillance, and this conviction is an invaluable instrument of social control.

We might ask here what exactly Bodin praises under the name of superstition. When Isocrates claims to admire the Egyptians for instituting animal worship as a kind of loyalty test, he is talking about superstition as an irrational, primitive belief. When Hieronymus Wolf reads Isocrates during the European Reformation, he denounces superstition as a false religion, an alienation from revealed truth. When Polybius praises superstition (τὴν δεσιδαιμονίαν), he is following Isocrates's example and reversing the values of his audience of Greek rationalists, who fail to appreciate the political advantage of a candid fear of the gods. Bodin seems to be talking about something more general or more fundamental. In his neo-Latin usage, *superstitio* means *divini numinis metus* or simply *numinis metus*, fear of god, which is necessary to supplement fear of the laws. In this sense, superstition means theism, which in turn means intimidation, while atheism is fearless and lawless. However, in the context of a plea for religious tolerance in the Wars of Religion, superstition means the minority religion, Calvinism. The majority is religious and the minority is superstitious, but if the majority persecutes the minority, they will convert from superstition to atheism and all hell will break loose. The Catholics need to tolerate Protestantism in France just as the Protestants need to tolerate Catholicism in the Netherlands. Only when your religion becomes the state religion or the majority religion does it cease to be a superstition in this political sense, while it remains a superstition in the more fundamental sense of theism. Calvinism, with its vernacular psalms and somber décor, is like the chickens in ancient Rome: it is a superstition that can be turned to the advantage of the state.

In all these examples from Bodin, the praise of superstition is subordinate to the even more paradoxical praise of tolerance. Tolerance is so widely associated with atheism and so deeply stigmatized in the Renaissance that it is quite plainly an *infamis materia* like the topics that Favorinus worked on. So what prevailing value does tolerance challenge? It must challenge the truth. If you believe that your religion is true, then you believe that everyone else's is false. To tolerate another religion is to be complicit in falsehood, an eternal falsehood. To advocate tolerance means that you don't care about the truth: to promote tolerance is to demote the truth.[47] Bodin claims quite remarkably that he doesn't care which is the true religion (though there can only be one).[48] Bodin won't take sides, and his parenthetical formula is vague enough to make everyone suspicious. When Machiavelli talks about miracles, he says they are celebrated in all religions, "even the false ones."[49] Religion is not based on truth but on carefully orchestrated credulity. Similarly, for Bodin, religion is not based on truth; it's based on fear. To say that your religion is true is faint praise. Bodin is Machiavellian in the sense that he disregards the criterion of truth, which is not to say that he always agrees with Machiavelli.

In his *Method of History* or *Methodus ad facilem historiarum cognitionem* of 1566, at the end of chapter 6, Bodin broaches the subject of the education of the prince or *institutio principis*, which is itself an important genre of Renaissance political philosophy. For Bodin, those charged with the education of the prince should focus not on foreign languages and other "pernicious and inept" subjects, as he calls them, but rather they should concentrate on religion.[50] For as long as the prince is so indoctrinated, or *informatus*, as to think that god is the judge and spectator of all his actions, he will do nothing criminal, nor will he even think anything shameful.[51] Such a prince will be an inspiration to his subjects and a model for them to follow. The situation of the prince is unique since, unlike his subjects, he cannot be deterred from crime by the fear of laws and magistrates. As Bodin asks, what magistrate, what laws, what powers will coerce the prince, unless he is held in check by fear of religion?[52] Here the prince plays the role assigned to the superstitious man in the passages we have already examined from the *De republica* and the *Colloquium*. He is *contained* or held in check by his religious belief that he is constantly under surveillance. While Coronaeus in the *Colloquium* says of the superstitious man, "hunc numinis metus in officio continet," the *Methodus* says, "princeps religionis metu contineatur." This passage from Bodin's first major work may in fact be his critique of Machiavelli. If the ruling class of ancient Rome used religion to keep the people in check, who kept them in check? Bodin reverses the terms: religion keeps the prince in check and he keeps everyone else in check. This version understands religion not as a trick to play on others but rather as a kind of training that works even on the trainers. No one is outside the system. No one except the theorist. In effect, only the theorist can speak in praise of something so all-encompassing as religion.

THE PATH OF PRAISE: MONTAIGNE

Compared to all the other writers sampled in this chapter, Michel de Montaigne may seem to take a fairly conventional approach to superstition and religion. Montaigne's religious position is often labeled fideism; he is loyal if not pious.[53] When he talks about superstition, he rarely expresses any enthusiasm or even much curiosity about how it works.[54] He is wary of understanding religion, because he seems to agree that understanding may inhibit belief. There is, however, one essay where Montaigne tries his hand at the functional analysis of religion as if he were impersonating Polybius or Machiavelli. There is one essay where he succumbs to the lure of social theory. This is the essay "De la gloire" (II, 16), which is about glory in the sense of honor and renown as incentives for virtue. So it is a reflection on ethics and on whether morality can be self-sufficient or whether it requires some external sanction like glory. The essay is generally understood to endorse "the primacy of the individual conscience" over the social sanction of honor. We can be virtuous all by ourselves even if no one is looking. This is basically the same question investigated by the other authors considered in this chapter, or rather it is an answer to that question which Isocrates and his colleagues would have found hopelessly naïve and politically disastrous. For glory, they substitute religion as the key incentive to virtue and inhibition to vice. So, when situated in the context outlined here, Montaigne's essay is really about religion and about how society has invented those stimuli, whether fear of god or desire for glory, that supplement our inadequate conscience and restrain our antisocial impulses. If human conscience really worked and if virtue were its own reward, who would need religion? The idealization of conscience is an atheistic impulse that usually retreats before the prospect of rampant crime.

"De la gloire" is an act of plagiarism in the guise of a critique. Just as Bodin pretended to argue against Machiavelli by using Machiavelli's arguments, so Montaigne poses as an indignant adversary of Cicero in an essay that from beginning to end conducts its argument with quotations and borrowings from Cicero's philosophical treatises.[55] If we had Cicero's lost work *De gloria* (advertised in *De officiis* 2.31), Montaigne assures us, then we could read some howlers, since Cicero was notoriously vainglorious: "I believe that if we had the books that Cicero had written on this subject, he would tell us some good ones; for that man was so frenzied with this passion that if he had dared, he would, I believe, have readily fallen into the excessive view into which others fell, that virtue itself was desirable only for the honor that always attended it: *There is little difference 'twixt buried idleness and hidden virtue*" (470). This hypothetical transgression is then illustrated with a quotation from Horace, not Cicero, before the essayist expresses his *dépit* that such a false opinion could ever have been entertained by one honored with the name of philosopher. This is surely a treacherous way to use one's sources, by imputing to them false opinions from lost works that are then rebutted with arguments taken from the extant works. The idea that virtue itself is valuable only for the honor it brings, which was conventional in Rome before Cicero challenged it, leads Montaigne to the ubiquitous question of witnesses: "If that were true, we should be virtuous only in public" (470). If we are only afraid of getting caught, "if impunity to us is justice," then morality is impossible. Citing a series of examples of unobserved moral integrity from Cicero's *De finibus*, Montaigne proposes himself as example: "What S. Peduceus did in faithfully returning the money that C. Plotius had entrusted to his sole knowledge, and what I have often done in the same way, I do not consider so laudable as I should consider it execrable for him to have failed to do it" (470). The adjective *laudable* or *loüable* (II, 16, 621) in this quote responds to a claim that Cicero makes in the *De officiis* that the honorable is by its very nature praiseworthy even if no one praises it.[56] What Cicero considers praiseworthy, Montaigne considers merely routine. In effect, the essayist stakes out a position more radical than his model. If Cicero says that the *honestum* is laudable, Montaigne says that praise sets too low a standard: honesty and integrity should be expected rather than applauded. Here he seems to evacuate completely the role of the audience or the witness from moral deliberations: we should all be trustworthy in the dark. Yet Montaigne is not a utopian thinker, and he understands the practical dimension, or indeed the practical urgency, of moral inquiry. Therefore he turns his attention to what was the most practical application of his topic in the context of the French Wars of Religion: the value of military glory.

Montaigne conducts his critique of glory as a critique of warfare, or the pursuit of glory in arms. Naturally, this critique implicates his own social class—the French nobility—and their claim to social preeminence. In a sense, "De la gloire" experiments with the proposition that social status can be adjudicated by conscience rather than by public recognition. If virtue does not require an audience, why should nobility? Conversely, if nobility must be performed in public, how can virtue be confined to the theater of conscience?[57] In a curious anachronism, the essay challenges the feudal ethos of military glory with a modified quotation from *De officiis* 1.14 (where Cicero discusses "something that, even though it be not generally ennobled, is still worthy of all honour"):[58] "Those who teach the nobility to seek only honor in valor, *as if what is not noted were not honorable*, what do they gain thereby but to instruct them never to hazard themselves unless they are seen, and to take good care that there are witnesses who can bring back news of their valor?" (471). If the nobility learns to fight courageously only in front of witnesses, ignoring the Ciceronian doctrine of *honestum*, which Montaigne was eager to use against Cicero, then they will learn to be cowards when no one is looking. Yet soldiers rarely have the leisure to inspect their comrades' conduct when their own life is at risk: in battle there can be a crowd without an audience. Moreover, as Montaigne adds in one of the most memorable phrases of the essay, soldiers are not always called on to perform in full view, or on stage, as it were: "On n'est pas tousjours sur le haut d'une bresche ou à la teste d'une armée, à la veuë de son general, comme sur un eschaffaut" (II, 16, 622). Sometimes we are caught "between the hedge and the ditch," where there are no spectators.

The use of theatrical metaphors such as "sur un eschaffaut" suggests the proximity of morality and performance while raising the question of whether virtue is better performed in public or in private. Cicero may have coined this metaphor, and inspired Montaigne's figurative language, when he proclaims, in the *Tusculan Disputations*, that there is no better theater for virtue than conscience.[59] Montaigne the soldier, sensitive to the indignity of unobserved heroism, consoles himself with the notion that virtue is its own reward. In war our virtuous deeds, however hidden from view, earn us the satisfaction of our own conscience: "We must go to war out of duty, and expect this reward, which cannot fail for all noble actions, however hidden they be, and even for virtuous thoughts: the contentment that a well-regulated conscience receives in itself from well-doing" (472). Here we are very close to Cicero's ideal of the theater of conscience, and Montaigne follows up his thought with the phrase "It is not for show that our soul must play its part, it is at home, within us, where no eyes penetrate but our own." In the theater of conscience, we perform for an audience of one. In the original 1580 version of the essay, this image of acting within, or "jouer son rolle au dedans" (II, 16, 623), is followed by a passage on the hypocrisy of war: "People are right to decry the hypocrisy that is found in war" (474). What can be easier, Montaigne asks, than for a coward to play the hero, even in a tight spot, or "à un dangereux pas," through the sheer force of effrontery? In effect, we cannot judge by appearances; we cannot bear witness to anyone's courage but our own: "That is why all these judgments that are founded on external appearances are marvelously uncertain and doubtful; and there is no witness so sure as each man to himself" (474). Morality is a performance that admits only one spectator and a trial that calls only one witness.

It is precisely at this juncture of his essay that Montaigne inserted on the Exemplaire de Bordeaux, some time between 1588 and 1592, an unexpected reference to the ring of Gyges, which he calls "l'anneau Platonique" (II, 16, 625 C). If the Platonic ring were available in warfare, he admits ruefully, there are plenty of soldiers who would hide when they ought to be seen, in order to avoid danger: "And if they had the use of the Platonic ring which made whoever wore it invisible if it was given a turn toward the palm of the hand, plenty of people would often hide when they ought to show themselves the most" (474). This unorthodox variation on a familiar topos stands in unsteady relation to the theatrical metaphor. With the ring of Gyges in hand, rather than play the hero under compulsion, the coward could shrink away from combat without endangering either his life or his reputation. The ring allows the coward to stay in character; it is an imaginary alternative to hypocrisy. The hypothetical popularity of the ring also suggests that glory and its opposite—shame—are still powerful sanctions on human behavior, providing an incentive to courage and a disincentive to cowardice. The many people who would eagerly claim such a ring are clearly indifferent to the lessons of "De la gloire" and the "primacy of the individual conscience" which has been recognized as the message of the text.[60] In this respect, the late interpolation to the essay represents a sort of disillusioned recognition that conscience cannot replace other systems of surveillance. Classical moral philosophy notwithstanding, the theater of one cannot enforce morality.

In the original version of the essay, Montaigne persists in accumulating arguments against glory and in favor of pursuing virtue for its own sake. His conclusive argument regards money and the aristocratic stigma against working for money. It would be fine, he allows, for artisans and professionals (non-nobles), to pursue glory as their *loyer* or salary, but a nobleman, he implies, cannot work for hire. "It might perhaps be excusable for a painter or another artisan, or even for a rhetorician or a grammarian, to toil to acquire a name by his works; but the actions of virtue are too noble in themselves to seek any other reward than from their own worth, and especially to seek it in the vanity of human judgments" (477). According to this paradoxical reasoning, glory is a sort of pay that disqualifies the nobleman. For Montaigne and his class, engaging in most forms of commerce or salaried employment is an act of *dérogeance* that can lead to the loss of noble privileges.[61] However, it is unlikely that Montaigne's audience would have been ashamed to achieve glory in arms, and few would have found his reasoning persuasive. He himself seems to have put so little faith in his critique of glory that, at this very moment in his argument, he reverses himself and recognizes the instrumental value of glory. Everything he has said in favor of internal moral sanctions and against external ones now appears to have been a utopian theory ill adapted to modern practice. Employing his favorite concessive adverb, he endorses the false opinion of glory: "Si toute-fois cette fauce opinion sert au public à contenir les hommes en leur devoir, qu'elle accroisse hardiment, et qu'on la nourrisse entre nous le plus qu'on pourra" (II, 16, 629).[62] After so many and such strenuous arguments against glory, the essayist capitulates: glory is a "false opinion" but an effective sanction because people believe in it, while conscience seems to be rather a feeble resource.

This concession, "si toute-fois," inspired a further concession, added to the 1588 addition, which reorients the discussion toward the rhetoric of praise and blame. "However, if this false opinion is of service to the public in keeping men within their duty; if the people are thereby roused to virtue; if princes are touched by seeing the world bless the memory of Trajan and abominate that of Nero; if it moves them to see the name of that great gallows bird, once so frightful and so dreaded, so freely cursed and reviled by the first schoolboy who deals with it, let it grow boldly and let it be fostered among us as much as possible" (477). Glory is useful if it can motivate princes to be like Trajan and unlike Nero. No one glorifies Nero (except Cardano). In the notes to his edition of the *Essais*, Pierre Villey suggests that Montaigne took this idea from the praise of history in the preface to Jean Bodin's *Methodus*, but it is more likely to derive from Machiavelli's *Discorsi* I, 10. In fact, both Bodin and Montaigne follow Machiavelli, but Montaigne follows more closely. *Discorsi* I, 10 is where Machiavelli extols history as the arbiter of praise and blame and attributes moral failure to the neglect or misunderstanding of history. Provided they study history and capitalize on the memories of antiquity, princes will emulate those rulers who are praised and shun the example of those who are blamed.[63] Among Roman emperors, Titus, Nerva, Trajan, Hadrian, Antoninus, and Marcus Aurelius earn praise, while Caligula, Nero, Vitellius, and a bunch of other crooks are blamed. Their history shows us the path of glory and of blame: "E se la istoria di costoro fusse bene considerata, sarebbe assai ammaestramento a qualunque principe a mostrargli la via della gloria o del biasimo."[64] Montaigne's revisions can be seen as a gloss on this passage. "La via della gloria o del biasimo" is the epideictic path. Epideixis reinforces moral values: praise of Trajan and blame of Nero train princes to be virtuous. Conversely, the praise of Nero obliges us to reexamine our values. Epideixis and ethics go together. In effect, the praise of glory is, on Montaigne's part, a rather reluctant praise of rhetoric.

Following this train of thought, the essay turns from rhetoric to religion in a late addition to the Exemplaire de Bordeaux. In this addition,

Montaigne recalls a passage from the *Laws* where Plato emphasizes the importance of εὐδοξία (950c4) or *gloria* in the Latin, "bonne reputation" (II, 16, 629 C) in the French. Plato says that even bad people are good judges of who is wicked and who is good, because they are endowed with a certain faculty that he calls θεῖον εὔστοχον (950b7–8) or divine sagacity. Montaigne renders it in Christian terms as "quelque divine inspiration." Montaigne finds this endorsement of εὐδοξία typical of Plato's opportunistic recourse to religious belief, which is a sleight of hand that he learned from his teacher, Socrates: "This person and his teacher are marvelous and bold workmen at bringing in divine operations and revelations everywhere that human power fails: *as the tragic poets have recourse to a god when they cannot unravel the end of their plot*" (477). Plato the social theorist knew how to make the most of religion, which reminds Montaigne of a line from Cicero's *De natura deorum* where the Epicurean Velleius compares the Stoics to the tragic poets.[65] The Stoics invoke divine intervention to explain what they don't understand, the way the tragic poets resort to the *deus ex machina* when they can't figure out how to end their play. This is an interesting expression of Epicurean cynicism redirected from Stoicism to Platonism, but Montaigne does not condemn Plato. He admires him the way that Machiavelli admires Papirius. They both knew how to use religion (because they didn't believe in it).

The original version of the essay, interrupted by Plato and Machiavelli, reiterates the need to make concessions to popular prejudice: "Since men, because of their inadequacy, cannot be sufficiently paid with good money, let false be employed too" (477). Naturally, we expect the false coin to mean glory, already designated as a false opinion. Yet from what follows Montaigne seems to be more interested in the false coin of religion. Since time immemorial, he declares, every polity has used falsehood and vain ceremony to keep the people in check. That is why cities claim a supernatural foundation; that is why clever rulers favor bastard religions; that is why the Roman king Numa pretended to consult the nymph Egeria. Here we are back to Livy, as read by Machiavelli. In *Discorsi* I, 11, Machiavelli maintained that there was never a lawgiver who didn't have recourse to god the same way that Numa did. "Così fece Licurgo, così Solone, così molti altri."[66] Montaigne completes the list, in another late addition to his essay:

> And the authority that Numa gave to his laws by claiming the patronage of this goddess, Zoroaster, lawgiver of the Bactrians and the Persians, gave to his in the name of the god Oromazis;

Trismegistus of the Egyptians, in the name of Mercury; Zamolxis of the Scythians, in the name of Vesta; Charondas of the Chalcidians, in the name of Saturn; Minos of the Candiots, in the name of Jupiter; Lycurgus of the Lacedaemonians, in the name of Apollo; Draco and Solon of the Athenians, in the name of Minerva. And every polity has a god at its head: falsely so the others, truly so the one that Moses set up for the people of Judea just out of Egypt. (477)

The exemption granted here to the Mosaic tradition, which alone among faiths honors the true god, cannot detract from the basic point of the argument: statesmen in all times and places favor religion for its instrumental value. Presumably the French kings are no exception. The metaphor of the false coin reminds us that religion depends for its authority on its currency, not its truth. We apprehend the truth of religious dogma only through the grace of god, as Montaigne recognizes, but we obey through a more immediate instinct. When Montaigne commends Christianity in his essay "De la coustume" (I, 23), he emphasizes its political efficacy: "The Christian religion has all the marks of the utmost justice and utility, but none more apparent than the precise recommendation of obedience to the magistrate and maintenance of the government" (87–88). Polybius couldn't have put it any better himself.

Although he professes the Christian faith, Montaigne's functional analysis of religion is nonsectarian. He discerns the same function in every polity, or "toute police." Every state circulates the false coin of religion, even though the name of god changes at the border. Montaigne even found in Jean de Joinville's chronicle of the Crusades an admiring reference to the stimulus that religion supplies to military valor among the Bedouin tribes: "The religion of the Bedouins, as Sire de Joinville tells us, held among other things that the soul of any one of them who died for his prince departed into another body happier, handsomer, and stronger than the first; on account of which they risked their lives much more willingly" (477–78). Plato's "noble lie" works even in the desert. In this way, Montaigne expresses his frank admiration for the salutary imposture of religion. Religion may be a hoax, but it works a lot better than conscience ever did to make people do their duty. Here we are fully immersed in the atmosphere of the Sisyphus fragment cited by Hieronymus Wolf in his commentary on Isocrates. Like the sophists and the Epicureans, Montaigne reflects critically on the function of religion in society, and like the sophists and unlike the Epicureans, he does not seem to want to disturb this function, in so far as it tends to conserve and enforce social norms. However, to describe the function of religion is already to weaken it, which is why Critias was considered an atheist. So how has "De la gloire" veered so far from moral idealism to a cynical sort of expediency? Or has it? Having struggled throughout the essay to vindicate the claims of conscience and the self-sufficiency of virtue, Montaigne finally recognizes that these values have little currency either among the nobility or among the people. Only counterfeit values, like glory among the French nobility or reincarnation among the Bedouins or fear of the gods in general, are potent enough to restrain bad behavior and spur on virtuous conduct. Religion and the traditional honor code may be, after all, the best surveillance system available to society.

The author of all those arguments in favor of disinterested virtue, the voice that prevails through most of "De la gloire," reemerges, somewhat meekly, in the very last sentence, added to the Exemplaire de Bordeaux: "Any person of honor chooses rather to lose his honor than to lose his conscience" (478).[67] This choice, alas, is but little documented in the course of history, and the ambivalence of honor in this last phrase reminds us that Cicero's *honestum* must compete with French *honneur*. Cicero's own dialogues do adduce some examples of those who chose the former over the latter, those who preferred to do the right thing in secret, and Montaigne's essay repeats some of those examples, as we have seen. Yet in his own time and place he can find no example other than himself. When he trains his critical eye on society, he only discerns self-interested virtue, and this self-interest is cultivated partly by the honor code and partly by religion. And so religion deserves some small measure of odious praise.

The conclusion of "De la gloire," with its play on the double meaning of "honneur" as both honor and reputation, makes a fitting prologue to the first essay from book 3, "De l'utile et de l'honneste." The alternative of *utile* and *honestum* is generally and rightly considered a topic of political theory because it frames the conflict between ethical imperatives and political expediency. What the Prince approves of, your conscience disapproves of. However, the same alternative is fundamental to the art of rhetoric. Book 1, chapter 3 of Aristotle's *Rhetoric* divides rhetoric into the three genres of deliberative, judicial, and epideictic, assigning to each its own end or τέλος. The end of deliberative rhetoric is the useful and the harmful (τὸ συμφέρον καὶ βλαβερόν), the end of judicial rhetoric is the just and the unjust (τὸ δίκαιον καὶ τὸ ἄδικον), and the end of epideictic rhetoric is the honorable and the shameful (τὸ καλὸν καὶ τὸ αἰσχρόν).[68] In that sense, the title of Montaigne's essay refers to the choice between deliberative and epideictic rhetoric, or between recommending what is useful and praising what is honorable. Interestingly, the Roman tradition modifies Aristotle's schema and confuses the clear division of rhetorical genres. Cicero's *De inventione* 2.156 rephrases *Rhetoric* 1.3.5–6 as follows:

> Nam placet in iudiciali genere finem esse aequitatem. . . . In deliberativo autem Aristoteli placet utilitatem, nobis et honestatem et utilitatem; in demonstrativo honestatem.

> For example, it is generally agreed that the end in the forensic type is equity. . . . In the deliberative type, however, Aristotle accepts advantage as the end, but I prefer both honour and advantage. In the epideictic speech it is honour alone.[69]

In this context, the title of Montaigne's essay translates the dual aim of deliberative rhetoric, according to Cicero's self-consciously utopian conflation of *honestas* and *utilitas*. Montaigne, as we may have mentioned, is not a utopian thinker, and for him the useful and the honorable are not natural allies. So we can count him as an Aristotelian in that one respect.

Essay III, 1 tries to strike a balance between realism and idealism, and while recognizing the utilitarian nature of politics, the essayist expresses a personal preference for the second term of his title, "l'honneste." In this way, he chooses epideictic over deliberative rhetoric. The first object of his praise is a rather unexpected candidate, Emperor Tiberius, who has only a very casual relationship with τὸ καλόν. According to Tacitus's *Annals*, Tiberius refused an offer to poison Rome's most formidable foe, Arminius, saying that Rome was accustomed to defeat its enemies by force rather than fraud. In other words, he chose the honorable over the useful and made himself, for once, eligible for praise.[70] In fact, his refusal of perfidy was all the more honorable for being disadvantageous to the state. When discussing the τέλος of praise and blame, Aristotle says that the encomiast will often praise an action precisely because it is not useful to the actor, as in the case of Achilles, who risked his life to avenge Patroclus.[71] Tiberius's uncharacteristic scruple was the more honorable for being the less useful to himself or Rome.

The rest of the essay is devoted primarily to examples from ancient and modern history of those who paid the price for allowing themselves to be used as the instruments of their rulers' perfidy, which tends rather to discourage a career in politics. After this litany of the wages of sin, there is one genuine, classic encomium at the end: the praise of Epaminondas, the Theban general and statesman. Montaigne praises Epaminondas for having lived a life of political and military conflict without ever yielding to the spirit of vengeance and cruelty and without ever betraying the principles of goodness and humanity, "la bonté et l'humanité" (III, 1, 801). Epaminondas is the very embodiment of τὸ καλόν and the very archetype of praise. Surely this is no odious praise, but rather the standard model, the rule to which we have unscrupulously preferred the exception. Indeed, Montaigne stays true to the ancient and modern theory of epideictic: he tries through his praise of Epaminondas to recreate a communion of values, "recréer une communion sur la valeur admise" in Perelman's parlance.[72] As Tim Hampton points out in his reading of III, 1, Montaigne uses Epaminondas to promote the spirit of concord and reconciliation amidst civil war.[73] After a quote from Cicero to the effect that duty to the state cannot override our other moral duties, we arrive at the climax of the essay, what Hampton calls a "quasi-oratorical moment."[74] Why quasi? Here is Montaigne's exhortation to his fellow Frenchmen to act like Epaminondas: "It is a lesson proper to the times. We have no need to harden our hearts with these plates of steel, it is enough to harden our shoulders; it is enough to dip our pens in ink without dipping them in blood. If it is greatness of heart and the effect of rare and singular virtue to despise friendship, private obligations, our word, and kinship, for the common good and obedience to the magistrate, truly it is enough to excuse us from this that it is a greatness that cannot lodge in the greatness of Epaminondas' heart" (609–10). After epideixis comes deliberation; after we praise, we advise. By rejecting the brutality of reason of state, Epaminondas teaches the French how to overcome the cycle of revenge and cruelty that has overtaken them and how to honor their shared values.

So Montaigne's essay and my book end with a classic instance of epideictic rhetoric in the service of consensus. Almost. In the very last paragraph, in order to reiterate the principle that all that is useful is not necessarily honorable, Montaigne offers the example of marriage. It is the most useful institution to society since it propagates the human race, but the most venerable social order, the clergy, is exempt. After all, he adds in the most tasteless analogy of the work, we send the least valuable animals out to stud.[75] So what does that mean? The idea that marriage is useful but not honorable is, in fact, a perfectly orthodox Pauline sentiment expressing the values of a social formation for which the author of the *Essais* has absolutely no sympathy. Earlier in the century, Erasmus provoked a furious reaction from monks and theologians with his *Encomium matrimonii*, which he classes among his declamations along with the *Praise of Folly*. Marriage is an object of odious praise but serious deliberation. In a way, "De l'utile et de l'honneste" reenacts the destabilizing ending of "De la gloire."

Conclusion

Why did Machiavelli praise *tumulti*? Why did he inscribe a positive value in a term marked by language with a negative value? For that matter, why did he deride the most pervasive ambient value of his society, Christianity? Why did Bodin reappraise *superstitio* at a positive value? Why did Montaigne advocate the circulation of false coin? For that matter, why did Cardano prefer Nero to the more respectable figures of Roman history? Up to now, we have emphasized the properly rhetorical object of these paradoxes, the effect they produce on the audience, the readers. Odious praise is identified by its surprising and disconcerting impact on the reader. This impact can in turn have some morally or logically therapeutic value by forcing us to reevaluate all the notions that we take for granted. As Montaigne says of custom, once the mask is lifted and we see things in a new light, our judgment will be completely overthrown and then reinstated on a firmer footing.[1] So odious praise is a kind of therapy for human judgment; it can enhance our faculty of judgment and supplant more traditional forms of education or instruction. Or it can further the educational program of rhetorical humanism by advertising the power of speech and of artfully constructed argument. In either case it offers a benefit to the reader that may exceed its entertainment value (and it had better do so for such tedious examples as the *De studio Socratis*).

But what about the author? What does Machiavelli want to understand when he revisits the upheavals of the early Roman Republic or when he lingers so affectionately over the manipulation of belief in the supernatural?

Here I want to invoke an outdated thesis from classical scholarship that was probably never fashionable to begin with, Rodolfo Mondolfo's massive and diffuse study of subjectivism in the ancient world, where he distinguishes between the objective and the subjective points of view in the religious conceptions of the Greeks.[2] In Mondolfo's terms, Machiavelli is not interested in the objective question of the existence or the nature of god. He is not interested in religious doctrine. Rather, he explores the subjective questions: why do people believe and how is their belief expressed and manipulated. Belief is a key to social coherence and to *buoni ordini*, in his untranslatable vocabulary. To investigate the subjective question, you need to void the objective question. To do social science, you need to dismiss theology, and this dismissal has always carried a powerful stigma. Mondolfo points to a lost work by Protagoras of Abdera known as the *Peri theon*. Only a fragment survives, cited by Diogenes Laertius, probably from a compilation rather than the original, and thus we only have the most indirect testimony to this tantalizing work.[3] Protagoras declares that he does not know if the gods exist or not and what their nature is because life is short and the question is obscure. After such a preamble, there isn't much to say on the objective questions of theology, so all that remains is the subjective question of what people believe about the gods and how their belief functions in society. This inquiry displaces the focus from the truth of such beliefs to their utility.[4] The work has all the hallmarks of odious praise, but of course it is lost to us. But it wasn't lost to Isocrates. Maybe Protagoras said, "Look at Egypt; they worship cats and it works for them." Finally, Protagoras's work may have the dubious distinction of being the first victim of book burning, so odious was its evasion of the unanswerable objective questions in favor of more useful psychological and sociological questions.[5] Thus one of the first instances of censorship involved one of the first experiments in social theory.

In effect, odious praise does what Socrates was praised and blamed for: it brings our thoughts down to earth to dwell on our social relations and institutions. Speroni criticizes Socrates for this redirection of human inquiry, but what he really holds against Socrates is his antisocial behavior, which defies the laws and customs of his own homeland.[6] Of Socrates's antithesis the sophist, he says that he is the type of the good citizen. Gorgias was a sophist and a civic orator. The sophist distinguishes "tra l'utile e l'onesto" because that is what the city does: it is a civic distinction.[7] All of this is an outrage to Platonic values, but there is more to it than that. The sophists represent an antiutopian tendency: they want to know about the society that they have to live in, not the one they want to live in. They want to understand human society, not to remake it. They are convinced that social reality is a valid object of inquiry, and so is Speroni. Montaigne seems to follow this same itinerary in his essay on glory, where he concedes that Cicero's *honestum* doesn't work since people respond only to an external sanction like the honor code or religious belief. He grudgingly acknowledges that society works on its own terms, not on the terms of idealistic moral philosophy.

In closing, I want to go back to a remark that Jean Bodin makes in his discussion of religious tolerance in his six books of the republic. I have already quoted the vernacular phrase above, where he refuses to define the best religion, and though there can only be one true religion, he won't tell us which one it is.[8] We just need to pick our superstition and stick to it. This is sort of like Protagoras updated for the confessional era. Odious praise is in some respects a protest against the Reformation and its fanatical assertion of the truth. Our *lodatori* want to void the question of truth. They are wary of the truth, since the truth, like Busiris, is fond of human sacrifice.

APPENDIX

Sperone Speroni, "Discorso dei lodatori," in Opere *(Venice, 1740), 3:405–6.*

Molti laudano molte cose assai vili e di nessun prezzo e molti ancora in prosa e in versi hanno ardimento di commendarne alcune altre per loro natura odiose, e ne' cui nomi sanza altrimenti distinguerli ogni lor biasimo, quasi in sol luce, da se medesimo si manifesta. E ciò fanno essi, come a me pare, perchè si veda l'onnipotenza de' loro ingegni, e sopraumani sian giudicati: e non si avveggono che in ciò facendo, essi vituperano se medesimi; avvenga che'l ragionar di tai cose, non che'l lodarle e magnificarle, sia gran vergogna di chi ne parla. Sono anche alcuni poco men vani de' sopra detti, li quali, mentre essi lodano qualche cosa, molto ne parlano ma poco o nulla ne provano. Ben dicono essi nelle lor lunghe orazioni, la tal persona è ricca, e nobile, e d'ogni bene così dell'animo come del corpo compitamente dotata: ma meglio sanno, e sallo ognuno che li ascolta, che quel lodato mai non fece opra o parola, che degna fosse d'alcuna laude. E' dunque ver, che essi parlano parte a guisa di adulatori, siccome sono, parte a guisa di ostentatori di una lor certa loquacità, perchè eloquenzia sia riputata. E di questi cotali nell'una lingua e nell'altra molto abbonda la nostra età. La qual cosa, se ben si stima, non è lodare; piuttosto è una maniera di vituperio di chi si crede che se ne debba onorare. Che'l dir d'altrui, che egli sia dotto, nè virtuoso (siano onorevoli, quanto si vogliono, la virtù e la scienza) se non lo prova la vita sua, non è sua gloria, anzi è il contrario, che ivi vuol la ragione, che sia verace la infamia, ove le laudi son simulate. Delle composizioni de'quali, come ad Aconzio disse Cidippe, "non ho giurato d'esser tua moglie, ma ho ben letto in un pomo tuo certe parole, che ciò giuravano" così può dirsi con verità, voi non lodate niuno, ma molte cose assai lodevoli con gran fatica avete insieme adunate; le quali quasi perle nelle botteghe de' giojellieri par che aspettino che alcun le compri, e sue le faccia con l'aver suo: in tanto stanno elle appese alle vostre ciancie. Or non è dubbio, che questi tali son della schiera de' molto miseri ed infelici sofisti; i quali attendendo, siccome fan tuttavia, anzi a parere che ad essere, meritamente non uomini, ma ombre d'uomini dalli intendenti son riputati. Perciocchè essi son quegli, che'l gran Platone in persona di quel buon Socrate, padre e maestro delle scienzie e delle virtù, ne' suoi divini dialogi or convincea disputando, ed or schernendo ammirava, sempre ammonendo con gentil modo la sua repubblica che da' costumi e dottrine loro non men dannose che vergognose guardar dovesse i suoi cittadini. De' quali antichi sofisti quasi ombra d'ombra, ora a' dì nostri rimane ancora qualche sembianza; e son costoro, di cui pur dianzi si ragionava, i quali se così biasimano come lodano; che così certo esser dee, quando ancora nell'altro genere uno istesso oratore con uno istesso artificio ora accusi ora iscusi, e quale accusa tale egli soglia iscusare, bene è beato colui e bene è degno di molta laude . . .

Many people praise many vile and worthless things, and many still in verse and prose have the nerve to commend other things which by their very nature are odious and in whose name, without other distinction, all their blame shines out like the light of the sun. And they do so, as far as I can tell, so that the omnipotence of their wit may be seen and they may be judged superhuman. And they don't even realize that by doing so, they blame themselves, since to discourse about such things, not to mention to praise them and to aggrandize them, is a shame to whoever speaks about them. There is another type, only slightly less vain than the first, who, while they praise something, say a great deal but prove little or nothing. Of course they claim, in their long orations, that so and so is rich and noble and endowed with every gift of body and spirit, but they know better, and so do their listeners, that the person praised never did, in word or deed, anything worthy of praise. And so it is true that they speak partly as flatterers, as indeed they are, and partly as showoffs of a certain loquacity of theirs, so that it may be taken as eloquence. Our age abounds in speakers like this, both in Latin and in the vernacular. But if you think about it, this isn't really praise but rather blame for whoever thinks he should be honored by it. For if someone else says that you're learned or virtuous (and let virtue and knowledge be as honorable as they like) if you don't prove it by your actions, it is not to your credit but to the contrary, because it is only reasonable that infamy be true where praises are false. And as far as their literary compositions are concerned, as Cydippa said to Acontius, "I didn't swear to marry you, but I read in your apple words to that effect,"[1] so the same could be said to them, you don't praise anyone, but you've strung together lots of praiseworthy things at great effort, which like pearls in the jewelry shop seem to be waiting for someone to buy them and make them his own with his money: just so they are hanging from your idle words. Now there is no doubt that such people are of the ranks of the miserable and unhappy sophists, who being attentive, as they still are, rather to appearance than to reality, are rightly held by those in the know to be not men but mere shadows of men. For they are the ones whom the great Plato, in the person of that good man Socrates, father and teacher of the sciences and the virtues, in his divine dialogues either refuted in argument or mockingly admired, always admonishing his city to protect its citizens from their customs and their doctrines, which were no less harmful than shameful. Of those ancient sophists you can still find some remnant in our own day and age, the shadow of a shadow as it were, and those are the ones I was just talking about. And if they blame the same way they praise, and why shouldn't they, since in the other genre, the very same orator uses the same trick to accuse and to excuse, and he accuses whom he usually excuses, then blessed is he and worthy of much praise . . .[2]

NOTES

INTRODUCTION

1. Commentary on *Georgics* 3.5 by Jodocus Willich in Virgil, *Universum Poema*, 89r: "aras) Quibus hospites mactavit, sed inhospitalitatis poenas dedit. Nam ab Hercule interfectus est."
2. Isocrates, *Isocrates I*, 51.
3. Virgil, *Georgics* 3.4–5.
4. Aulus Gellius, *Noctes Atticae* 2.6: "illaudatus quoque igitur finis est extremae malitiae."
5. Virgil, *Opera Virgiliana* 86r: "Sed enim tot inter opiniones primas obtinere videtur Isocratis oratio dicentis, eum qui Busiridem laudare conatus fuerat, id demum effecisse, ut et vituperabilis et odio magis dignus, ob eam commendationem videretur."
6. Petronius, *Satyricon* 141, in *Satiricon*, 176: "Omnes qui in testamento meo legata habent, praeter libertos meos hac condicione percipient quae dedi, si corpus meum in partes conciderint et astante populo comederint."
7. Ibid., in *Satiricon*, 177: "Apud quasdam gentes scimus adhuc legem servari, ut a propinquis suis consumantur defuncti, adeo quidem ut obiurgentur aegri frequenter, quod carnem suam faciant peiorem."
8. "Quod si exemplis vis quoque probari consilium, Saguntini oppressi ab Hannibale humanas edere carnes, nec hereditatem expectabant."
9. Bodin, *Les six livres*, 635: "aussi pourroit on loüer les maladies: comme Favorin loua grandement la fievre quarte: qui seroit confondre la difference du bien et du mal, du proffit et dommage, de l'honneur et deshonneur, du vice et de vertu, brief ce seroit mesler le feu et l'eau, le ciel et la terre."
10. Du Bellay, *Regrets et autres œuvres poëtiques*, 218.
11. Pernot, *Epideictic Rhetoric*, 104.
12. Euripides, *Heraclidae* 203 and *Iphigenia at Aulis* 980, cited in Pernot, *Epideictic Rhetoric*, 115.
13. Lucian, *How to Write History* 12, cited in Pernot, *Epideictic Rhetoric*, 116.
14. Montaigne, *Complete Essays of Montaigne*, 83.
15. Perelman and Olbrechts-Tyteca, "Logique et rhétorique."
16. Ibid., 11–12.
17. Cassin, *L'effet sophistique*, 201–2.
18. O'Malley, *Praise and Blame in Renaissance Rome*, 139.
19. Cox, "Machiavelli and the *Rhetorica ad Herennium*," 1111.
20. Cope, *Rhetoric of Aristotle with a Commentary*, 1:159, is more sensitive to the differences between the two treatises: "The definition of virtue here given compared with the celebrated one of Eth. Nic. II 6,

init., and the detailed treatment of the list of virtues and the meagre and incomplete account here given of them, contrasted with the elaborate and ingenious analysis of them in the third and fourth books of the same work, is a most striking illustration of the difference between the point of view and method of treatment in the popular Rhetoric and comparatively scientific Ethics."

21. "As we call the rash courageous, the spendthrift generous, the miser thrifty."

22. Johannes Sturmius, *Scholia in libros III Rhetoricorum*, 97r°: "Ponit tria genera hominum et primum deterrimum est, Scythicum videlicet, apud hos enim laudabile erat hospites occidere. Lacones) Hoc est genus medium quia apud Lacedaemonios laudabatur res militaris sed furta concedebantur, non vituperabantur. Et nullum est genus hominum apud quos non sit aliquid laudabile." Note that the Scythians seem to have inherited Busiris's strange enthusiasm for hospicide.

23. Isocrates, *Opera omnia*, 2:278: ὅσοι δὲ τῶν θείων πραγμάτων οὕτω προέστησαν ὥστε καὶ τὰς ἐπιμελείας καὶ τὰς τιμωρίας δοκεῖν εἶναι μείζους τῶν συμβαινόντων, οἱ δὲ τοιοῦτοι πλεῖστα τὸν βίον τὸν τῶν ἀνθρώπων ὠφελοῦσιν. Renaissance editions of Isocrates have the following variant: εἶναι δοκεῖν ἀκριβεστέρας τῶν συμβαινόντων.

24. Wolf, *Hieronymi Wolfii*, 64I: "De quo praefatur in genere, et locum communem tractat de utilitate religionis, et ita quidem ut tractatio illa magis ad superstitiones pertineat quam ad veram pietatem. Inter quas qui nihil interesse censent, in maximo errore versantur, et in extremam incidunt impietatem."

CHAPTER I

1. Isocrates, *Isocrates I*, 50.
2. Ibid., 35.
3. For the problematic relationship between epideictic and consensus, with further bibliography, see MacPhail, "Philosophers in the New World."

4. Isocrates, *Isocrates I*, 35.
5. Gorgias, *Encomium of Helen*, 21: "The man who says rightly what ought to be said should also refute those who blame Helen, a woman about whom both the belief of those who have listened to poets and the message of her name, which has become a reminder of the calamities, have been in unison and unanimity. I wish, by adding some reasoning to my speech, to free the slandered woman from the accusation."
6. Isocrates, *Isocrates I*, 51.
7. Aristotle, *On Rhetoric*, 82.
8. Livingstone, *Commentary on Isocrates' "Busiris,"* 36.
9. Stokes, "Three Defences of Socrates," 266: "Polycrates then gave the whole matter a particular political twist involving Alcibiades and Critias."
10. Striker, *Essays on Hellenistic Epistemology and Ethics*, 3. John Burnet, in his commentary on the *Apology*, would rather emphasize the cordiality. He even goes so far as to claim, unaccountably, "Socrates is nowhere represented as an enemy of the sophists." Plato, *Euthyphro, Apology of Socrates, Crito*, 164.
11. See Ostwald, "Sophists and Athenian Politics," 37.
12. According to Bailly, *Dictionnaire grec-français*, s.v. δεινός. The TLG gives the same example from Sophocles, *OT* 545.
13. See Vickers, *In Defence of Rhetoric*, 136.
14. Montaigne, *Essais*, 183: "n'ayants ordre, suite ny proportion que fortuite." Hereafter, the Essays will be cited by book, chapter, page (in Villey and Saulnier edition) = I, 28, 183. Frame's translation will be cited merely by page number.
15. ASD IV-3:74: "Mihi porro semper gratissimum fuit, ὅττικεν ἐπ' ἀκαιρίμαν γλῶτταν ἔλθῃ dicere." She uses the Greek version of adage 473, *Quicquid in lingua venerit.*
16. Isocrates, *Isocrates I*, 35.
17. Plato, *Five Dialogues*, 43.
18. "An aliter defensionem Socratis et eorum qui pro patria ceciderant laudem scripsisset? Quae certe sunt oratoris opera."

19. "Sequitur quaestio an utilis rhetorice. Nam quidam vehementer in eam invehi solent, et, quod sit indignissimum, in accusationem orationis utuntur orandi viribus" (2.16.1).

20. See commentary by Winterbottom and Reinhardt cited in MacPhail, *Sophistic Renaissance*, 65.

21. Aristotle, *De sophisticis elenchis* 165a21–23: ἔστι γὰρ ἡ σοφιστικὴ φαινομένη σοφία οὖσα δ' οὔ, καὶ ὁ σοφιστὴς χρηματιστὴς ἀπὸ φαινομένης σοφίας ἀλλ' οὐκ οὔσης.

22. Philostratus, *Flavii Philostrati opera*, 5.

23. Cassin, *Effet sophistique*, 452, calls this classificatory system a "taxonomie renversante" because it reverses the conventional distinction between real and apparent.

24. This is one of the *Apophthegmata Laconica* collected by Plutarch and reworked by Erasmus. ASD IV-4:89: "cum sophista quispiam appararet recitare librum et Antalcidae percontanti quod esset argumentum respondisset 'Herculis encomium,' 'Quis' inquit 'illum vituperat?' supervacaneum existimans in eo laudando sumere operam, quem uno ore praedicarent omnes."

25. We now have an invaluable resource to help us in the study of Speroni: Katinis, *Sperone Speroni*. In the appendix, Katinis transcribes and translates the last two of these three discourses, and I will cite them from his transcription.

26. Speroni, *Opere*, 3:405: "Molti laudano molte cose assai vili e di nessun prezzo e molti ancora in prosa e in versi hanno ardimento di commendarne alcune altre per loro natura odiose, e ne' cui nomi sanza altrimenti distinguerli ogni lor biasimo, quasi in sol luce, da se medesimo si manifesta." I have transcribed and translated the whole text of the *Discorso* in the Appendix.

27. Ibid.

28. Ibid., 3:406.

29. Ibid.

30. Cicero, *Tusculanae disputationes* 5.10: "Socrates autem primus philosophiam devocavit e caelo et in urbibus conlocavit et in domus etiam introduxit et coegit de vita et moribus rebusque bonis et malis quaerere." See also adage 585, *Aedibus in nostris quae prava aut recta geruntur*, which was supposed to be one of Socrates's favorite sayings (ASD II-2:108).

31. Erasmus collects this saying as adage 569 and again in the *Apophthegmata* as saying 23 of book 3 (ASD IV-4:203).

32. Katinis, *Sperone Speroni*, 150: "come par che egli le consideri, quando parla contra i sofisti."

33. Ibid., 151: "Queste cose dirai contra Socrate per li sofisti."

34. Ibid. "He was not consistent with himself."

35. ASD IV-3:72: "Lubitum est enim paulisper apud vos Sophistam agere, non quidem huius generis, quod hodie nugas quasdam anxias inculcat pueris ac plusquam muliebrem rixandi pertinaciam tradit, sed veteres illos imitabor qui, quo infamem Sophorum appellationem vitarent, sophistae vocari maluerunt."

36. Katinis, *Sperone Speroni*, 155: "Chi è sapiente da senno, se non colui che conosce la sua ignoranzia, come diceva di sé Socrate?"

37. Ibid., 156: "Sofista è lo esser nostro, perché non è e pare essere: non è, perché il presente dello essere è instante indivisibile, che fu piuttosto, e forse non sarà, che non è; e solo lo immortale è veramente."

38. Montaigne, *Complete Essays of Montaigne*, 455.

39. Nancy Siraisi manages to integrate Cardano's epideictic orations with his historical thought and his medical training in "Anatomizing the Past," 21–24.

40. For the third, *The Praise of Gout*, see Tomarken, *Smile of Truth*, 62–64.

41. Cardano, *Opera omnia*, 200A: "Adeo damnatur Nero ut iam in adagium versum sit" and 208A: "Itaque reor hoc Adagium, Nerone crudelior."

42. Ibid., 179A: "Si quis contradicere vel illum laudare tentet, paradoxa dicere videatur."

43. "Quid est enim aliud omnis historia, quam Romana laus?" he asks in the *Invectiva contra eum qui maledixit Italie.* Petrarca, *Invectives*, 416.

44. For Siraisi, "Anatomizing the Past," 21, "However the treatise is interpreted, its most salient feature is surely the reversal of conventional judgement—not only of Nero, but also of Tacitus."

45. For a more comprehensive reading of the *Encomium Neronis*, with extensive bibliographical references, see Van der Poel, "Cardano's *Neronis encomium*."

46. Cardano, *Opera omnia*, 179A: "Quod si illud Antisthenis dictum aureum secum pensitarent, idem esse laudari ab improbis et vituperari a probis, vel vituperari ab improbis, a probis laudari, non minimum laudis haec vituperatio afferre posset."

47. LB IV:326F: "At quid mali feci?"

48. Plutarch, *Moralia* 536B. This is fragment 26 in Antisthenes, *Antisthenis fragmenta*, 31.

49. ASD IV-2:321: "Itaque vir malus est et is, qui malum laudat, et is, qui a bono vituperatur. Usque adeo a talibus nec flecti poterat nec capi servans praeceptum illud, quod Antisthenaeus Hercules praecepit filiis, ne quam haberent gratiam iis, a quibus laudarentur." Cardano seems to be following Erasmus's version.

50. Cardano, *Opera omnia*, 183A: "Haec igitur et non plura optimi principis officia esse, nemo non videt, tametsi nullus Glauco vel Polemarchus nostra dicta tanquam aliena probet."

51. ASD IV-3:68: "Cum Busiridem laudarit Polycrates et huius castigator Isocrates, iniusticiam Glauco, Thersiten et quartanam febrim Favorinus, calvicium Synesius, muscam et parasiticam Lucianus."

52. Cardano, *Opera omnia*, 219B.

53. Ibid., 220B: "Non defuturos etiam esse puto qui me accusent, quod in bonos omnes hac laudationis specie debacchatus sim: praesertim in Augustum, Ciceronem et Senecam."

54. Ibid.: "falsa hominum opinio."

55. Ibid., 208B: "Vides iudicia? vides errores hominum?" and 199B: "O iudicia hominum, o stultitiam!"

56. "L'action est louable, non pas l'homme" (II, 1, 336).

57. Cardano, *Opera omnia*, 151A: "Cum Socratem tamquam pessimum virum habituri sint mortales: Neronem vero ut optimum Principem collaudaturi?"

58. Ibid., 151B: "Nemo ante me illum damnavit? Imo, nemo sapiens, nemo probus illum approbavit."

59. Ibid.: "Dehortatur Socrates mortales ab omnium disciplinarum studio, avertitque nos ab optimo opere: ille idem suadet, ut morali disciplinae incumbamus, hoc inane."

60. Ibid., 152A–B.

61. Ibid., 153A.

62. Ibid., 154A.

63. Ibid., 154B: "adeo corrupta sunt, hominum iudicia."

64. Ibid., 157B: "quid dicas de Alcibiade?" as if he's talking to Plato.

65. Ibid., 158B: "Quid dicam de Phavorino?"

66. We will cite from Labé, *Œuvres complètes*. Translations are from Labé, *Complete Poetry and Prose*, 46–131.

67. See Lauvergnat-Gagnière, "Rhétorique dans le *Débat de Folie et d'Amour*," and Marie-Madeleine Fontaine, "L'ordinaire de la folie." Fontaine in particular is helpful on the intertextual relations between the *Débat* and the *Moriae encomium* while also pointing out a possible connection to Speroni's dialogue on jealousy.

68. Labé, *Œuvres complètes*, 82: "Apolon, qui ha si long tems ouy les causeurs à Romme, ha bien retenu d'eus à conter tousjours à son avantage. Mais Folie, comme elle est tousjours ouverte, ne veut point que j'en dissimule rien : et ne vous en veut dire qu'un mot, sans art, sans fard et ornement quelconque."

69. Ibid., 84–85: "Folie m'a defendu que ne la fisse miserable, que ne vous suppliasse pour lui pardonner, si faute y avoit : m'a defendu le plorer, n'embrasser vos genous,

vous adjurer par les gracieus yeus, que quelquefois avez trouvez agreables venans d'elle, ny amener ses parens, enfans, amis, pour vous esmouvoir à pitié."

70. Plato, *Five Dialogues*, 38.

71. Labé, *Œuvres complètes*, 88: "il sera estimé, loué, prisé, et suivi d'un chacun."

72. ASD IV-3:102: "Principio si rerum usu constat prudentia, in utrum magis competet eius cognominis honos, in sapientem, qui partim ob pudorem partim ob animi timiditatem nihil aggreditur, an in stultum, quem neque pudor, quo vacat, neque periculum, quod non perpendit, ab ulla re deterret?"

73. Labé, *Œuvres complètes*, 88: "Que dureroit mesme le monde, si elle n'empeschoit que lon ne previt les facheries et hazars qui sont en mariage ? Elle empesche que lon ne les voye et les cache : à fin que le monde se peuple tousjours à la maniere acoutumee. Combien dureroient peu aucuns mariages, si la sottise des hommes ou des femmes laissoit voir les vices qui y sont?"

74. ASD IV-3:94: "nec amicus amicum nec maritum uxor . . . diutius ferat, nisi vicissim inter sese nunc errent, nunc adulentur, nunc prudentes conniveant."

75. ASD IV-3:96–98: "Qui quidem [philosophi] quam sint ad omnem vitae usum inutiles, vel Socrates ipse, unus Apollinis oraculo sapiens, sed minime sapienter iudicatus, documento esse potest, qui nescio quid publice conatus agere summo cum omnium risu discessit."

76. The endless bibliography on Montaigne and Socrates seems to have begun already in 1581 when Montaigne was granted Roman citizenship and recognized by his Roman hosts as *Socrates Gallicus*. See Perona, "Introduction," 10n7. More recently (than 1581), an entire volume has been devoted to *Le Socratisme de Montaigne*.

77. Katinis, *Sperone Speroni*, 153.

78. Porteau, "Sur un paradoxe de Montaigne."

79. Ibid., 346: "Autrefois, 'le maître des maîtres' disputait moins pour enseigner ses disciples que pour exercer leurs âmes. Notre Français est de la lignée de Socrate. Il entend éperonner les esprits."

80. Montaigne, *Complete Essays of Montaigne*, 97.

81. "Vers d'Euripide, pris dans Stobée" (I, 25, 138n1).

82. Nauck, *Tragicorum Graecorum Fragmenta*, 652.

83. ASD II-2:44–45. The epigram cited in Suetonius's *Life of Tiberius* is obviously not meant in praise: "aspice felicem sibi, non tibi, Romule, Syllam."

84. Plato, *Five Dialogues*, 80.

85. "Or il ne faut pas attacher le sçavoir à l'ame, il l'y faut incorporer" (I, 25, 140).

86. Ficino, *Opera omnia*, 2:1315: "quasi eloquentia sine sapientia sit ensis acutus in manibus furiosi." Around the same time, Giovanni Pico della Mirandola used the same figure in his letter to Ermolao Barbaro, which we will examine at greater length in our chapter 3: "insipiens eloquentia, uti gladius in furentis manu, non obesse maxime non potest." See Pico, *Ioannes Picus Mirandulanus*, 820.

87. Ep. 2449, in Erasmus, *Opus epistolarum*, 9:183. Though neglected by Montaigne's editors, this testimony is cited by Gadoffre, *La révolution culturelle*, 24.

88. Ep. 2449 Allen ll. 39–41: "Pulcherrimam Spartam sortiti estis, nihil superest nisi ut eam pro sua quisque facultate certatim exornetis."

89. For a quite handy summary of Montaigne's own social status and his family's transition from the merchant bourgeoisie to the hereditary nobility, see Desan, "From Eyquem to Montaigne."

90. For a wider survey of laconism in the *Essais*, see MacPhail, "Montaigne and the Praise of Sparta."

91. Plato, *Protagoras*, 7.

92. Gorgias, *Encomium of Helen*, 24: "The power of speech bears the same relation to the ordering of the mind as the ordering of drugs bears to the constitution of bodies. Just as different drugs expel different humours from the body, and some stop it from being ill but others stop it from living, so too some speeches cause sorrow,

some cause pleasure, some cause fear, some give the hearers confidence, some drug and bewitch the mind with an evil persuasion."

93. See Scodel, "Affirmation of Paradox," 220, on the image of the poisonous medicine in III, 12.

94. Plato, *Phaedrus and the Seventh and Eighth Letters*.

95. It is a *difformation* disguised as a *reformation* (III, 12, 1043 C). Montaigne does not explicitly target the Reformation in the 1588 text.

96. "Il a faict grand faveur à l'humaine nature de montrer combien elle peut d'elle mesme" (III, 12, 1038 B).

97. For other examples, see Smith on lexical paradox in Montaigne: "'J'honnore le plus ceux que j'honnore le moins.'"

98. For *bêtise* in the sense of animality and for Montaigne's ideal of *abêtissement*, see Giocanti, *Penser l'irrésolution*, 365–419.

99. For a proper reading of this speech within an essay, see Langer, "Ce qui sauve la vie."

100. Like Plato in his seventh letter, according to Montaigne: "luy qui, par la sincerité de sa conscience, merita envers la faveur divine de penetrer si avant en la Chrestienne lumiere, au travers des tenebres publiques du monde de son temps" (III, 12, 1043 C).

101. "Et en son plus haut essay renoncé à la verité et naiveté, ornemens de son parler, pour se parer du fard des figures et feintes d'une oraison apprinse?" (III, 12, 1054 C).

102. "Il représente . . . la pure et premiere impression de nature" (III, 12, 1054–55 B).

CHAPTER 2

1. "Enimvero re dein tota diligentius pervestigata, meas esse partes et item cuiuscunque latini professoris existimavi, Ciceronis gloriam, qua vel maxime contra Graecos stamus, etiam vice capitis omni contentione defensare." Poliziano, *Opera*, 225. The *Miscellanea* was first published in 1489, when Poliziano was still alive.

2. Cicero, *De finibus* 1.10: "sed ita sentio et saepe disserui, Latinam linguam non modo non inopem, ut vulgo putarent, sed locupletiorem etiam esse quam Graecam."

3. Cicero, *On Ends*, 221. Cicero, *De finibus* 3.5: "Et quoniam saepe diximus, et quidem cum aliqua querela non Graecorum modo sed eorum etiam qui se Graecos magis quam nostros haberi volunt, nos non modo non vinci a Graecis verborum copia sed esse in ea etiam superiores."

4. Cicero, *Tusculan Disputations*, 185. *Tusculanae disputationes* 2.35: "O verborum inops interdum, quibus abundare te semper putas, Graecia!"

5. Poliziano, *Opera*, 224: "nobilem illam Marci Tullii Ciceronis exclamationem."

6. *Suasoriae* 7.10: "omnes pro libris Ciceronis solliciti fuerunt, nemo pro ipso."

7. Ibid.: "Iniuriam illum facturum populo Romano cuius linguam in locum principem extulisset, ut insolentis Graeciae studia tanto antecederet eloquentia, quanto fortuna."

8. Poliziano, *Opera*, 224: "Ob id igitur subiratus latinae copiae genitori et principi Graecus magister, etiam dictitare ausus est (quod nunc quoque vix aures patiuntur) ignarum fuisse non philosophiae modo Ciceronem, sed etiam (si diis placet) Graecarum literarum."

9. Ibid.: "Sed enim nemo est (aiebat) in Aristotelis lectione paulo frequentior, quin sciat Entelechian esse potius Aristoteleum verbum, neutiquam significans quod Cicero putat, continuatam motionem, et perennem, sed perfectionem potius, aut consummationem quampiam."

10. Ibid.: "Vix enim dici potest, quam nos aliquando, id est, Latini homines, in participatum suae linguae, doctrinaeque non libenter admittat ista natio. Nos enim quisquilias tenere literarum, se frugem: nos praesegmina, se corpus: nos putamina, se nucleum credit."

11. Lamers, *Greece Reinvented*, 185.

12. Sabbadini, "Vita e opere di Francesco Florido Sabino," 353.

13. Poliziano, *Opera*, 224.

14. Gellius, *Attic Nights*, 1:409.

15. Poliziano, *Opera*, 225: "tum ostendendum, ex eo quod obiicitur, augeri Ciceronis praeconium, nedum decrescat."

16. Ibid., 227: "Principio igitur quaero ego ab istis, quonam maxime argumento Entelechian potius quam Endelechian scriptum collegerint ab Aristotele? Tam enim verbum novum hoc, quam illud: nec minus altero significari animus, quam altero potest: nec Aristoteles ipse perfectionem potius, quam motionem illam indicari continuam nova voce pronunciat. Crediderint ita sane Porphyrius, Themistius, Simiplicius, aut siqui compares: quae autem tandem invidia est, etiam aliter quam posteriores opinatum, si stare ipse sic quoque tuerique gradum bene et fortiter potest?"

17. Garin, "Ἐνδελέχεια e Ἐντελέχεια," 180.

18. Poliziano, *Opera*, 227: "Quo circa nihil est quod iam dubitemus, quin de sinceritate primaeva lectionis istius, praesertim tantillo discrimine, vel libera sit in utramque partem suspicio, vel (si alterutri accedendum) tutius Ciceronem sit praeferri."

19. Ibid.: "Quid autem prohibet, quominus Cicero ipse videre matricem quoque librorum Aristotelis, qui fuerint ipsius aetate publicati: si non incorruptam, certe (sicuti diximus) conscribellatam potuerit?" I have no idea what *conscribellatam* means, and neither do the Latin dictionaries that I consulted. By *matrix*, Poliziano may have in mind, though he may not, the exoteric works to which he refers earlier in the chapter: "Nam peripatetici veteres . . . paucos modo, quos vocant exotericos habuerunt."

20. Bignone, *Aristotele perduto*. See especially "Appendice al capitolo III: Una nuova meta nella riconquista dell'Aristotele perduto" (1:202–51). It was Garin, not Bignone, who noticed Poliziano's intuition into the authority of Cicero as a witness to the lost Aristotle.

21. Poliziano, *Opera*, 227: "eam novo huic Aristotelis vocabulo interpretationem iure accommodare sit ausus, quae cum Platonis in Phaedro sententia, super animae motu sempiterno, atque (ut Varro inquit) dio, consentiret: de qua ipse quoque vel in Tusculanis quaestionibus, vel in sexto reipublicae volumine, commeminerit."

22. Ibid.: "Quando et Philoponus in Aristotelis vita, et Simplicius in comentariis de anima, et in extremo Peri hermenias libro Boetius ipse germanas esse, et compares utriusque philosphi sententias asseverant, etiamque libros septem composuisse Porphyrius traditur . . . quod et Picus hic Mirandula meus in quadam suarum disputationum praefatione tractavit, et vero verius esse copiosissimo opere (credo) pulcherrimoque pervincet (nisi me tamen gustus fefellit) quod de Platonis hac ipsa, quam dicimus, et Aristotelis concordia, noctes atque dies molitur et cudit." See Garin, "Ἐνδελέχεια e Ἐντελέχεια," 180. For Bettinzoli, *La lucerna di Cleante*, 160: "la *praefatio* pichiana non è altro che *l'Oratio de hominis dignitate*."

23. Poliziano, *Opera*, 228: "Etiam ipsemet, in quo praecipue diverticulo calumniam patitur, largissime cumulatissimeque praestiterit."

24. Ep. 1479 to Haio Herman, dated August 31, 1524, in Erasmus, *Opus epistolarum*, 5:519: "Oderunt Christi nomen."

25. Scott, *Controversies over the Imitation of Cicero*, 19n13. McLaughlin, *Literary Imitation*, 202, dates it more precisely to 1485.

26. "Sed cum Ciceronem, cum bonos alios multum diuque legeris . . . tum demum velim (quod dicitur) sine cortice nates, atque ipse tibi sis aliquando in consilio." In DellaNeva, *Ciceronian Controversies*, 4. Page numbers in parentheses refer to this bilingual Latin English edition. Erasmus remembers this saying as adage 742, *Sine cortice nabis* (ASD II-2:262).

27. DellaNeva, *Ciceronian Controversies*, 7–9. "Et primum de iudicio libenter fatebor, cum viderem eloquentiae studia tamdiu deserta iacuisse et sublatum usum forensem et quasi nativam quandam vocem deesse hominibus nostris, me saepe palam affirmasse nihil his temporibus ornate

varieque dici posse, nisi ab iis qui aliquem sibi praeponerent ad imitandum. Cum et peregrini expertes sermonis alienas regiones male possint sine duce peragrare" (6–8).

28. ASD I-2:704: "amnis e fonte cordis tui promanans."

29. Ep. 1479. For this Academy, see Gouwens, "Ciceronianism and Collective Identity," 173–95.

30. Ep. 1479 Allen l. 110: "De stili formula nunquam fui superstitiose sollicitus" and l. 158: "Postremo, quod me negant orthodoxum, ad id crimen respondebo."

31. Ep. 1479 Allen l. 120: "Oderunt Christi nomen."

32. Ep. 1479 Allen ll. 176–78: "Novi enim quantum absint a Christianismo, qui in bonis litteris velut ad scopulos Sireneos consenescunt, praesertim apud Italos." The CWE translation seems to be mistaken: "I know how little Christianity there is about those who, in their enthusiasm for literature, are dashing themselves to pieces, as it were, on the rocks of the Sirens, and this is especially so in Italy." *Consenescere* means to grow old, following Aulus Gellius, *Noctes Atticae* 16.8.

33. In his quarrel with Etienne Dolet, Francesco Florido imitates Erasmus's use of *consenescere* in order to deride those who grow old in imitation of Cicero. See Telle, *Erasmianus sive Ciceronianus*, 82n10.

34. Ep. 1706 Allen ll. 37–44. Erasmus returns to the Ciceronian-Lutheran analogy in two letters addressed to Viglius Zuichemus: epistle 2604, ll. 23–25 and epistle 2682, ll. 10–13.

35. Ep. 1719 Allen ll. 51–52.

36. Ep. 1720 Allen ll. 48–51.

37. Ep. 1720 Allen l. 54. Bonamico apparently did not live up to this invidious epithet, as may be inferred from Erasmus's correspondence. See the entry on him in Bietenholz, *Contemporaries of Erasmus*, 1:166.

38. For more details, see Marcel Bataillon, *Érasme et l'Espagne*, chap. 5, and Charles Fantazzi's introduction to the newly published CWE 75.

39. Ep. 1791 Allen ll. 37–43.

40. Ep. 1791 Allen l. 60: "omnium Transmontanorum eloquentissimum."

41. Ep. 1791 Allen l. 67.

42. DellaNeva, *Ciceronian Controversies*, 2: "Mihi vero longe honestior tauri facies aut item leonis quam simiae videtur, quae tamen homini similior est." DellaNeva's note *ad locum* reminds us of the long genealogy of this figure of speech.

43. ASD I-2:583: "un schéma complet de ce qui va devenir le *Ciceronianus*."

44. Ep. 1885 Allen l. 114: "In harena moriendum Erasmo."

45. Ep. 1885 Allen ll. 129–31: "Apud hos prope turpius est non esse Ciceronianum quam non esse Christianum."

46. Ep. 1885 Allen l. 133.

47. We can think of Saint Augustine's use of *peregrinatio* to describe the passage from the city of man to the city of god. The citizen of the city of god is only a pilgrim in this world ("isto peregrinus in saeculo" [*City of God* 15.1]) or in the pilgrimage of this life ("in huius vitae peregrinatione" [15.6]).

48. ASD I-2:656: "Idem affectus et me quondam habuit, sed ab eo morbo revalui . . . ὁ λόγος τῷ λόγῳ mihi medicatus est."

49. Chomarat, *Grammaire et rhétorique*, 842: "un des aspects bien connus de la pensée d'Erasme, et à vrai dire de maints humanistes, c'est la critique du monachisme, qui, faisant fi des différences individuelles, soumet tous les moines à une règle uniforme."

50. CWE 28:356, from adage 671, *Olet lucernam*.

51. Pigman, "Imitation and the Renaissance Sense of the Past."

52. ASD I-2:646 and notes 418–23 in CWE 28:568.

53. Ep. 541 cited in Telle, *Erasmianus sive Ciceronianus*, 38.

54. Adage 1444, *Cum diis pugnare*: "θεομαχεῖν, id est cum diis pugnare, dicuntur qui vel naturae repugnant, vel adversus fatalem necessitatem reluctantur" (ASD II-3:434).

55. Chomarat, *Grammaire et rhétorique*, 833: "Erasme seul forme en toute clarté la notion de personnalité."

56. Ibid, 838: "le titre honorifique et infâmant de cicéronien."

57. Telle, *Erasmianus sive Ciceronianus*, 37: "Se trouver dans ce catalogue était aussi onéreux que de ne pas y figurer."

58. See Telle, *Erasmianus sive Ciceronianus*, 85.

59. Florido, *Succisivae lectiones* I, 2, 1000–1013.

60. The *Apologia* will be cited from the copy of the 1537 edition in the Bibliothèque de l'Arsenal in Paris: 4-BL-4573. Page numbers in parentheses refer to this edition.

61. Marullus, *Michaelis Marulli carmina*, 8–9. The version quoted in Florido, *Apologia*, 42, shows only one variant: *Musaeo lepore* for *lepore Musaeo*. This variant is not taken from Crinito, and it is not clear if it is due to Florido's source or to his negligence.

62. Marullus, *Poems*, 12.

63. Florido, *Apologia*, 48: "At nec sanum iudicium tibi admodum debuit."

64. See Fantazzi's introduction to his translation.

65. Crinito, *De honesta disciplina*, 440.

66. Ibid.: "Factum est iudicium nuper a nostro Marullo de poetis Latinis egregie profecto et prudenter." It is not clear why Poliziano's disciple refers to his master's archenemy as "noster Marullus."

67. "Tum quicunque Crinitum, tuae laudis cupidissimum, non esse Aesopi corniculam iudicarit, is nihil se non invita Minerva dicere aut facere minime ambigat." Earlier, Florido used the variant form "adversa Minerva" (12).

68. Julius Caesar Scaliger would later use the epithet *graculus* against Erasmus in his *Poetices libri septem*, proving that Erasmus is like rhetoric itself: you need him if you want to attack him. See Tournoy, "Erasmus: 'gracculus' or 'graeculus'?," 405–6.

69. In his prologue, Florido deplores the fact that Latin now seems foreign to Italians, "Latinam linguam Italis externam videri posse" (4).

70. Among bilingual authors, Florido mentions Pietro Bembo and Jacopo Sannazaro: "Quamvis enim in utraque lingua celeberrimi fuerunt, eo tamen aliis praestantiora sunt, quae Romane scripserunt, quo Latinus sermo est vulgari nobilior, elegantior, atque absolutior" (63), which may have provoked Du Bellay's counterclaim in *La Deffence et Illustration de la Langue Françoyse* (1970), 189–90: "Je me contenteray de nommer ce docte cardinal Pierre Bembe, duquel je doute si onques homme immita plus curieusement Ciceron, si ce n'est paraventure un Christofle Longueil. Toutesfois par ce qu'il a ecrit en Italien, tant en vers comme en prose, il a illustré et sa Langue et son nom trop plus qu'ilz n'estoint au paravant."

71. Ep. 1791 Allen ll. 49–53.

72. "Erasmum Roterodamum alterum orbis iubar, maximumque rei literariae decus, si laudare velim, vereor ne omnes me insanire proclament: tam multa enim, tamque erudite scripsit, ut ex antiquis plurimos non adaequarit modo, sed longo etiam post se intervallo reliquerit" (77).

73. Florido, *Apologia*, 79: "minime ambigentes, nisi vulgarem hunc sermonem seculo incommode obtrusissent, brevi fieri potuisse, ut Latinus in pristinum statum redigeretur, ac omnibus etiam vel cauponibus fieret communis."

74. Dolet, *La manière*, 7: "Seigneur tout humain, je te requiers de prendre ce mien labeur en gré: et s'il ne reforme totallement nostre langue, pour le moins pense que c'est commencement qui pourra parvenir à fin telle, que les estrangers ne nous appelleront plus Barbares."

75. Marie Madeleine Fontaine proposes a new date for the first edition of the *Deffence*, somewhere between February 15 to April 6, 1550, in "Les relations entre Charles Fontaine et Barthélemy Aneau," 149–86.

76. Villey, *Les sources italiennes*. Villey reprints the *Dialogo delle lingue* in the first appendix to his work.

77. Florido, *Apologia*, 78.

78. Villey, *Les sources italiennes*, 115.

79. Ibid., 140: "non d'invidia, ma d'odio, non di fatica, ma di fastidio, et degna finalmente di dovere essere non appresa, ma ripresa."
80. Speroni, *Dialogo delle Lingue*, 41.
81. See, for example, Gérard Defaux's histrionic denunciation of Du Bellay's condescension to the past in "Du Bellay, Ronsard, Sainte-Beuve et le mythe humaniste du progrès."
82. Du Bellay, *La Deffence et Illustration de la Langue Françoyse* (1970), 28: "Est-ce là defense et illustration, ou plustot offense et denigration?" Chamard reprints the text of the *Quintil* in his notes. Unlike the *Deffence*, the *Quintil* does not seem to have been translated into English.
83. "Mon amy, on voit tout à clair que tu forges icy des repreneurs à plaisir, souz la personne desquels tu cuides couvrir et dissimuler la censure que toy mesme fais de tels personnages, lesquels tu ne oses nommer ne reprendre ouvertement" (94).
84. "Voila bien defendre et illustrer la langue Françoise, ne y recevoir que cinq ou six bons poetes, si cinq douzaines d'autres ne s'y opposoient, à tresbon droit, et pour le moins la grande douzaine" (97).
85. Du Bellay, "*Regrets*" *with* "*The Antiquities of Rome*," 358; "Ceux qui penseront que je soye trop grand admirateur de ma Langue, aillent voir le premier livre des *Fins des Biens et des maulx*, fait par ce pere d'eloquence Latine Ciceron, qui au commencement dudict livre, entre autres choses, repond à ceux qui deprisoint les choses ecrites en Latin, et les aymoint myeux lire en Grec. La conclusion du propos est qu'il estime la Langue Latine non seulement n'estre pauvre, comme les Romains estimoint lors, mais encor' estre plus riche que la Greque" (84).
86. "Je ne veux pas donner si hault loz à notre Langue, pour ce qu'elle n'a point encores ses Cicerons et Virgiles" (84–85).
87. "J'ay bien voulu (lecteur studieux de la Langue Françoyse) demeurer longuement en cete partie, qui te semblera (peut estre) contraire à ce que j'ay promis: veu que je ne prise assez haultement ceux qui tiennent le premier lieu en nostre vulgaire, qui avoy' entrepris de le louer et deffendre" (101).
88. "Toutesfoys je croy que tu ne le trouveras point etrange, si tu consideres que je ne le puis mieux defendre, qu'atribuant la pauvreté d'iceluy, non à son propre et naturel, mais à la negligence de ceux qui en ont pris le gouvernement" (101–2).
89. Chamard, *Histoire de la Pléiade*, 1:205–21: "l'attaque et la défense de la *Deffence*." See also the "dossier de la *Deffence*" put together by Jean-Charles Monferran, including Speroni and Quintil, for his edition of *La Deffence, et illustration de la langue françoyse* (2001), 187–383.
90. See Tucker, *Homo viator*, 239–67. The theme of exile is already present in the *Deffence* according to Ferguson, "Exile's Defense."

CHAPTER 3

1. As reported in the chronicle of Gaspare Veronese according to J. Vahlen in Valla, *Opera omnia*, 2:341.
2. Camporeale, *Christianity, Latinity and Culture*, 166–70.
3. Valla, *Encomion*, 298.
4. Ibid., 300.
5. Ibid., 302.
6. Rabelais, *Œuvres complètes*, 245.
7. Ibid., 224: "Car *Panta* en Grec vault autant à dire comme tout, et *Gruel* en langue Hagarene vault autant comme alteré."
8. Valla, *Encomion*, 302: "tamen me iuste ab eo vel reprehendi vel admoneri."
9. Ibid.: "Perstringendae enim sunt illae apud hos patres conscriptos, non explicandae, ne taedium afferant."
10. Ibid., 304.
11. Ibid., 305.
12. Ibid., 306: "Denique, ut finem comparationis faciam, ille optimam fratrum regulam scripsit, hic plurimos ac praestantissimos libros."
13. Ibid.: "et certe non plures transmittit in caelum scriptis suis Thomas quam Dominicus sua regula."

14. Ibid.: "Cur autem eumdem possint omnibus praeponere, hinc demonstrabant quod dicerent eum ad probationem theologiae adhibere logicam, metaphysicam atque omnem philosophiam, quam superiores doctores vix primis labiis degustassent."

15. Ibid., 308.

16. Colossians 2:8 "non per philosophiam ac inanem fallaciam," quoted in Valla, *Encomion*, 310. According to Camporeale, Valla interpreted Paul as rejecting "the hollow abstraction and argumentation of philosophy" (*Christianity, Latinity and Culture*, 186). Valla had already appealed to this verse from Paul's letter to the Colossians in his *De voluptate*, as Brian Vickers reminds us in "Valla's Ambivalent Praise of Pleasure," 318.

17. Valla, *Encomion*, 308: "illi latinissimi fuerunt, recentes autem omnes paene barbari.."

18. Ibid., 310.

19. Ibid.: "Hic est verus et, ut dicitur, germanus theologandi modus, haec vera dicendi et scribendi lex."

20. Ibid., 312.

21. Ibid.

22. Ibid., 314.

23. Ibid.: "ipse gemino sono theologiae pariter ac philosophiae canere delectatus est."

24. Valla, *In Quartum Librum Elegantiarum Praefatio*, in Garin, *Prosatori*, 612: "quorum culpa non ex minima parte latinae litterae iacturam naufragiumque fecerunt."

25. Ibid., 614: "Porro quinam sunt isti libri in quibus venena eloquentiae occultantur? Certe nullos ego scio non eloquentes nisi tuos tuorumque similium, quibus nec robur ullum adest, nec splendor."

26. For this ideal of "sapientia et eloquentia," see Vickers, *In Defence of Rhetoric*, 163–64.

27. Valla, *Praefatio*, 616: "Nolo hoc in loco comparationem facere inter philosophiam et eloquentiam."

28. Ibid.: "multum usus atque ornamenti divinis accedit rebus."

29. Ibid., 620: "Quod ceteri omnes Latini Graecique fecerunt, Hilarius, Ambrosius, Augustinus, Lactantius, Basilius, Gregorius, Chrysostomus aliique plurimi, qui in omni aetate praetiosas illas divini eloquii gemmas auro argentoque eloquentiae vestierunt."

30. Ibid.: "Non modo non reprehendendum est studere eloquentiae, verum etiam reprehendendum non studere."

31. Ibid.: "Qui vero eleganter loqui nescit, et cogitationes suas litteris mandat, in theologia praesertim, impudentissimus est; et si id consulto facere se ait, insanissimus."

32. Ibid., 622: "At ego malim apes quam formica esse. . . . Quae probatum iri bonae mentis iuvenibus, nam senes desperandi sunt, confidimus."

33. In the *Novum Organum*, aphorism 84 of book 1 proposes the paradox that the moderns are the true ancients because they benefit from a greater store of observation and experience than their predecessors. Bacon, *Works*, 1:190.

34. In Poliziano's *Opus epistolarum*, part of his *Opera omnia* of 1498, this is letter 2 of book 9 (IX, 2) and carries no date. The letter is transcribed in Mario Martelli, "Il 'Libro delle epistole' di Angelo Poliziano," 221–22, with some slight variants. Martelli dates it to "poco primo del 23 maggio 1494" on the basis of external evidence, especially the chronology of Ricci's career in the Florentine Republic.

35. Collected by Erasmus as adage 834 (CWE 32:200).

36. Latininity, splendor, beauty, style, charm, ornament, and majesty.

37. Martelli, "Il 'Libro delle epistole,'" 222: "Quae displicere non debet propterea quod eloquentiam destruit: destruit enim sic eloquenter, ut adstruat hoc ipso, quod destruit. Ita nihil eloquentiam destruere praeter eloquentiam potest, ideoque nec ipsa potest, quoniam scilicet hoc quoque potest, quod omnino non potest." The last clause should perhaps be rendered "unless it can do what cannot be done."

38. Martelli doubts whether this was Poliziano's own editorial decision, because Barbaro's first letter, of April 5, 1485, is unflattering to Pico, but I find his reasoning unpersuasive.

39. Breen, *Christianity and Humanism*, 13; Barbaro, *Epistolae*, 1:86: "sordidi, rudes, inculti, barbari."

40. Pico, *Ioannes Picus Mirandulanus*, 806: "dum barbaros hos philosophos insectaris . . . ita me puduit piguitque studiorum meorum—iam enim sexennium apud illos versor—ut nihil minus me fecisse velim quam in tam nihili facienda re tam laboriose contendisse."

41. Garin, *L'umanesimo italiano*, 120, 121.

42. Valcke, "Jean Pic et le retour au 'style de Paris.'"

43. Farmer, *Syncretism in the West*, 34.

44. Martelli, "Il 'Libro delle epistole,'" 225.

45. Pico, *Ioannes Picus Mirandulanus*, 808: "Nam quod aliud rhetoris officium, quam mentiri, decipere, circumvenire, praestigiari? . . . Eritne huic cum philosopho affinitas, cuius studium omne in cognoscenda et demonstranda ceteris veritate versatur?"

46. Ibid.: "Est ob hanc causam legere res sacras rustice potius quam eleganter scriptas, quod nihil sit magis dedecens et noxium in omni materia, in qua de vero cognoscendo agitur, quam universum istud dicendi genus elaboratum."

47. Ibid., 810; Breen, *Christianity and Humanism*, 18: "We search after the what of writing, we do not search after the how—that the style be without flourish and without flower." Breen does not capture the flourish of this ironic refusal of rhetoric.

48. Martelli, "Il 'Libro delle epistole,'" 225–26.

49. Pico, *Ioannes Picus Mirandulanus*, 816: "Dic, quaeso, quid movet fortius et persuadet quam sacrarum lectio litterarum?"

50. Valla's annotations to the New Testament, now known as the *Collatio*, were first published by none other than Erasmus himself as *Laurentii Vallensis in Latinam Novi Testamenti interpretationem ex collatione Graecorum exemplarium Adnotationes* in 1505.

51. Pico, *Ioannes Picus Mirandulanus*, 820.

52. Gray, "Renaissance Humanism," 211–12.

53. Breen, *Christianity and Humanism*, 24; Pico, *Ioannes Picus Mirandulanus*, 822.

54. Pico, *Ioannes Picus Mirandulanus*, 822; Breen, *Christianity and Humanism*, 24: "But I have given freely of myself in this matter, as in something of ill repute; so that, like those who praise the quartan fever, I might test my abilities."

55. Pico, *Ioannes Picus Mirandulanus*, 822: "Quamvis, dicam libere quod sentio, movent mihi stomachum grammatistae quidam, qui cum duas tenuerint vocabulorum origines, ita se ostentant, ita venditant, ita circumferunt iactabundi, ut prae seipsis pro nihilo habendos philosophos arbitrentur. Nolumus, inquiunt, hasce vestras philosophias; et quid mirum? nec Phalernum canes."

56. Moss, *Renaissance Truth*, 70: "the only time when Pico speaks in his own voice is when he expresses exasperated contempt for grammarians of the humanist sort who think their philological expertise gives them leave ignorantly to discount the works of philosophers."

57. Breen, *Christianity and Humanism*, 25.

58. Ibid., 25; Pico, *Ioannes Picus Mirandulanus*, 822: "non esse facile dictu quid laudum tu tibi vindices, qui sis inter philosophos eloquentissimus, inter eloquentes, ut dicam graece, φιλοσοφότατος."

59. Breen, *Christianity and Humanism*, 26–27; Barbaro, *Epistolae*, 1:101: "ut hostis pro hoste, socius contra socium, ipse contra te ipsum stare patrocinarique simulares."

60. Breen, *Christianity and Humanism*, 27; Barbaro, *Epistolae*, 102: "Proinde ab amicis, quos habeo Patavii, certior factus sum apologiam tuam, quae Scytharum et

Teutonum est inscribi coepta, quasi Typhonis et Eumenidum laudatio, molestissimam accidisse maiori eorum parti, quos defendis, aliis aliter factum tuum interpretantibus."
61. Breen, *Christianity and Humanism*, 38.
62. Or stepmother's (ibid., 28). "Mihi quidem videtur flere ad tumulum novercae." Erasmus collects this saying as adage 810, *Flere ad novercae tumulum*.
63. Moss admits it: "Indeed Pico's letter is disquieting, even for a modern reader" (68).
64. Quintilian, *Institutionum oratoriarum*, 131°: "Sic exercendi ingenii gratia Picus Mirandula iusto pene volumine barbariem defendens, eloquentiam insectatur, idque potissimum efficit eloquentiae viribus: unde huic potissimum ab Hermolao Barbaro et abunde responsum est Apologia."
65. Quintilian, *Institutio oratoria* 2.17.4: "Equidem illos qui contra disputaverunt non tam id sensisse quod dicerent quam exercere ingenia materiae difficultate credo voluisse, sicut Polycraten, cum Busirim laudaret et Clytaemestram: quamquam is, quod his dissimile non esset, composuisse orationem quae est habita contra Socraten dicitur."
66. ASD IV-3:68: "si nugae seria ducant."
67. ASD IV-3:68: "alius diu consarcinata oratione rhetoricen aut philosophiam laudat."
68. ASD IV-3:69–70: "pulchrum esse a stulticia vituperari, quam cum loquentem fecerimus, decoro personae serviendum fuit."
69. Ep. 304 Allen ll. 21–22: "Etiam si verissima scripserit, nonne demenciae est nihil aliud se fatigando quam odium querere?" The CWE translation doesn't serve my turn: "but even if what he says were perfect truth, surely it is madness to wear oneself out with the sole purpose of making oneself unpopular" (CWE ll. 23–26).
70. Ep. 304 Allen l. 28.

71. Chomarat, *Grammaire et rhétorique*, 973–82.
72. ASD IV-3:178: "proinde sacrarum quoque literarum testimoniis, si videtur, laudes nostras fulciamus sive, ut docti solent, fundemus, principio veniam a theologis praefatae, ut nobis fas esse velint."
73. ASD IV-3:186: "de vita tollendum haereticum."
74. ASD IV-3:190: "Sed posteaquam semel τὴν λεοντήν induimus, age doceamus et illud, felicitatem Christianorum, quam tot laboribus expetunt, nihil aliud esse quam insaniae stulticiaeque genus quoddam; absit invidia verbis, rem ipsam potius expendite."
75. ASD IV-3:192: "Nempe spiritus absorbebit corpus. . . . Deinde spiritus a mente illa summa mire absorbebitur. . . . Ita ut iam totus homo extra se futurus sit, nec alia ratione felix futurus nisi quod extra sese positus."
76. Ep. 337 Allen ll. 538–42: "Iam vero in ipsa rei tractatione quid est omnino quod non pie, quod non circumspecte sit dictum ac reverentius etiam quam ut conveniat Moriae? Sed ibi malui paulisper oblivisci decori quam non satisfacere dignitati rei; malui rhetoricen offendere quam laedere pietatem."
77. Ep. 304 CWE ll. 71–74.
78. Ep. 337 Allen ll. 326–29.
79. Ep. 337 Allen l. 670: "bonas litteras metuunt et suae timent tyrannidi."
80. See Moss, *Renaissance Truth*.

CHAPTER 4

1. Isocrates, *Isocrates I*, 55.
2. Livingstone, *Commentary on Isocrates' "Busiris,"* 151.
3. "De quo praefatur in genere, et locum communem tractat de utilitate religionis, et ita quidem ut tractatio illa magis ad superstitiones pertineat quam ad veram pietatem. Inter quas qui nihil interesse censent, in maximo errore versantur, et in extremam incidunt impietatem, omnia esse commenticia quae de providentia Dei, de immortalitate

animorum, de piorum praemiis, de suppliciis impiorum dicuntur, opinantes. Quare huiusmodi sententiae cum iudicio legendae sunt, et verus Dei cultus divinitus patefactus, ab ethnicorum superstitionibus infinito intervallo seiungendus." Wolf, *Hieronymi Wolfii*, 641.

4. Isocrates, *Isocrates I*, 55.

5. Wolf, *Hieronymi Wolfii*, 642: "Quarum bestiarum nunc omnia plena sunt, ob superstitionis in manifestum Epicurismum et impietatem conversionem. Medium tenuere beati, inquit Poeta: sed vulgus, quod proverbio dicitur, diabolum imitatur, vel ultramodum procedendo, ut factum est in superstitionibus, vel intra modum resistendo, ut nunc fit, omni honesta disciplina profligata, et studio religionis neglecto." Wolf was a German Lutheran.

6. Sextus Empiricus, *Adversus Mathematicos* 9.54.

7. For text, translation, and commentary of the Sisyphus fragment, see Davies, "Sisyphus and the Invention," 16–32.

8. Plutarch, *Moralia* 880E–F; Livy, *Ab urbe condita* 1.19.4; and Statius, *Thebaid* 3.661, cited in Wolf, *Hieronymi Wolfii*, 641.

9. Polybius, *Histoires Livre VI*, 139.

10. Wolf, *Hieronymi Wolfii*, 643.

11. Dionisotti, *Machiavellerie*, 138–39.

12. Sasso, *Niccolò Machiavelli*, 36, n. 21.

13. Though not always faithful to Livy. For this aspect, see Martelli, *Machiavelli et gli storici antichi*.

14. The term is taken from Preus, "Machiavelli's Functional Analysis." Before Preus, Alberto Tenenti focused his discussion of Machiavelli's religion on "la sua analisi funzionale delle credenze religiose" in "La religione di Machiavelli," 715. Viroli espouses a completely opposite view of Machiavelli's religion in *Il Dio di Machiavelli*.

15. Machiavelli, *Il Principe*, 138–41.

16. Ibid., 140: "così fece Licurgo, così Solone, così molti altri."

17. Ibid.: "E come la osservanza del culto divino è cagione della grandezza delle repubbliche, così il dispregio di quello è cagione della rovina di esse."

18. Sasso, *Niccolò Machiavelli*, 553: "non è più soltanto uno strumento di dominio"

19. Machiavelli, *Principe*, 142: "Come costoro cominciarono dipoi a parlare a modo de' potenti, e che questa falsità si fu scoperta ne' popoli, diventarono gli uomini increduli ed atti a perturbare ogni ordine buono."

20. Najemy, "Papirius and the Chickens."

21. Rhetorical analysis of Machiavelli has been overwhelmingly oriented toward *The Prince*. Viroli, *Redeeming the Prince*, chap. 3, reads *The Prince* as an exercise in deliberative rhetoric, a protreptic oration. Tinkler studies both deliberative and epideictic aspects of *The Prince* in "Praise and Advice." Kahn, *Machiavellian Rhetoric*, discusses the "rhetorical politics" of both *The Prince* and the *Discourses* without regard to the different genres of rhetoric. The most recent example of this trend, but not the last, is Skinner, *From Humanism to Hobbes*, with the inevitable chapter on *The Prince*, understood in terms of judicial rhetoric.

22. Machiavelli, *Il Principe*, 135: "Ed è impossibile che quelli che in stato privato vivono in una republica, o che per fortuna o per virtù ne diventono principi, se leggessono le istorie, e delle memorie delle antiche cose facessono capitale, che non volessero quelli tali privati vivere nella loro patria più tosto Scipioni che Cesari, e quelli che sono principi, più tosto Agesilai, Timoleoni, Dioni, che Nabidi, Falari e Dionisii: perché vedrebbono questi essere sommamente vituperati, e quelli eccessivamente laudati."

23. Ibid., 134: "Intra tutti gli uomini laudati, sono i laudatissimi quelli che sono stati capi e ordinatori delle religioni."

24. Tinkler, "Praise and Advice," 205, seems to recognize Machiavelli's penchant for odious praise: "His memorably shocking paradox is that to pursue utility at the expense of honor is itself honorable, praiseworthy."

25. Gentillet, *Anti-Machiavel*, 12; Gentillet, *Discours*, 7: "Il en a pris en cest endroit à Machiavel, comme il fit une fois

au Philosophe Phormio, lequel estant un jour en son auditoire faisant sa leçon en l'escole des Peripateticiens en Grece, y voyant entrer et arriver Annibal de Carthage, (lequel y fut mené par aucuns siens amis, pour ouyr l'eloquence de ce Philosophe) se mit incontinent à parler et disputer avec un beau babil des loix de guerre, et du devoir d'un bon Chef, par devant ce grand Capitaine."

26. Cicero, *De oratore* 2.75: "Nec mihi opus est Graeco aliquo doctore, qui mihi pervulgata praecepta decantet, cum ipse numquam forum, numquam ullum iudicium aspexerit."

27. Ibid., 2.76: "Hoc mihi facere omnes isti, qui de arte dicendi praecipiunt, videntur; quod enim ipsi experti non sunt, id docent ceteros."

28. Gentillet, *Discours*, 9 (marginal heading): "Calomnies de Machiavel, contre les Rois et peuple de France."

29. Ibid., 184: "Le Prince doit soustenir ce qui est faux en la Religion."

30. Ibid., 186: "par raison naturelle."

31. Ibid., 187: "Machiavel et les Machiavelistes, lesquels on conoit assez estre tous vrais Epicuriens."

32. Ibid., 214: "par la propre confession de Machiavel, les hommes deviennent meschans en toute meschanceté et desbordement, des qu'ils commencent à estre sans Religion. Pourquoy donc est-ce que Machiavel enseigne tout ouvertement l'Atheisme?" His answer is that Machiavelli wants people to be *méchant*, but that seems a little simplistic. Gentillet is the wrong reader. Machiavelli is writing for those who interpret, not those who believe.

33. For a rare overview of Bodin's complex achievement, see Lloyd, *Jean Bodin*.

34. Bodin, *Six Books*, A70; Bodin, *Les six livres*, a iii v to a iv r: "Macciavel: lequel a mis pour deux fondemens des Republiques, l'impieté et l'injustice, blasmant la religion comme contraire à l'estat: et toutesfois au Polibe gouverneur et lieutenant de Scipion l'Africain, estimé le plus sage Politique de son aage, ores qu'il fust droit Atheiste,

neantmoins il recommande la religion sur toutes choses, comme le fondement principal de toutes Republiques . . . quand il dit que les Romains n'ont iamais rien eu de plus grand que la religion."

35. The text that first drew my attention to the primordial importance of *République* IV, 7 for Bodin's thought is Roellenbleck, "Jean Bodin et la liberté de conscience."

36. Bodin, *Les six livres*, 634: "Premierement nous poserons ceste maxime, que les factions et particularités sont dangereuses, et pernicieuses en toute sorte de Republique."

37. Machiavelli, *Il Principe*, 115–17: "Io non voglio mancare di discorrere sopra questi tumulti che furono in Roma dalla morte de' Tarquini alla creazione de' tribuni, e dipoi alcune altre cose contro la opinione di molti, che dicono Roma essere stata una republica tumultuaria. . . . Io dico che coloro che dannano i tumulti intra i nobili e la plebe, mi pare che biasimino quelle cose che furono prima causa del tenere libera Roma. . . . E se i tumulti furono cagione della creazione de' tribuni, meritano somma laude."

38. Gentillet, *Discours*, 555: "Ceste raison ressemble à l'argument d'un certain philosophe, duquel Aulugelle se mocque, qui vouloit soustenir que la fievre quartaine est une bonne chose, parce qu'elle fait devenir les gens sobres et temperans, et les garde de trop boire et manger."

39. Bodin, *Les six livres*, 652.

40. Ibid., 653.

41. Ibid., 654: "Il ne voulut pas forcer ny punir les Arrians, quoy qu'il fust leur ennemi, ains au contraire il permit à chacun de vivre en liberté de conscience, et fit ordonner deux Evesques en chacune ville, iaçoit qu'il eust faict quelques edicts contre les Arrians, qu'il tint en souffrance, ne voulant qu'ils fussent executés."

42. Ibid.: "Mais le Roy des Turcs garde sa Religion aussi bien que Prince du monde, et ne force personne, ains au contraire permet à chacun de vivre selon sa conscience."

43. Ibid., 655: "la plus forte superstition du monde n'est pas à beaucoup pres si detestable que l'atheïsme."

44. Bodin, *De republica libri sex*, 485: "Et quemadmodum ex omni civitatum genere nullum deterius est anarchia, in qua nemo paret, nemo imperat, sed in summa scelerum omnium impunitate ac licentia vivitur: sic etiam nulla pestis civitatibus gravior accidere potest numinis carentia, quam Graeci ἀθεισμὸν vocant: et certe non parum peccant qui πολυθεότητος et ἀθεότητος eandem poenam statui putant oportere: aut θεῶν ἀπειρίαν τὸν αὐτοκράτορα θεον ἀναιρεῖν. Nam superstitio quantacunque fuerit, homines tamen in legum ac magistratuum metu et in mutuis vitae officiis continet: impietas autem adversus numina omnem ex anima peccandi metum penitus evellit."

45. Bodin, *Colloquium*, 124: "Coronaeus: Illud omnibus persuasum esse opinor, multo praestabilius esse falsam quam nullam habere religionem, ut in omnibus rerum publicarum gentibus nullum perniciosius est ἀναρχία, in qua nemo imperat, nemo paret, nulla praemia bonis, nulla supplicia peccatis irrogantur. Sic nulla est tanta superstitio, quae metu divini numinis improbos in officio continere et naturae lege quodammodo tueri non possit, cum praemia bonis, supplicia peccatis irrogari divino judicio persuasum habeant."

46. Ibid., 182–83: "Coronaeus: Superstitio, quantacumque sit, quovis atheismo tolerabilior est; nam qui superstitione aliqua obligatur hunc numinis metus in officio quodammodo ac naturae legibus continet, atheum vero, qui nihil nisi testem metuit aut judicem, ad omnia scelera proclivi lapsu ruere oportet."

47. Characteristic is Fridericus's role in the *Colloquium*, 118: "Qui religionum discrepantium varietatem admittit, verae religionis eversionem moliri videtur." Fridericus does not seem to be the voice of Bodin.

48. Bodin, *Les six livres*, 654: "Ie ne parle point icy laquelle des Religions est la meilleure, (combien qu'il n'y a qu'une Religion, une verité, une loy divine publiee par la bouche de Dieu)"; *Six Books*, 537: "I will not here take upon me to determine which of them is the best (howbeit that there can be but one such, one truth, and one divine law, by the mouth of god published)."

49. Machiavelli, *Il Principe*, 142: "E perché questo modo è stato osservato dagli uomini savi, ne è nato l'opinione dei miracoli che si celebrano nelle religioni eziandio false."

50. Bodin, *Methodus*, 344: "Consequens est ad unius Principis institutionem optimi sapientiae magistri ac moderatores, maximis propositis praemiis conquirantur: non qui peregrina lingua id quod inepte ac perniciose antea factum vidimus, sed qui religione vera molles Principis animos leniter imbuant."

51. Ibid.

52. Ibid., 345: "Propterea quod improbos ab injuriosa facinorosaque vita magistratuum metus, non religio deterret: Principem vero quis magistratus, quae leges, quae imperia coercebunt, nisi religionis metu contineatur?"

53. This is the classic position advocated by Popkin, *History of Scepticism*.

54. One exception is the "Apologie," where he cites Socrates's saying that superstition follows pride like its father (II, 12, 498) and insinuates that Protestantism is a superstition. See Legros, "Plutarque, Amyot, Montaigne et la 'superstition.'"

55. For a representative sampling of these borrowings, see Supple, *Essais de Montaigne*, 62–63.

56. Cicero, *De officiis* 1.14: "honestum . . . dicimus, etiamsi a nullo laudetur, natura esse laudabile."

57. This question was debated by Arlette Jouanna and Étienne Vaucheret in *Les Écrivains et la politique*, a volume commemorating the four hundredth anniversary of Montaigne's appointment as mayor of Bordeaux in 1581. In her paper "Montaigne et la noblesse" (113–23), Jouanna insists on the social construction of "la vertu noble," whereas Vaucheret wonders if nobility is

not first and foremost "un problème de morale et de conscience personnelle" (125).
58. Cicero, *On Duties*, 17. In Latin, "quod etiamsi nobilitatum non sit, tamen honestum sit," which Montaigne changes to "quasi non sit honestum quod nobilitatum non sit" (II, 16, 622).
59. *Tusculanarum disputationum libri* 2.64: "nullum theatrum virtuti conscientia maius est."
60. Supple, *Arms Versus Letters*, 189.
61. Arlette Jouanna provides a concise discussion of "la dérogeance," with further bibliography, in the chapter "Hiérarchie et noblesse" in *La France du XVIe siècle*, 57-69.
62. This is the text of the 1580 edition, before the interpolation of three more *si* clauses in the 1588 edition: "[B] si le peuple en est esveillé à la vertu; si les Princes sont touchez de voir le monde benir la memoire de Trajan et abominer celle de Neron; si cela les esmeut de voir le nom de ce grand pendart, autresfois si effroyable et si redoubté, maudit et outragé si librement par le premier escolier qui l'entreprend: [A] qu'elle accroisse hardiment" (II, 16, 629).
63. Machiavelli, *Il Principe*, 135.
64. Ibid., 136.
65. *De natura deorum* 1.53: "ut tragici poetae confugiunt ad deum, cum explicare argumenti exitum non possunt."
66. Machiavelli, *Il Principe*, 140.
67. "Toute personne d'honneur choisit de perdre plustost son honneur, que de perdre sa conscience" (II, 16, 630 C).
68. Aristotle, *Rhetoric* 1358b20–29.
69. Cicero, *De inventione*, 322–25.
70. "Il quitta l'utile pour l'honneste" (III, 1, 790).
71. Aristotle, *Rhetoric* 1359a1–6.
72. Perelman and Olbrechts-Tyteca, "Logique et rhétorique," 11.
73. Hampton, *Fictions of Embassy*, 62–71.
74. Ibid., 71.
75. "Comme nous assignons au haras les bestes qui sont de moindre estime" (III, 1, 803).

CONCLUSION

1. "Qui voudra se desfaire de ce violent prejudice de la coustume, il trouvera plusieurs choses receues d'une resolution indubitable, qui n'ont appuy qu'en la barbe chenue et rides de l'usage qui les accompaigne; mais, ce masque arraché, rapportant les choses à la verité et à la raison, il sentira son jugement comme tout bouleversé, et remis pourtant en bien plus seur estat" (I, 23, 117).
2. Mondolfo, *La comprensione*.
3. This is the fragment known as DK 80 B4 conserved in Diogenes Laertius, *Lives of the Philosophers* 9.51.
4. Mondolfo, *La comprensione*, 96: "È molto probabile che Protagora non potesse continuare a trattare il suo tema se non come relativo alle opinioni umane, secondo il suo principio dell'uomo misura di tutte le cose; e probabilmente anche applicando il criterio pragmatistico dell'utilità in sostituzione del criterio della verità oggettiva."
5. See Piccirilli, "Il primo caso."
6. Katinis, *Sperone Speroni*, 151: "Queste cose dirai contra Socrate per li sofisti, e contra la maniera della sua vita da lui tenuta contra le leggi e costumi della sua patria."
7. Ibid., 154. It is also what Montaigne does and what Aristotelian rhetoric does.
8. Bodin, *Les six livres*, 654, quoted above in chapter 4, section 3 *in fine*.

Appendix

1. Ovid, *Heroides* epistles 20 and 21. Acontius put an apple with writing on it in the lap of Cydippa. Speroni could have found this in adage 1370, *Malis ferire*, an adage of bribery.
2. The text breaks off here without telling us who is *beato*, if not the one who is the object of blame. By this logic Socrates is blessed since Speroni, one of the new sophists, blames him elsewhere.

BIBLIOGRAPHY

PRIMARY SOURCES

Antisthenes. *Antisthenis fragmenta.* Edited by Fernanda Decleva Caizzi. Milan: Cisalpino, 1966.

Aristotle. *Aristotelis ars rhetorica.* Edited by Rudolf Kassel. Berlin: de Gruyter, 1976.

———. *On Rhetoric.* Translated by George Kennedy. New York: Oxford University Press, 2007.

———. *Topica et Sophistici Elenchi.* Edited by W. D. Ross. Oxford Classical Texts. Oxford: Clarendon Press, 1958.

Augustine. *De civitate Dei.* Edited by Bernhard Dombart and Alphonse Kalb. 2 vols. Bibliotheca Teubneriana. Stuttgart: Teubner, 1993.

Bacon, Francis. *The Works of Francis Bacon.* Edited by James Spedding, R. L. Ellis, and D. D. Heath. 7 vols. London, 1857–59. Reprint, New York: Garrett Press, 1968.

Barbaro, Ermolao. *Epistolae, Orationes et Carmina.* Edited by Vittore Branca. 2 vols. Florence: Bibliopolis, 1943.

Bodin, Jean. *Colloquium Heptaplomeres de rerum sublimium arcanis abditis.* Edited by Ludwig Noack. Stuttgart: Frommann, 1966.

———. *De republica libri sex.* Paris: Jacques Du Puys, 1586.

———. *Methodus ad facilem historiarum cognitionem.* Paris: Martin Le Jeune, 1566.

———. *The Six Books of a Commonweale: A Facsimile Reprint of the English Translation of 1606.* Edited by Kenneth Douglas McRae. Cambridge, MA: Harvard University Press, 1962.

———. *Les six livres de la République.* Paris: Jacques Du Puys, 1583. Reprint, Aalen: Scientia, 1961.

Cardano, Girolamo. *Opera omnia.* Vol. 1. Lyon: Huguetan et Ravaud, 1663.

Cicero. *De inventione.* Translated by H. M. Hubbell. Loeb Classical Library. Cambridge, MA: Harvard University Press, 2014.

———. *On Duties.* Translated by Walter Miller. Loeb Classical Library. Cambridge, MA: Harvard University Press, 2014.

———. *On Ends.* Translated by Harris Rackham. Loeb Classical Library. Cambridge, MA: Harvard University Press, 2014.

———. *Tusculanae disputationes.* Edited by Max Pohlenz. Bibliotheca Teubneriana. Stuttgart: Teubner, 1967.

———. *Tusculan Disputations.* Translated by J. E. King. Loeb Classical Library. Cambridge, MA: Harvard University Press, 2014.

Cope, Edward Meredith. *The Rhetoric of Aristotle with a Commentary.* Edited by John Edwin Sandys. 3 vols. Cambridge: Cambridge University Press, 1877. Reprint, Salem, NH: Ayer, 1988.

Crinito, Pietro. *De honesta disciplina.* Edited by Carlo Angeleri. Rome: Fratelli Bocca, 1955.

DellaNeva, JoAnn. *Ciceronian Controversies.* I Tatti Renaissance Library. Cambridge, MA: Harvard University Press, 2007.

Dolet, Etienne. *La maniere de bien traduire d'une langue en aultre.* Lyon, 1540. Reprint, Geneva: Slatkine, 1972.

Du Bellay, Joachim. *La Deffence, et illustration de la langue françoyse.* Edited by Jean-Charles Monferran. Geneva: Droz, 2001.

———. *La Deffence et Illustration de la Langue Françoyse.* Edited by Henri Chamard. Paris: Didier, 1970.

———. *Les Regrets et autres œuvres poëtiques suivis des Antiquitez de Rome Plus un Songe ou Vision sur le mesme subject.* Edited by J. Jolliffe and M. A. Screech. Geneva: Droz, 1979.

———. *"The Regrets" with "The Antiquities of Rome," Three Latin Elegies, and "The Defense and Enrichment of the French Language."* Edited and translated by Richard Helgerson. Philadelphia: University of Pennsylvania Press, 2006.

Erasmus, Desiderius. *Collected Works of Erasmus.* In progress. Toronto: University of Toronto Press, 1974.

———. *Desiderii Erasmi Roterodami opera omnia.* Edited by Jean Le Clerc. 10 vols. Leiden: P. van der Aa, 1703–6.

———. *Opera omnia Desiderii Erasmi Roterodami.* In progress. Amsterdam: North Holland, Elsevier, and Brill, 1969.

———. *Opus epistolarum Des. Erasmi Roterodami.* Edited by P. S. Allen et al. 12 vols. Oxford: Clarendon Press, 1906–58.

Ficino, Marsilio. *Opera omnia.* 2 vols. Basel: Henricpetri, 1576. Reprint, Turin: Bottega d'Erasmo, 1959.

Florido, Francesco. *Apologia in Marci Actii Plauti aliorumque poetarum et linguae latinae calumniatores.* Lyon: Sébastien Gryphe, 1537.

———. *Succisivae lectiones.* In *Lampas sive fax artium liberalium,* edited by Janus Gruterus, 1:996–1222. Frankfurt, 1602.

Garin, Eugenio, ed. *Prosatori Latini del Quattrocento.* Milan: Ricciardi, 1952.

Gellius, Aulus. *Attic Nights.* Translated by John C. Rolfe. 3 vols. Loeb Classical Library. Cambridge, MA: Harvard University Press, 1946–52.

Gentillet, Innocent. *Anti-Machiavel: A Discourse upon the Means of Well Governing.* Edited by Ryan Murtha. Translated by Simon Patericke. Eugene, OR: Resource Publications, 2018.

———. *Discours sur les moyens de bien gouverner et maintenir en bonne paix un royaume ou autre principauté . . . contre Nicolas Machiavel.* Geneva: Jacob Stoer, 1576.

Gorgias. *Encomium of Helen.* Edited by D. M. MacDowell. London: Bristol Classical Press, 1982.

Isocrates. *Isocrates I.* Edited by David Mirhady and Yun Lee Too. Austin: University of Texas Press, 2000.

———. *Opera omnia.* Edited by Basilius Mandilaras. 3 vols. Bibliotheca Teubneriana. Munich: K. G. Saur, 2003.

Labé, Louise. *Complete Poetry and Prose. A Bilingual Edition.* Edited and translated by Deborah Lesko Baker. Chicago: University of Chicago Press, 2006.

———. *Œuvres complètes.* Edited by François Rigolot. Paris: Flammarion, 1986.

Machiavelli, Niccolò. *Il Principe e altre opere politiche.* Edited by Delio Cantimori. Milan: Garzanti, 1981.

Marullus, Michael. *Michaelis Marulli carmina*. Edited by Alessandro Perosa. Zurich: Thesaurus Mundi, 1951.

———. *Poems*. Translated by Charles Fantazzi. I Tatti Renaissance Library. Cambridge, MA: Harvard University Press, 2012.

Montaigne, Michel de. *The Complete Essays of Montaigne*. Translated by Donald Frame. Stanford: Stanford University Press, 1958.

———. *Les Essais*. Edited by Pierre Villey and V.-L. Saulnier. Paris: Presses Universitaires de France, 1978.

Nauck, August. *Tragicorum Graecorum Fragmenta*. 2nd ed. Leipzig: Teubner, 1889.

Petrarca, Francesco [Petrarch]. *Invectives*. Edited by David Marsh. I Tatti Renaissance Library. Cambridge, MA: Harvard University Press, 2003.

Petronius. *Le Satiricon*. Edited by Alfred Ernout. Paris: Les Belles Lettres, 1950.

Philostratus. *Flavii Philostrati opera*. Edited by Carl Ludwig Kayser. 2 vols. Bibliotheca Teubneriana. Leipzig: Teubner, 1870–71.

Pico della Mirandola, Giovanni. *Ioannes Picus Mirandulanus Hermolao Barbaro suo s*. In *Prosatori Latini del Quattrocento*, 804–22. Edited by Eugenio Garin. Milan: Ricciardi, 1952.

Plato. *Euthyphro, Apology of Socrates, Crito*. Edited by John Burnet. Oxford: Clarendon Press, 1924.

———. *Five Dialogues*. Translated by G. M. A. Grube. Indianapolis: Hackett, 1981.

———. *Phaedrus and the Seventh and Eighth Letters*. Translated by Walter Hamilton. New York: Penguin, 1973.

———. *Protagoras*. Translated by Stanley Lombardo and Karen Bell. Indianapolis: Hackett, 1992.

Poliziano, Angelo. *Opera, quae quidem extitere hactenus, omnia*. Basel: Apud Nicolaum Episcopium Iuniorem, 1553.

Polybius. *Histoires Livre VI*. Edited by Raymond Weil. Paris: Les Belles Lettres, 1977.

Quintilian. *Institutionum oratoriarum libri XII*. Paris: Josse Bade, 1538.

Rabelais, François. *Œuvres complètes*. Edited by Mireille Huchon. Bibliothèque de la Pléiade. Paris: Gallimard, 1994.

Seneca Rhetor. *Declamations*. Translated by Michael Winterbottom. 2 vols. Loeb Classical Library. Cambridge, MA: Harvard University Press, 2014.

———. *Oratorum et rhetorum sententiae divisiones colores*. Edited by Adoph Kiessling. Bibliotheca Teubneriana. Stuttgart: Teubner, 1967.

Speroni, Sperone. *Dialogo delle Lingue*. Translated by Helene Harth. Munich: Wilhelm Fink, 1975.

———. *Opere*. Edited by Forcellini. 5 vols. Venice: Domenico Occhi, 1740.

Sturm, Johann. *Scholia in libros III Rhetoricorum*. Strasbourg: T. Rihelius, 1570.

Valla, Lorenzo. *Encomion Sancti Thomae Aquinatis*. In *Christianity, Latinity and Culture: Two Studies on Lorenzo Valla*, edited by Patrick Baker and Christopher Celenza, 297–315. Leiden: Brill, 2014.

———. *In Quartum Librum Elegantiarum Praefatio*. In *Prosatori Latini del Quattrocento*, edited by Eugenio Garin, 612–22. Milan: Ricciardi, 1952.

———. *Opera omnia*. Edited by Eugenio Garin. 2 vols. Basel, 1540. Reprint, Turin: Bottega d'Erasmo, 1962.

Virgil. *Opera Virgiliana cum decem commentis docte et familiariter exposita*. Lyon: Jacques Mareschal, 1528.

———. *P. Virgilii Maronis Universum Poema . . . cum Iodocique Vuillichii eruditis super Georgica commentariis*. Venice: Giovanni Maria Bonelli, 1558.

Wolf, Hieronymus. *Hieronymi Wolfii in omnia Isocratis opera, et vitam eiusdem a diversis autoribus descriptam Annotationes.* Basel: Oporinus, 1570.

SECONDARY SOURCES

Bailly, Anatole. *Dictionnaire grec-français.* 16th ed. Paris: Hachette, 1950.
Bataillon, Marcel. *Érasme et l'Espagne. Recherches sur l'histoire spirituelle du XVIᵉ siècle.* Geneva: Droz, 1998.
Bettinzoli, Attilio. *La lucerna di Cleante. Poliziano tra Ficino e Pico.* Florence: Olschki, 2009.
Bietenholz, Peter. *Contemporaries of Erasmus.* 3 vols. Toronto: University of Toronto Press, 1985–87.
Bignone, Ettore. *L'Aristotele perduto e la formazione filosofica di Epicuro.* 2 vols. Florence: La Nuova Italia, 1973.
Breen, Quirinus. *Christianity and Humanism: Studies in the History of Ideas.* Edited by Nelson Peter Ross. Grand Rapids, MI: Eerdmans, 1968.
Camporeale, Salvatore. *Christianity, Latinity and Culture: Two Studies on Lorenzo Valla.* Edited by Patrick Baker and Christopher Celenza. Leiden: Brill, 2014.
Cassin, Barbara. *L'effet sophistique.* Paris: Gallimard, 1995.
Chamard, Henri. *Histoire de la Pléiade.* 4 vols. Paris: Didier, 1961.
Chomarat, Jacques. *Grammaire et rhétorique chez Érasme.* Paris: Les Belles Lettres, 1981.
Cox, Virginia. "Machiavelli and the *Rhetorica ad Herennium*." *Sixteenth Century Journal* 28, no. 4 (1997): 1109–41.
Davies, Malcolm. "Sisyphus and the Invention of Religion (Critias TrGF 1 (43) F19 = B25 DK)." *Bulletin of the Institute of Classical Studies* 36, no. 1 (1989): 16–32.
Defaux, Gérard. "Du Bellay, Ronsard, Sainte-Beuve et le mythe humaniste du progrès." In *Histoire et littérature au siècle de Montaigne: Mélanges offerts à Claude-Gilbert Dubois*, edited by Françoise Argod-Dutard, 285–99. Geneva: Droz, 2001.
Desan, Philippe. "From Eyquem to Montaigne." In *The Oxford Handbook of Montaigne*, 17–39. New York: Oxford University Press, 2016.
Dionisotti, Carlo. *Machiavellerie. Storia e fortuna di Machiavelli.* Turin: Einaudi, 1980.
Farmer, Stephen. *Syncretism in the West: Pico's 900 Theses (1486); The Evolution of Traditional Religious and Philosophical Systems.* Tempe, AZ: Medieval and Renaissance Texts and Studies, 1998.
Ferguson, Margaret. "Exile's Defense: Du Bellay's *La Deffence et illustration de la langue françoyse.*" *Publications of the Modern Language Association* 93, no. 2 (1978): 275–89.
Fontaine, Marie-Madeleine. "L'ordinaire de la folie." In *La folie et le corps*, edited by Jean Céard, 179–96. Paris: Presses de l'École Normale Supérieure, 1985.
———. "Les relations entre Charles Fontaine et Barthélemy Aneau et le débat du *Quintil Horatian* ou comment dater les premières œuvres de Du Bellay." In *Charles Fontaine: Un humaniste parisien à Lyon*, 149–86. Geneva: Droz, 2014.
Gadoffre, Gilbert. *La révolution culturelle dans la France des humanistes.* Geneva: Droz, 1997.
Garin, Eugenio. "Ἐνδελέχεια e Ἐντελέχεια nelle discussion umanistiche." *Atene e Roma* 39 (1937): 177–87.
———. *L'umanesimo italiano.* Bari: Laterza, 1993.
Giocanti, Sylvia. *Penser l'irrésolution. Montaigne, Pascal, La Mothe Le Vayer: Trois itinéraires sceptiques.* Paris: Honoré Champion, 2001.
Gontier, Thierry, and Suzel Mayer, eds. *Le Socratisme de Montaigne.* Paris: Classiques Garnier, 2010.
Gouwens, Kenneth. "Ciceronianism and Collective Identity: Defining the

Boundaries of the Roman Academy, 1525." *Journal of Medieval and Renaissance Studies* 23, no. 2 (1993): 173–95.

Gray, Hanna H. "Renaissance Humanism: The Pursuit of Eloquence." In *Renaissance Essays*, edited by Paul Oskar Kristeller and Philip P. Wiener, 199–216. New York: Harper and Row, 1968.

Hampton, Timothy. *Fictions of Embassy: Literature and Diplomacy in Early Modern Europe*. Ithaca: Cornell University Press, 2009.

Jouanna, Arlette. *La France du XVIe siècle, 1483–1598*. Paris: Presses Universitaires de France, 1996.

———. "Montaigne et la noblesse." In *Les Écrivains et la politique dans le sud-ouest de la France autour des années 1580: Actes du colloque de Bordeaux, 6–7 novembre 1981*, 113–23. Bordeaux: Presses Universitaires de Bordeaux, 1982.

Kahn, Victoria. *Machiavellian Rhetoric: From the Counter-Reformation to Milton*. Princeton: Princeton University Press, 1994.

Katinis, Teodoro. *Sperone Speroni and the Debate over Sophistry in the Italian Renaissance*. Leiden: Brill, 2018.

Lamers, Han. *Greece Reinvented: Transformations of Byzantine Hellenism in Renaissance Italy*. Leiden: Brill, 2016.

Langer, Ullrich. "Ce qui sauve la vie, est-ce vraiment une 'rhétorique'? ('De la phisionomie')." In *Montaigne: Une rhétorique naturalisée? Actes du colloque international tenu à University of Chicago (Paris) les 7 et 8 avril 2017*, edited by Déborah Knop, Blandine Perona, and Philippe Desan, 117–30. Paris: Champion, 2019.

Lauvergnat-Gagnière, Christiane. "La Rhétorique dans le *Débat de Folie et d'Amour*." In *Louise Labé, les voix du lyrisme*, edited by Guy Demerson, 53–67. Paris: Editions du CNRS, 1990.

Legros, Alain. "Plutarque, Amyot, Montaigne et la 'superstition.'" In *Moralia et Œuvres morales à la Renaissance*, edited by Olivier Guerrier, 275–91. Paris: Champion, 2008.

Livingstone, Niall. *A Commentary on Isocrates' "Busiris."* Leiden: Brill, 2001.

Lloyd, Howell. *Jean Bodin: "This Pre-eminent Man of France": An Intellectual Biography*. Oxford: Oxford University Press, 2017.

MacPhail, Eric. "Jean Bodin and the Praise of Superstition." *Rhetorica* 36, no. 1 (2018): 24–38.

———. "Montaigne and the Praise of Sparta." *Rhetorica* 20, no. 2 (2002): 193–211.

———. "Philosophers in the New World: Montaigne and the Tradition of Epideictic Rhetoric." *Rhetorica* 30, no. 1 (2012): 22–36.

———. *The Sophistic Renaissance*. Geneva: Droz, 2011.

Martelli, Mario. "Il 'Libro delle epistole' di Angelo Poliziano." *Interpres* 1 (1978): 184–255.

———. *Machiavelli et gli storici antichi: Osservazioni su alcuni luoghi dei Discorsi sopra la prima deca di Tito Livio*. Rome: Salerno, 1998.

McLaughlin, Martin. *Literary Imitation in the Italian Renaissance*. New York: Oxford University Press, 1995.

Mondolfo, Rodolfo. *La comprensione del soggetto umano nell'antichità classica*. Florence: La Nuova Italia, 1958.

Moss, Ann. *Renaissance Truth and the Latin Language Turn*. Oxford: Oxford University Press, 2003.

Najemy, John. "Papirius and the Chickens, or Machiavelli on the Necessity of Interpreting Religion." *Journal of the History of Ideas* 60, no. 4 (1999): 659–81.

O'Malley, John W. *Praise and Blame in Renaissance Rome: Rhetoric, Doctrine, and Reform in the Sacred Orators of the Papal Court, c. 1450–1521*.

Durham: Duke University Press, 1979.
Ostwald, Martin. "The Sophists and Athenian Politics." In *Democrazia e antidemocrazia nel mondo greco*, edited by Umberto Bultrighini, 35–52. Alessandria: Edizioni dell'Orso, 2005.
Perelman, Chaïm, and Lucie Olbrechts-Tyteca. "Logique et rhétorique." *Revue Philosophique de la France et de l'Étranger* 140 (1950): 1–35.
Pernot, Laurent. *Epideictic Rhetoric: Questioning the Stakes of Ancient Praise*. Austin: University of Texas Press, 2015.
Perona, Blandine. "Introduction: Montaigne: Une rhétorique naturalisée?" In *Montaigne: Une rhétorique naturalisée? Actes du colloque international tenu à University of Chicago (Paris) les 7 et 8 avril 2017*, edited by Déborah Knop, Blandine Perona, and Philippe Desan, 9–20. Paris: Champion, 2019.
Piccirilli, Luigi. "Il primo caso di autodafé letterario: Il rogo dei libri di Protagora." *Studi Italiani di Filologia Classica*, 3rd ser., 15 (1997): 17–23.
Pigman, G. W. "Imitation and the Renaissance Sense of the Past: The Reception of Erasmus' *Ciceronianus*." *Journal of Medieval and Renaissance Studies* 9 (1979): 155–77.
Poel, Marc van der. "Cardano's *Neronis encomium*: Literary Trifle or Political Treatise?" *Studi Umanistici Piceni* 25 (2005): 283–96.
Popkin, Richard. *The History of Scepticism from Erasmus to Descartes*. New York: Harper and Row, 1968.
Porteau, Paul. "Sur un paradoxe de Montaigne." In *Mélanges de littérature, d'histoire et de philologie offerts à Paul Laumonier par ses élèves et ses amis*, 329–46. Paris: Droz, 1935.
Preus, Samuel. "Machiavelli's Functional Analysis of Religion: Context and Object." *Journal of the History of Ideas* 40, no. 2 (1979): 171–90.
Roellenbleck, Georg. "Jean Bodin et la liberté de conscience." In *La liberté de conscience (XVIe–XVIIe siècles): Actes du Colloque de Mulhouse et Bâle (1989)*, edited by Hans Guggisberg, Frank Lestringant, and Jean-Claude Margolin, 97–106. Geneva: Droz, 1991.
Sabbadini, Remigio. "Vita e opere di Francesco Florido Sabino." *Giornale Storico della Letteratura Italiana* 8 (1886): 333–63.
Sasso, Gennaro. *Niccolò Machiavelli*. Vol. 1, *Il pensiero politico*. Bologna: Il Mulino, 1993.
Scodel, Joshua. "The Affirmation of Paradox: A Reading of Montaigne's 'De la Phisionomie' (III: 12)." *Yale French Studies*, no. 64 (1983): 209–37.
Scott, Izora. *Controversies over the Imitation of Cicero in the Renaissance*. Davis, CA: Hermagoras Press, 1991.
Siraisi, Nancy. "Anatomizing the Past: Physicians and History in Renaissance Culture." *Renaissance Quarterly* 53, no. 1 (2000): 1–30.
Skinner, Quentin. *From Humanism to Hobbes: Studies in Rhetoric and Politics*. Cambridge: Cambridge University Press, 2018.
Smith, Paul J. "'J'honnore le plus ceux que j'honnore le moins': Paradoxe et discours chez Montaigne." In *Le paradoxe en linguistique et en littérature*, edited by Ronald Landheer and Paul J. Smith, 173–97. Geneva: Droz, 1996.
Stokes, Michael. "Three Defences of Socrates: Relative Chronology, Politics and Religion." In *Xenophon: Ethical Principles and Historical Enquiry*, edited by Fiona Hobden and Christopher Tuplin, 243–67. Leiden: Brill, 2012.
Striker, Gisela. *Essays on Hellenistic Epistemology and Ethics*. Cambridge: Cambridge University Press, 1996.

Supple, James. *Arms Versus Letters: The Military and Literary Ideals in the "Essais" of Montaigne.* Oxford: Clarendon Press, 1984.

———. *Les Essais de Montaigne: Méthode(s) et méthodologies.* Paris: Champion, 2000.

Telle, Émile. *L'Erasmianus sive Ciceronianus d'Etienne Dolet.* Geneva: Droz, 1974.

Tenenti, Alberto. "La religione di Machiavelli." *Studi Storici* 10, no. 4 (1969): 709–48.

Tinkler, John. "Praise and Advice: Rhetorical Approaches in More's *Utopia* and Machiavelli's *The Prince.*" *Sixteenth Century Journal* 19, no. 2 (1988): 187–207.

Tomarken, Annette. *The Smile of Truth: The French Satirical Eulogy and Its Antecedents.* Princeton: Princeton University Press, 1990.

Tournoy, Gilbert. "Erasmus: 'gracculus' or 'graeculus'?" *Humanistica Lovaniensia* 52 (2003): 405–6.

Tucker, George Hugo. *Homo Viator: Itineraries of Exile, Displacement and Writing in Renaissance Europe.* Geneva: Droz, 2003.

Valcke, Louis. "Jean Pic et le retour au 'style de Paris': Portée d'une critique littéraire." *Rinascimento* 32 (1992): 253–73.

Vickers, Brian. *In Defence of Rhetoric.* New York: Oxford University Press, 1989.

———. "Valla's Ambivalent Praise of Pleasure: Rhetoric in the Service of Christianity." *Viator* 17 (1986): 271–319.

Villey, Pierre. *Les sources italiennes de la "Deffense et illustration de la langue Françoise" de Joachim Du Bellay.* Paris: Champion, 1908.

Viroli, Maurizio. *Il Dio di Machiavelli e il problema morale di Italia.* Rome: Laterza, 2005.

———. *Redeeming the Prince.* Princeton: Princeton University Press, 2013.

INDEX

Achilles, 107
Agrippa, Henricus Cornelius, 30
Albert the Great, 69, 73
Alciati, Andrea, 48, 58
Alcibiades, 12–13, 15, 26
Ambrose, 69
Anaxagoras, 95
Aneau, Barthélemy, 61
Anselm of Canterbury, 69
Antalcidas, 19, 23, 58
Antisthenes, 24
Antoninus Pius, 103
Anytus, 31
Apion, 69
Argyropoulos, John, 39, 41–43, 48, 56, 58, 75
Arian heresy, 95
Aristophanes, 30
Aristotle, 6–7, 12, 17–18, 39, 41–45, 79, 81, 106–7
   Nicomachean Ethics, 6
   Poetics, 23
   Rhetoric, 6–7, 12, 44, 106–7
   Sophistic Refutations, 17–18, 20
Arminius, 107
Augustine, 49
Aurelius, Marcus, 103
Averroes, 73

Bacon, Francis, 71
Bade, Josse, 53, 76
Barbaro, Ermolao, 8, 58, 65, 72–77
Basil of Caesarea, 69, 79
Becket, Thomas, 66
Bede, 69
Bembo, Pietro, 59–60
Bernard of Clairvaux, 69
Beroaldo, Filippo, 58
Bignone, Ettore, 44
Bodin, Jean, 4, 85, 89, 92–99, 103, 111, 113
   Colloquium Heptaplomeres, 96, 98
   De republica libri sex, 96, 98
   Les six livres de la République, 4, 93–97, 113
   Methodus ad facilem historiarum cognitionem, 89, 98, 103
Boethius, 69
Bonamico, Lazzaro, 48, 59
Bonaventure, 69
Brutus, Marcus Iunius, 39
Budé, Guillaume, 53, 58
Busiris, 1–2, 8, 19, 25, 30, 45, 63, 77, 83–84, 113

Caligula, 103
Callicles, 13
Camerarius, Joachim, 76
Camporeale, Salvatore, 66
Capito, Wolfgang, 51
Cardano, Girolamo, 7, 13, 23–27, 103, 111
   De Socratis studio, 25–27, 111
   Encomium Neronis, 23–26
Carneades, 94–95
Casembroot, Leonard, 48
Cassin, Barbara, 5
Castiglione, Baldesar, 49, 59
Catullus, 55
Charles VIII, 35

INDEX

Chamard, Henri, 63
Chomarat, Jacques, 53, 78–79
Christ, 26, 45–46, 49, 78–81
Chrysostom, John, 69, 79
Cicero, 7–9, 20, 25, 31, 39–63, 75–76, 85, 88, 91, 99–101, 104, 106–8, 113
  Brutus, 53
  De divinatione, 40, 88
  De finibus, 7, 39–40, 42, 57, 62, 100
  De gloria, 99
  De inventione, 107
  De natura deorum, 85, 104
  De officiis, 99–100
  De oratore, 76, 91
  Tusculan Disputations, 20, 40–41, 101
Claudius Pulcher, Appius, 89
Colocci, Angelo, 47
Cortesi, Paolo, 46–47, 50
Creon, 14
Crinito, Pietro, 55
Critias, 13, 15, 85, 106

Derrida, Jacques, 36
Diogenes Laertius, 112
Dionisotti, Carlo, 87
Dionysius II, 36
Dolet, Etienne, 54, 59
Dominic, Saint, 67
Dorp, Maarten van, 8, 71, 78–79, 81–82
Du Bellay, Guillaume, 59
Du Bellay, Joachim, 4–5, 54, 56–57, 59–63
  Deffence et Illustration de la Langue Françoyse, 7, 19, 56–57, 59–63
  Les Regrets, 4
Duns Scotus, John, 69, 73, 79

Epaminondas, 108
Epicurus, 92
Epicureanism, 39, 84, 92, 104-6
Erasmus, Desiderius, 8, 24–33, 37, 45–54, 56–59, 63, 65, 68, 71, 77–82, 109
  Adages, 14, 24, 29, 31, 33, 50–52, 56, 72, 79–80, 134
  Apophthegmata, 24, 58
  Correspondence, 32–33, 47–50, 71, 78, 81–82
  De ratione studii, 47
  Dialogus Ciceronianus, 8, 45–54, 56
  Enchiridion, 50
  Encomium matrimonii, 109
  Julius exclusus e coelo, 17
  Panegyricus, 77
  Praise of Folly, 8, 14, 22, 25, 27–29, 71, 77–82, 109
Euathlus, 43

Eumolpus, 3
Euripides, 4, 31, 85
Eurystheus, 2
Euthydemus, 13
Evenus of Paros, 13

Favorinus of Arles, 4, 18, 23, 27, 74, 77, 94–95, 97
Ficino, Marsilio, 32
Florido, Francesco, 8, 54–59, 61, 63
  Apologia in Marci Actii Plauti aliorumque poetarum et linguae latinae calumniatores, 54–59
  Succisivae lectiones, 54

Garin, Eugenio, 44–45, 73
Gaza, Theodorus, 58
Gellius, Aulus, 2–3, 18, 27, 43, 47, 74, 94
Gentillet, Innocent, 90–94
Glaucon, 24–25
Gorgias, 3, 11–14, 16, 22–23, 27, 36, 112
Gray, Hanna, 74–75
Gregory I (the Great), Pope, 69
Gregory Nazianzen, 69
Gruget, Claude, 59
Gyges, 96, 101–2

Hadrian, 103
Haio Herman, 47
Hampton, Timothy, 108
Hannibal, 90–91
Harth, Helene, 60
Helen of Troy, 18
Héroët, Antoine, 61
Hercules, 1–2, 19, 23–24, 58
Hilary of Poitiers, 69
Hippias, 13–14, 34
Homer, 77
Horace, 55, 79, 99

Isidore of Seville, 69
Isocrates, 1–3, 8–9, 11–12, 18–19, 27, 38, 63, 77, 83–86, 92, 96–97, 105, 112
  Busiris, 1–2, 8, 11–12, 15, 19, 77, 83–86, 96
  Helen, 11–12, 16
  Panathenaicus, 14

Jerome, 49, 68–70, 77, 79
Joinville, Jean de, 105
Julian the Apostate, 19

Knott, Betty, 54

Labé, Louise, 27–29

La Boétie, Etienne de, 35
Lactantius, 69
Lamers, Han, 42
Landino, Cristoforo, 58
Lascaris, Janus, 60, 87
Libanius, 13, 19
Livingstone, Niall, 13
Livy, 58, 85, 87, 104
Longueil, Christophe de, 48–49
Lucan, 56
Lucian, 5
Lucretius, 55
Luther, Martin, 47–49
Lycurgus, 87, 105
Lyra, Nicolas de, 80
Lysias, 38

Machiavelli, Niccolò, 9, 85, 87–94, 97–99, 103–4, 111
Marot, Clément, 61
Martelli, Mario, 73–74
Marullus, Michael, 54–57, 61
Meletus, 15
Mesnard, Pierre, 49
Miller, Clarence, 29, 78
Mondolfo, Rodolfo, 112
Montaigne, Michel de, 3, 5, 7, 9, 13, 25, 29–38, 44, 85, 87, 89, 91, 98–109, 111, 113
    I, 23 "De la coustume et de ne changer aisément une loy reçue," 5, 105, 111
    I, 25 "Du pedantisme," 29–35, 91
    I, 28 "De l'amitié," 14
    I, 31 "Des Cannibales," 3
    II, 1 "De l'inconstance de nos actions," 25
    II, 12 "Apologie de Raymond Sebond," 23, 29, 133
    II, 16 "De la gloire" 87, 99–106, 109, 113
    III, 1 "De l'utile et de l'honneste," 22, 106–9
    III, 12 "De la phisionomie," 35–38
    III, 13 "De l'experience," 89
More, Thomas, 53, 77, 81
Mosellanus, Petrus, 76–77
Moses, 105

Najemy, John, 89
Nero, 23–26, 103
Nerva, 103
Numa Pompilius, 85, 87–88, 104

Olbrechts-Tyteca, Lucie, 5
Olivar, Pedro Juan, 48–49, 57
O'Malley, John, 5–6

Ovid, 4, 56, 77

Papirius Cursor, Lucius, 89, 104
Patroclus, 107
Paul, Saint, 67–69, 78–81, 109
Penelope, 22
Perelman, Chaïm, 5, 108
Perotti, Niccolò, 58
Pernot, Laurent, 4
Peter of Verona, 66
Petrarch, 24, 57
Petronius, 3
Philip of Macedon, 88
Philostratus, 18
Phormio, 90–91
Pibrac, Guy du Faur de, 93
Pico della Mirandola, Giovanni, 8, 44–45, 65, 71–77
Pio, Alberto, prince of Carpi, 53, 58
Plato, 7, 13–38, 44, 76, 104–5, 116
    Apology of Socrates, 13–17, 21, 26–30, 35, 37–38
    Crito, 21
    Gorgias, 17, 32, 76
    Hippias Maior, 34
    Laws, 104
    Menexenus, 17
    Meno, 31–32, 34
    Phaedrus, 44
    Protagoras, 18, 22, 32, 34–35
    Republic, 25
    Seventh Letter, 36–37
    The Sophist, 14, 18, 22
Plautus, 54–56
Pliny the Elder, 58, 69
Pliny the Younger, 4, 6
Plutarch, 23–25, 31, 34, 44, 85
Poliziano, Angelo, 39–49, 56, 58, 63, 71–73, 75–77
    Miscellaneorum centuria prima, 39, 41–45, 48
    Opus epistolarum, 46–47, 71–72
Polus of Agrigentum, 13
Polybius, 9, 85–87, 94, 97, 99, 105
Polycrates, 1–3, 7–8, 11–13, 15, 19, 26, 63, 77
Pomponazzi, Pietro, 60
Pontano, Giovanni, 49, 57
Porteau, Paul, 30
Prodicus, 13–14
Propertius, 56
Protagoras, 13, 31, 35, 43, 112–13
pseudo.-Dionysius the Areopagite, 66, 69

Quintilian, 6, 17, 19, 21, 29, 38, 76–77

Rabelais, François, 50, 66–67
Ricci, Bernardo, 71–72
Romulus, 87

Sabbadini, Remigio, 42
Sadoleto, Jacopo, 58
Saint-Gelais, Mellin de, 61
Sallust, 66
Sasso, Gennaro, 87
Savonarola, Girolamo, 88
Scève, Maurice, 61
Seneca Rhetor, 41
Servius, 58
Sextus Empiricus, 85
Sisyphus, 85–86, 105
Socrates, 7, 12–38, 43, 104, 112, 116
Solon, 87, 105
Sophocles, 14
Speroni, Sperone, 7, 13, 19–23, 26–27, 30, 59–61, 112–13, 115–17
   Contra Socrate, 20–21, 26
   Dialogo delle lingue, 19, 59–60
   Discorso dei lodatori, 19–20, 115–17
   In difesa dei sofisti, 21–23
Statius, 85
Stobaeus, Johannes, 31
Stokes, Michael, 13
Strabo, 44
Striker, Gisela, 13
Sturm, Johann, 6–7
Suetonius, 23–24, 31

Tacitus, 23–24, 45, 107
Telle, Émile, 53
Terence, 55–56
Theodorus of Byzantium, 13
Theodosius I (the Great), 95
Thomas Aquinas, 65–70, 73
Thrasybulus, 12
Thrasymachus, 13
Tiberius, 69, 107
Tibullus, 55–56
Titus, 103
Toussain, Jacques, 32
Trajan, 4, 103
Trebizond, George of, 58

Valeriano, Pierio, 2
Valla, Lorenzo, 8, 58, 65–71, 73–74, 79
   Elegantiarum linguae Latinae libri sex, 70–71
   Encomion Sancti Thomae Aquinatis, 65–70
Vergara, Francisco de, 49
Villey, Pierre, 31, 59, 103
Virgil, 2, 55, 58, 62, 77
   Aeneid, 58
   Culex, 77
   Georgics, 2
Vitellius, Aulus, 103

Wolf, Hieronymus, 8, 83–86, 92 97, 105

Xenophon, 15

Zoroaster, 104

Lightning Source UK Ltd.
Milton Keynes UK
UKHW041516070422
401195UK00002B/94